Financial Reform in Japan

Financial Reform in Japan

Causes and Consequences

Maximilian J.B. Hall

Senior Lecturer in Economics, Loughborough University, UK

Edward Elgar
Cheltenham, UK • Northampton, MA, USA

© Maximilian J.B. Hall, 1998

All rights reserved. No part of this publication may be reproduced, stored in a retrieval system or transmitted in any form or by any means, electronic, mechanical or photocopying, recording, or otherwise without the prior permission of the publisher.

Published by
Edward Elgar Publishing Limited
Glensanda House
Montpellier Parade
Cheltenham
Glos GL50 1UA
UK

Edward Elgar Publishing, Inc.
6 Market Street
Northampton
Massachusetts 01060
USA

A catalogue record for this book
is available from the British Library

Library of Congress Cataloguing in Publication Data

Hall, Maximilian.
    Financial reform in Japan : causes and consequences / Maximilian
J.B. Hall.
    Includes bibliographical references and index.
    1. Finance—Japan.   2. Financial institutions—Japan–
–History—20th century.   3. Financial institutions—Deregulation–
–Japan.   4. Banks and banking—Japan.   5. Capital market—Japan.
6. Money market—Japan.   7. Japan—Economic conditions—1945–1989.
8. Japan—Economic conditions—1989–   9. Japan—Economic
policy—1945–1989.   10. Japan—Economic policy—1989–   I. Title.
HG187.5.J3H35   1999
332'.0952—dc21   98–34330
                                                                                        CIP

ISBN 1 85898 887 X

Typeset by Manton Typesetters, 5–7 Eastfield Road, Louth, Lincolnshire, LN11 7AJ, UK
Printed and bound in Great Britain by Bookcraft (Bath) Ltd.

Contents

List of exhibits   vii
List of charts   ix
List of abbreviations   xi
Preface   xiii
Acknowledgements   xiv

PART 1   FINANCIAL STRUCTURE AND THE REFORM DEBATE

1   The Japanese financial system   3
2   Pressures for reform   20

PART 2   FINANCIAL REFORM

3   Financial deregulation: 1975–97   67
4   Financial reform under the 'big bang' programme   139
5   Supervisory reform   159
6   Reform of the Bank of Japan   189

PART 3   THE CONSEQUENCES OF FINANCIAL REFORM FOR PUBLIC POLICY

7   Implications of financial liberalization for the conduct of monetary policy   201
8   Implications of financial liberalization for prudential policy   214

Index   223

List of exhibits

1.1	The Japanese financial system	4
1.2	The Japanese banking system	7
1.3	The structure of Japan's financial markets	13
2.1	'Bad' loans of the Japanese banking sector: 1992–97	30
2.2	'Bad' loans of Japanese banks by industry grouping: 1995–97	33
2.3	Other balance sheet trends for Japanese banks: total assets, loans and bad loans: 1995–97	34
3.1	Internationalization of the yen: 1980–95	68
3.2	Internationalization of the yen: the programme of deregulation post-1978	71
3.3	Liberalization of time-deposit rates in Japan	83
3.4	Relaxation of controls on money market certificates	85
3.5	Liberalization of the Japanese money market: the programme of financial deregulation in the interbank market	90
3.6	Liberalization of the Japanese money market: the programme of financial deregulation in the open market	94
3.7	Liberalization of the public bond market: the programme of deregulation	102
3.8	Foreign securities companies' operations in Japan at 31 December 1988	116
3.9	A comparison of the relative merits of different options for reforming Article 65	122
3.10	The 'five formulas' for reform in Japan	125
3.11	The development of cross-entry by financial institutions under the Financial System Reform Act of 1993	128
4.1	Financial reform under Japan's 'big bang' and the timetable for reform	140
4.2	Revisions to the Foreign Exchange and Foreign Trade Control Law approved in 1997	148
4.3	Japan's version of prompt corrective action	154
5.1	Chronology of the emergence and resolution of 'problem' banks in Japan: 1991–97	160
5.2	Balance sheet profile of the seven *jusen* companies at 19 December 1995	168

5.3   Current institutional landscape governing the regulation and
      supervision of financial institutions in Japan   184
6.1   Changes made to the Bank of Japan Law of 1942   192
7.1   The transmission mechanism of monetary policy in postwar
      Japan   202
7.2   Reserve ratio requirements imposed on Japanese banks   204

List of charts

2.1	GDP growth rate: 1970–98	48
2.2	Public sector debt ratio: 1970–96	49
2.3	Export and import of goods and services: 1970–98	50
2.4	Unemployment ratio: 1970–98	51
2.5	Corporate bankruptcies: 1970–98	52
2.6	Short-term interest rates: 1970–98	53
2.7	Lending margin: 1970–98	54
2.8	Land price indices of urban areas: 1970–97	55
2.9	Nikkei stock average: 1970–98	56
2.10	Loans and discounts outstanding by type of financial institution: 1970–98	57
3.1	Classification of Japanese banks' associated companies	110
5.1	*Jusen* disposal scheme	169
5.2	Deposit insurance reform: 1996	173
5.3	Framework of emergency measures for stabilizing the financial system	175
5.4	Relationships between the Financial Supervisory Agency, Ministry of Finance, Bank of Japan and Deposit Insurance Corporation	183
5.5	Japan premium: 1995–98	186
7.1	Provision of liquidity by the Bank of Japan: October 1997–May 1998	210

List of abbreviations

ABS	Asset-backed securities
BA	Bankers' acceptance
BIS	Bank for International Settlements
BoJ	Bank of Japan
BOJ-NET	Bank of Japan netting
CCPC	Co-operative Credit Purchasing Company
CDs	Certificates of deposit
CP	Commercial paper
DIC	Deposit Insurance Corporation
EMU	European and Monetary Union
EPA	Economic Planning Agency
EU	European Union
FAIR	Foundation for Advanced Information and Research
FBAJ	Federation of Bankers' Associations of Japan
FDIC	Federal Deposit Insurance Corporation
FOREX	Foreign exchange
FRNs	Floating-rate notes
FSA	Financial Supervisory Agency
FSRC	Financial System Research Council
FTC	Fair Trade Commission
GDP	Gross domestic product
HLAC	Housing Loan Administration Corporation
JASDAQ	Japanese Securities Dealers' Automated Quotation
JCIF	Japan Centre for International Finance
LDP	Liberal Democratic Party
LIBOR	London Inter-Bank Offered Rate
M&A	Mergers and acquisitions
MMCs	Money market certificates
MoF	Ministry of Finance
MPT	Ministry of Posts and Telecommunications
MTNs	Medium-term notes
OECD	Organization for Economic Co-operation and Development
OTC	Over-the-counter
PCA	Prompt corrective action

RCB   Resolution and Collection Bank
RTGS   Real time gross settlement
SEC   Securities and Exchange Council
SESC   Securities and Exchange Surveillance Commission
SICAFC   Savings Insurance Corporation for Agricultural and Fishery
           Co-operatives
SPCs   Special-purpose companies
TBs   Treasury bills
TIBOR   Tokyo Inter-Bank Offered Rate
TIRAL   Temporary Interest Rate Adjustment Law
TSE   Tokyo Stock Exchange

Preface

This book is concerned with the evolution of financial reform in postwar Japan, with an emphasis being placed on the period 1975–98. It provides comprehensive and detailed coverage of the causes and nature of the financial liberalization adopted in Japan during this period, as well as its consequences for public policy. It also includes the recent reforms adopted in respect of Japan's central bank, the Bank of Japan, as well as the various supervisory initiatives adopted to help stablize the Japanese financial system in the face of a variety of 'shocks', mainly of internal origin. By providing an overview of the local financial system and detailed discussion of the evolution of financial markets in Japan, the analysis is placed firmly within an institutional context; and the politics, as well as the economics, of the financial liberalization programme adopted are presented to widen the appeal of the text.

M.J.B.H.

Acknowledgements

First, I should like to acknowledge gratefully the financial support received from the British Academy and the Japan Society for the Promotion of Science which enabled me to visit Japan to collect material for the text and to interview interested parties. The latter – comprising regulators, practitioners, trade associations, credit rating agencies and academics – also deserves a vote of thanks for its willing co-operation. In this respect, my host in Japan, Professor Hisashi Harui, of Kwansei Gakuin University, deserves a special mention for co-ordinating my interviews, as does Mr Kazumasa Okubo, of the Ministry of Finance, for opening doors for me at the relevant ministries and for keeping me up to date with official documentation relevant to my studies.

Finally, I should like to thank Gloria Brentnall for slaving tirelessly on the word processor on my behalf to produce so promptly a manuscript suitable for publication.

PART 1

Financial Structure and the Reform Debate

1.   The Japanese financial system

JAPANESE FINANCIAL INTERMEDIARIES

Classification of Japanese Financial Intermediaries

The various financial intermediaries operating in Japan may be classified largely along functional lines as shown in Exhibit 1.1. In principle, banking business is separated from securities business, deposit banking from trust business and, within the commercial banking sector, long-term from short-term finance. Further *de facto* separation, often secured through 'administrative guidance', results in additional functional segmentation in the form of the isolation of insurance business from banking and securities business, and foreign exchange business from deposit-taking (all depository institutions have to obtain authorization from the Ministry of Finance (MoF), in accordance with the Foreign Exchange and Foreign Trade Control Law, before engaging in foreign currency operations). And further functional segmentation within the banking sector arises because of the founding charters of the various specialist banks. For example, the *shinkin* banks (including the Zenshinren Bank) and the Shokochukin Bank all specialize in the provision of finance to small- and medium-sized companies; and the Norinchukin Bank specializes in meeting the financial needs of the agricultural, forestry and fisheries industries.

As noted below, the separation of long-term from short-term finance within the private banking sector is achieved by law and the use of administrative guidance. The former results in the operation of two types of long-term credit institutions, long-term credit banks and trust banks, which specialize in the provision of long-term loans to industry and whose sources of funds are severely restricted (leading to a heavy reliance of the long-term credit banks on debentures and of the trust banks on loan trust accounts). The latter is used to limit the maturity composition of ordinary banks' borrowed funds – no *legal* controls on the maturity composition of either deposits or loans exist – and to limit the issue of financial debentures by institutions other than long-term credit banks.[1]

The separation of banking from trust business, initially because of conflict-of-interest concerns but, after the Second World War, as a means of enforcing

Exhibit 1.1   The Japanese financial system

The banking sector[1]

Non-bank deposit-taking intermediaries
    Private   credit co-operatives (including the National Federation of
            Credit Co-operatives) (364)[2]
            agricultural co-operatives (and their credit federations) (2297)
            fishery co-operatives (and their credit federations) (1283)
    Public   the Post Office (postal savings)

Non-depository institutions
    Private   insurance companies: life assurance companies (44)
                            non-life insurance companies (33)
                            various mutual aid (*kyosai*) co-operatives
            securities investment trust management companies (40)
            securities finance companies (225)
            consumer credit institutions
            venture capital firms
            securities companies
            money market dealers
    Public   Trust Fund Bureau, Special Account for Post Office Life
            Insurance and Postal Annuity, Industrial Investment Special
            Account
            Overseas Economic Co-operation Fund
            People's Finance Corporation
            Small Business Finance Corporation
            Small Business Credit Insurance Corporation
            Environmental Sanitation Business Finance Corporation
            Agriculture, Forestry and Fishery Finance Corporation
            Housing Loan Corporation
            Finance Corporation of Local Public Enterprises
            Hokkaido and Tohoku Development Corporation
            Okinawa Development Finance Corporation
            Government-related funding bodies

Notes:
[1]   See Exhibit 1.2 for a further breakdown.
[2]   Figures in parentheses represent the number of financial institutions in each category as of
    end February 1997.

Sources: Derived from Federation of Bankers' Associations of Japan (FBAJ) (1989), Figure 1.
1, pp. 18–19; FBAJ (1997), p. 1.

the separation of short- from long-term finance, was also secured by the joint use of legal provisions and administrative guidance. Under the Law Concerning Concurrent Operation of Savings Bank Business or Trust Business by Ordinary Banks of 1943, ordinary banks and long-term credit banks were permitted to engage in trust business, under licence from the MoF, in accordance with the Trust Business Law of 1922.[2] Administrative guidance (first adopted in 1958) has been used, however, to confine trust business to long-term financial institutions and, under the Loan Trust Law of 1952, non-trust banks engaging in trust operations are prohibited from obtaining long-term funds through the offering of loan trusts. The decision taken in 1985 to allow foreign banks to undertake trust business in Japan does undermine the principle of separation, though.

The final major form of functional segmentation – the separation of banking from securities business – was effected for the first time in statute with the enactment of the Securities and Exchange Law of 1948. Article 65 of this law prohibits banks, in principle, from engaging in securities business other than for their own investment purposes or in pursuance of trust contracts. The underwriting and trading of public bonds, however, was exempted from the provisions, although administrative guidance ensured that all such activities except the underwriting of government bonds remained prohibited until the 1980s.

As for the separation of banking from trust business, the principle of separation of banking and securities business in Japan established in 1948 has since been breached with the admission in 1985 of securities subsidiaries of foreign banks into the Japanese marketplace. And the mushrooming in the securities operation of Japanese banks' overseas subsidiaries (and, indeed, in the banking operations of Japanese securities companies' overseas subsidiaries) since the mid-1980s further calls into question the rationale for continued enforcement of the remaining separation in domestic markets (this and other related issues are addressed in more detail in Chapter 4).

Evolution of the Banking Sector

The roots of the present-day structure can be traced back to the beginning of the Meiji Restoration period in 1868. The system set up at that time was based on the national banking system of the USA, characterized by the existence of a large number of issuing banks. Accordingly, under the National Bank Act of 1872, a number of privately owned national banks were permitted to start operations, functioning largely as issuing banks. By 1879, the date at which a halt was called to the establishment of national banks, there were over 150 such banks in existence and they operated side by side with other types of company also engaged in banking businesses. Indeed, it was from the latter group's ranks that the first private bank emerged when the Mitsui Gumi Company formed the Mitsui Bank in 1876. This bank, along with most of the other private banks and banking companies formed after 1876, subsequently converted to ordinary bank status in accordance with the Banking Act of 1890. For the national banks, this process was accelerated by their loss of issuing authority following the founding of the Bank of Japan in 1882. The result was that the Japanese banking system operated along the lines of the British system, rather than that of the USA, before the turn of the nineteenth century.

Another important historical feature of the Japanese banking system is the absorption of the savings bank system into the banking system proper. The savings bank system was established as long ago as 1890 under the Savings Bank Act, and the savings banks were initially protected by the Savings Bank Law of 1921 which prohibited ordinary banks from engaging in savings banking business (that is, the taking of small deposits, their investment in securities – primarily government bonds – and the payment of compound interest). This prohibition remained in force until 1943, but by the end of the Second World War only five savings banks remained. And by 1948 each of these five institutions had either converted into or merged with an ordinary bank, marking the demise of the species as a separate entity. After 1949 savings banking business became the preserve of the ordinary banks, a position formalized in 1981 with the revision of the Banking Law which, for the first time, gave official blessing to the joint offering of commercial and savings banking business.

The Japanese Banking Sector: A Classification System

Banking institutions in Japan may be categorized according to the system adopted in Exhibit 1.2. In this approach, the central bank, ordinary banks, specialized banks and government-owned banks are separately identified. Even this list, however, does not embrace all deposit-taking intermediaries operating in Japan: credit co-operatives (including the National Federation of Credit Co-operatives), agricultural co-operatives (and their credit federations) and fishery co-operatives (including their credit federations) from the private sector, and the Post Office from the public sector, all play their part (see Federation of Bankers' Associations of Japan (FBAJ), 1989, pp. 27–35; and Suzuki, 1987, ch. 5, for further details); and it includes three institutions (that is, the central bank and the government-owned banks) which do not accept deposits from the general public. Nevertheless, for illustrative purposes, it is perhaps the most sensible taxonomic approach to adopt, although clearly historical precedent further reduces the degree of functional separation secured.

Exhibit 1.2   The Japanese banking system

Central bank	The Bank of Japan
Private banks	
Ordinary banks	City banks (10)
	Regional banks (64)
	'Second Association' of regional banks (65)
	Foreign banks (92)
Specialized banks	
long-term financial institutions	Long-term credit banks (3)
	Trust banks (33)
in finance for small- and medium-sized corporations	*Shinkin* banks/Zenshinren Bank (413)
	Labour banks/Rokinren Banks (48)
	Shokochukin Bank
in serving the agricultural, forestry and fisheries industries	Norinchukin Bank
Public (non-depository) sector banks	Japan Development Bank
	Export–Import Bank of Japan

Note: The figures in parentheses represent the number of banks in each category as of end February 1997.

Sources: Federation of Bankers' Associations of Japan (FBAJ) (1989), ch. 1; Suzuki (1987), ch. 5; FBAJ (1997), p. 1.

The central bank

The Bank of Japan (the 'Bank') was established as the central bank of Japan in October 1882 and currently operates under the Bank of Japan Law of 1998. Legally, it functions as a special corporation outside the framework of government, with 55 per cent of its capital held by the government and the remainder by the private sector. Control over the Bank is exercised by a policy board comprising the Bank's governor, two vice-governors and six other ('expert') members.

As prescribed in Article 1 of the above-mentioned law, the main role of Bank today is to 'contribute to the development of a sound national economy through the maintenance of price stability' and to 'contribute to the maintenance of an orderly credit system by securing smooth funds settlements for financial institutions'. This is to be achieved primarily through appropriate manipulation of the money supply and money market conditions, the proximate goals of which are a stable currency and price stability. The other traditional macroeconomic goals – full employment, economic growth and external balance – are also considered important, however.

Apart from conducting monetary policy, the Bank also performs a range of other duties traditionally expected of a central bank. These embrace, *inter alia:* note issuance; banker to the government; banker to the banking system; foreign exchange market intervention; and government bond and money market activities. (For recent reform of the Bank of Japan see Chapter 6.)

Private banks

The first group of privately owned banks, the ordinary banks, operate in accordance with the Banking Law under licence from the MoF. They concentrate on the provision of short-term finance facilities, operating as traditional Western-style deposit bankers in both domestic and foreign markets. Their customer base embraces small, medium-sized and multinational corporations, together with private individuals.

Statistically, the ordinary banks are broken down into three separate groupings: city banks; regional banks; and foreign banks.

City banks This group comprises the nationwide branching institutions. Traditionally suppliers of short-term funds to large corporations, they have recently focused on developing the longer-term end of their business. Additionally, they have been forced to cultivate clients from amongst the smaller corporate fry and the personal sector because of the downturn in their traditional customers' demand for bank credit. This downturn arose for a number of reasons, chief among which were an increasingly liquid trading situation and the opportunities created by developments in the capital market – the so-called process of securitization – which were themselves partly the result of official deregulatory moves (for example, to allow for the establishment of a commercial paper market and to open up the corporate bond market during the 1980s). Apart from borrowing from the Bank of Japan, they fund themselves in the deposit and short-term financial markets. They are widely engaged in securities-type operations – despite the legal restrictions separating commercial banking and securities business in Japan (see Chapter 4) – both at home and abroad, and most have a significant international dimension to their operations (the largest are the largest banks in the world, by deposit or asset size).

Regional banks The second grouping of ordinary banks comprises the regional banks, which are divided into regional banks proper and the 'Second Association' of regional banks. They are smaller in scale than the city banks and usually confine their operations to the principal cities of the prefectures in which their head offices are located. Accordingly, their local ties are strong, with the bulk of their lending going to small or medium-sized companies in the locality. The bulk of their deposits are time deposits of an initial term of one year or more, with over 50 per cent accruing from individuals. Apart from making business loans, they invest heavily in the stock market and are important lenders in the local money market.

Foreign banks   There are more than 90 foreign banks operating in Japan, forming the third and final grouping of ordinary banks. Licensed by the MoF in respect of their branching operations (prior notification suffices in the case of representative offices), they have traditionally been heavily involved in foreign currency transactions and trade finance and so have also had to acquire the status of authorized foreign exchange banks. Their share of the Japanese banking market has always been small, but this may pick up in the next few years as a result of the new opportunities created by the 'big bang' reforms (see Chapter 4). Low margins on corporate lending activities led some to eschew this business and instead to focus on investment banking and risk management, both for themselves and for clients. Other advisory services offered relate to foreign real-estate investment and mergers and acquisitions; and leasing and securitization activities are also regarded as potentially profitable. For tax reasons, however, incentives remain for the banks to book outside the country the deals agreed in Japan. On the liabilities side, they are forced to rely heavily on eurocurrency borrowings from their main branch offices as their limited branch networks (the source of the city banks' major funding advantage), like the local money market, fail to deliver funds in sufficient quantity. Despite deregulation – which, although ending their monopoly on the provision of foreign currency loans to Japanese residents, did provide them with access to trust banking and broadened their funding base through a broadening of the interbank market, the establishment of an offshore market and expansion in the yen swap market – foreign banks have still found it difficult to penetrate domestic markets to date.

Specialized banks   The first group of specialized banks,[3] the *long-term financial institutions,* comprise both long-term credit banks and trust banks. The *long-term credit banks,* of which there are three in number, were established under the Long-Term Credit Bank Law of 1952 to engage in long-term finance in order to achieve a separation between short- and long-term finance and to reduce the long-term funding burden imposed on the ordinary banks by the demands of industry. They are distinguishable from ordinary banks in their funding operations, their lending operations and in the size of their branch networks. On the funding side, they alone are permitted to issue debentures – either five-year interest-bearing debentures or one-year discount debentures – up to a maximum of 30 times their own capital, but must confine their deposit-taking to their borrowing clientele, public bodies, corporations which entrust bond subscriptions to them, and other clients; on the lending side, the average term to maturity of their loans is considerably longer (partly because of the limitation placed on their provision of short-term working capital for industry: it cannot exceed the volume of deposits solicited); and the size of their branch networks is considerably smaller.

The other group of long-term banking institutions comprises the *trust banks*. These institutions are ordinary banks established under the Banking Law but given extended powers in accordance with the 1943 law permitting concurrent ordinary bank and trust operations (that is, the Law Concerning Joint Operation of Ordinary Banks, Savings Bank Business and Trust Business), as revised in 1981. Excluding the subsidiaries of foreign banks – nine were admitted in 1985 by the MoF on condition that they incorporate locally – there are currently 33 institutions operating as trust banks in Japan. They obtain most of their funds from trusts (particularly the loan trusts peculiar to Japan – see Suzuki, 1987, ch. 3) and, in respect of their trust accounts, satisfy much of the large Japanese corporations' capital investment finance needs. They also offer savings and deposit accounts and tap the money markets. Apart from their trust and banking operations, they are active in funds management (especially *tokkin* funds,[4] but also pension funds), and provide real-estate broking and stock transfer services. Following an easing of the restrictions on the proportion of trust assets which can be invested outside Japan[5] they have become significant investors in overseas markets where they are also engaged in securities underwriting and distribution as well as lending operations.

Finance for small and medium-sized companies is the domain of a third group of specialized banks. This group comprises the *shinkin* banks (including the Zenshinren Bank), the labour banks (including the Rokinren Bank) and the Shokochukin Bank.[6]

The *shinkin* banks, operating in accordance with the 1951 Shinkin Bank Law (as last revised in 1981), are non-profit-making co-operatives with a strong local bias. Their membership comprises local residents and small to medium-sized companies (that is, those with a capitalization of up to ¥400 million and employing up to 300 staff), and the minimum subscription per member is fixed by law. Their business comprises the taking of deposits and instalment savings from both members and non-members, lending and discounting bills for members, as well as effecting funds transfers and engaging in foreign exchange operations. The amount of lending to non-members which they can undertake is limited to 20 per cent of their total lending (excluding lending to financial institutions), and a single loan limit of 20 per cent of net worth (or ¥800 million, whichever is smaller) applies. They are also allowed to undertaken certain ancillary operations, the most important of which are securities-related.

Each *shinkin* bank is a member of the Zenshinren Bank, which acts as the national federation of *shinkin* banks. As stipulated in Article 54 of the Shinkin Bank Law, this bank may engage in: deposit-taking, lending and funds transfer for its members; deposit-taking and lending with non-members, as permitted by the MoF; deposit-taking for national and regional government bodies and other non-profit-making organizations; and, as ancillary business, securities-related activities and agency services for public financial institutions. Since 1981, the Zenshinren Bank has also been allowed to undertake foreign exchange operations and to accept the short-term surplus funds from its members. Like its members, it, too, is subject to loan exposure rules – loans to one borrower may not exceed 25 per cent of net worth, with a lower limit of 20 per cent applying if the borrower is a non-member.

The final group of specialist bank institutions (that is, with the term 'bank' used in their title) serving the small to medium-sized company sector in Japan are the *labour banks*. These institutions operate along co-operative lines in accordance with the Labour Bank Law of 1953. Their *raison d'être* is to raise the living standards of labourers by promoting the activities of bodies such as labour unions and consumer co-operatives. They are relatively unsophisticated intermediaries, mainly involved in deposit-taking, the generation of instalment savings and lending. Ceilings are placed on the extent to which they can fund themselves from outside their membership (20 per cent of total deposits) and on the amount of their lending to non-members (20 per cent of total loans, excluding loans to financial institutions). Surplus funds are usually lent to affiliated associations or invested in public corporation bonds.

Like the *shinkin* banks, the labour banks have their own central national organization, the Rokinren Bank, which was set up in 1955. Its major activities of deposit-taking and lending mirror those of its member institutions, although it has also developed systems to maximize efficiency in funds transfer and management for the benefit of its members.

The final specialist institution involved in servicing the small to medium-sized company sector in Japan is the Shokochukin Bank. Founded in 1936 under the Shokochukin Bank Law to provide financial assistance to the unions of small and medium-sized companies and to rectify temporary local fund imbalances between them, the bank is currently involved in lending to and taking deposits from its subscribers, their members and others, including individuals, non-profit-making organizations, government bodies, financial institutions, foreign enterprises and electricity, power and gas companies. Its chief source of funds, however, is debenture issues – it is allowed to raise up to 20 times its net worth through this medium – some of which are underwritten by the government. A revision to the governing law in 1985 also allows them to undertake certain securities-related activities.

The fourth area of operation for the specialist Japanese banks is the servicing of the financial needs of the *agricultural, forestry and fisheries industries.* The most powerful institution operating in this field, and the only one with the term 'bank' included in its title, is the Norinchukin Bank. This bank's capital was subscribed by private agricultural, forestry and fishery organizations according to its founding law (the Norinchukin Bank Law of 1923), and its funding base comprises deposits (mainly taken from its subscribers, especially agricultural organizations) and the proceeds from debenture issues (limited to 30 times its net worth). In principle, these funds are to be used for the purpose of lending to subscribers, although surplus funds are also lent to non-subscribers that are eligible to subscribe and to a range of other organizations and individuals. Surplus funds are invested in short-term securities, and securities-related (sanctioned under an amendment of the Norinchukin Bank Law in 1981) and money market activities have assumed a greater significance in recent years. Indeed, the Norinchukin Bank is an important provider of funds to the interbank markets and is the largest institutional investor in the private sector through its securities holdings.

Public sector banks
There are just two wholly publicly owned banks operating in Japan today – as explained above, the government also holds stakes in the Shokochukin Bank and the Norinchukin Bank – the Japan Development Bank and the Export–Import Bank of Japan. Neither, however, is permitted to take deposits, as this would breach the prohibition in principle on competing with private sector institutions. This has not prevented their share of total intermediation from rising dramatically in recent years, however. (For further information see Suzuki, 1987, pp. 291–4.)

JAPANESE FINANCIAL MARKETS

The present-day structure of Japan's financial markets is illustrated in Exhibit 1.3. At the end of the Second World War, however, the situation was very different. The chief structural characteristics were that of a hollow, underdeveloped marketplace with indirect finance (that is, bank intermediation) the dominant force.

As far as the *money market* was concerned, development centred around the interbank market which, at that time, comprised only a call market. Moreover, rates in this market were strictly controlled. Freely negotiated money rates did not arrive on the scene until the fledgling bond *gensaki* (that is, 'repo') market materialized in 1949. The lack of a secondary market in government bonds led securities companies, the major holders, to initiate

Exhibit 1.3 The structure of Japan's financial markets[a]

The money market
Interbank markets:	the call market (1902)
	the bill market (commercial bills – May 1971)
	the 'Tokyo dollar' call market (April 1972)
'Open'[b] markets:	bond repurchase agreement (bond[c] *gensaki*) market (1949)[d]
	the (negotiable) certificates of deposit (CD) market (May 1979 for issuing; May 1980 for secondary market trading)
	the (yen-denominated) bankers' acceptance (BA) market (June 1985)
	the 'Treasury bill' (i.e. short-term government bond) market (February 1986)
	the commercial paper (CP) market (November 1987)
	the euroyen market[e]

The Tokyo offshore market (December 1986)

The capital market
Bond markets:	the government bond market (postwar reopening – the primary market, 1949; the secondary market, 1966)
	the market for other 'public' bonds
	the market for corporate bonds: bank debenture issues
	'other' (public subscription and private placement)

Equity markets[f]
Futures and options markets:	bond futures (October 1985)[g]
	stock (index) futures (June 1987)[h]
	financial futures and options (interest, currency, other) (June 1989)[i]
	stock index options (October l989)[j]
	US Treasury bond futures options (May 1990)[g]
	government bond futures options (May 1990)[g]
	options on euroyen futures (July 1991)[i]

The foreign exchange markets (July 1952)

Notes:
[a] The dates when trading started are shown in parentheses.
[b] That is, in which, in principle, the non-financial sector may participate.
[c] There is also *gensaki* trading in CDs. This started in July 1981.
[d] The market did not fully mature until 1967, although it took until 1976 for the market to be legalized by the MoF.
[e] Prior to the abolition of the limits on the conversion of foreign currency into yen in June 1984 a separate yen conversion (broadly defined, spot foreign exchange position plus inter-office euroyen accounts) market was distinguished.
[f] Stock exchanges are located in Tokyo, Osaka, Nagoya, Kyoto, Hiroshima, Fukuoka, Niigata and Sapporo, with Tokyo accounting for over 80 per cent of trading by volume and value.
[g] These are traded on the Tokyo Stock Exchange (TSE).
[h] The date when trading first started on the Osaka Securities Exchange. (Stock index futures trading began on the TSE in September 1988.)
[i] Trading takes place on the Tokyo International Financial Futures Exchange, established in April 1989.
[j] Trading takes place on the Tokyo and Nagoya Stock Exchanges.

Sources: Federation of Bankers' Associations of Japan (FBAJ) (1989), ch. 6; FBAJ (1992), p. 14; Japan Centre for International Finance (1988), parts II, III and V; Suzuki (1987), part II, ch. 4.

sale–repurchase agreements with agricultural financial institutions. But even here the market did not become well established until 1967. The deepening of the money market did not begin to occur until the mid-1970s, when the newly established markets began to blossom, although the 'deregulation and internationalization' measures adopted thereafter (see Chapter 3) eventually led to rapid growth in most segments of the market.

In respect of the *capital market,* a similar picture emerges. The government bond market was not reopened until 1949, and secondary trading remained virtually non-existent, despite the reopening of trading on the Tokyo and Osaka Exchanges in 1966, partly because of the dearth of supply – public sector deficits were not significant until the mid-1970s – partly because of the marketing tactics adopted by the monetary authorities whereby the bonds (treasury bills, in the form of 'discount bonds', were not issued until 1986) taken up at issue by the underwriting syndicate (comprising mainly banks and securities companies) were bought back by the Bank of Japan after one year, and partly because the low yield paid on the bonds meant that pre-maturity sales would result in capital losses. By choice, the Bank of Japan also preferred to secure its monetary policy objectives through the use of 'direct' controls (see Chapter 7) rather than open market operations, so little pressure emerged for change from this source until the efficacy and efficiency of such a system began to be called into question in the mid-1970s. This, as noted earlier, was also the time when the emergence of sizeable public sector deficits began to put a strain on the chosen method for getting the associated government bond issues absorbed in the marketplace. Once again, deregulation and internationalization measures did not result in the emergence of a broad and active secondary market in government bonds until the mid-1980s.

The postwar corporate debenture market was also subdued, partly because of the restrictive issuing practices and controls involving, *inter alia,* demanding eligibility standards for prospective issuers, limitations on the size of issues, collateral requirements (under the so-called 'collateral rule'), anti-competitive underwriting practices and restrictions on the private placement of bonds. Despite later modifications to issuing practices and relaxation of the allied restrictions (see Chapter 3), the market for straight corporate bonds (as opposed to 'convertibles', which benefited from the rising stock market) remained depressed during the 1970s and 1980s, partly because of the attractions of the overseas market (restrictions on the issuing of foreign bonds were lifted in November 1975), with bullish views on the yen predominating.

A final reason for the hollowness of Japan's postwar capital market was its isolation from the rest of the world, a position secured by close regulation of all financial market participants and extensive foreign exchange controls, which were not substantially relaxed until 1980. As regards non-resident activity in the Japanese capital markets, *samurai* bond issues (yen-denominated bonds issued in Japan by non-residents) did not make an appearance until 1970, with *shogun* bond issues (foreign-currency-denominated issues by non-residents) first putting in an appearance in 1972. And non-resident eurobond issues arrived even later, in 1977, with the market stagnating until 1984.

THE TRADITIONAL STRUCTURE OF FINANCIAL REGULATION IN JAPAN

In addition to the functional separation achieved by the use of law and administrative guidance, all financial intermediaries were burdened to a greater or lesser extent by a plethora of regulations affecting most aspects of their operations. As far as private depository institutions were concerned, such restrictions impinged, *inter alia*, on: their sources and uses of funds; the terms on which they could borrow and lend (that is, restrictions on yield, maturity and minimum denomination had to be observed, along with collateral requirements); the activities in which they could engage; their branching and merger activities; and their investment decisions in respect of holdings of other companies' stock (under the Anti-Monopoly Law of 1947). (See Suzuki, 1987, pp. 239–304 for a discussion of how private, non-depository financial intermediaries were affected.) In addition, the requirements of monetary policy necessitated the imposition of yet further restrictions in the form of reserve deposit requirements, credit ceilings on borrowing from the Bank of Japan, and lending (that is, 'window') 'guidance', both qualitative and quantitative. (These requirements are discussed in Chapter 7.) Once again, a mixture of legal requirements (such as banking law and Cabinet and ministerial ordinances which are used to enforce it) and moral suasion (in the guise of MoF circulars and administrative notices) were used to secure the authorities' objectives.

Apart from the prohibitions applied under the foreign exchange, securities and trust laws which have already been noted, the scope of (ordinary) private banks' domestic activities is determined by banking law, as interpreted by the Banking Bureau at the MoF. Under the current Banking Law of 1981, basic (that is, 'typical') banking business is defined as the taking of deposits or instalment savings, the lending of funds or discounting of bills, and funds transfer (Article 10: clause 1). In addition, ordinary banks are permitted to engage in 'ancillary' and 'peripheral' business (in the latter case, only through associated companies, which may also undertake some ancillary business, such as factoring, the provision of credit guarantees, and credit card and mortgage certificate business, and act as agents for the banks), and in 'permissible' securities (Article 11) and trust (Article 12) business. (For further details see Chapter 4.)

Apart from the rules governing the range of ordinary banks' permissible peripheral and ancillary business activities, there are also rules concerning the size of the equity stake that the parent bank may take in an associated company and the physical separation of the company's office from that of the parent bank. Accordingly, parental shareholdings must not exceed 5 per cent, and the company's office is not allowed to be located in the same building as the parent bank's office.

The range of permissible *securities* activities listed in Article 11 comprises various activities associated with the undertaking of business in government and other forms of bond. This includes both underwriting and the offering of bonds for subscription or sale. Notwithstanding this, however, banks must still obtain permission from the MoF to engage in such securities activities, in accordance with Article 65 of the Securities and Exchange Law (see Chapter 4). Apart from these activities, further activities in the securities field are sanctioned under Article 10 of the Banking Law under the heading of permissible ancillary business, as noted above.

Finally, banks are allowed to engage in *trust business* under the Law Concerning Concurrent Operation of Trust Business by Ordinary Banks of 1981 (previously, the Law Concerning Concurrent Operation of Savings Bank Business or Trust Business), in accordance with the Trust Business Law of 1992. They may also participate in mortgage debenture trust business, bond registration business and the lottery business in accordance with the Mortgage Debentures Trust Law, the Law for Registration of Corporate Debentures and the Law for Establishment of Certificates with Prizes, respectively.

Having established the allowable scope of banks' activities, it is also worthwhile to highlight the controls and restrictions imposed on banks' borrowing and lending terms in the early postwar period. The relevant piece of legislation at this time was the Temporary Interest Rate Adjustment Law (TIRAL) which superseded the deposit-rate accords operated by the regional banking associations (see Suzuki, 1987, pp. 40–41) in 1947. Under the TIRAL, which was designed to eliminate destructive interest-rate competition and to contribute towards the achievement of price stability, the Policy Board of the Bank of Japan, on the advice of the MoF, would set upper limits on interest rates for all private financial institutions, abolishing or changing them as deemed necessary. As far as *deposit rates* were concerned, ten types of deposit were initially distinguished, although this was reduced to four in 1970: current deposits (which yield no interest); term deposits; deposits for tax payment; and 'other' deposits. Even after this date, though, guidelines were still used by the Bank of Japan to control the rates paid on the other types of deposit (including savings accounts) previously distinguished (see Suzuki, 1987, p. 149). Since the mid- 1970s, however, the number of TIRAL-exempt (as determined by the MoF) deposit or deposit-like instruments (such as money market certificates) has increased to include, *inter alia*, certificates of deposit (CDs), non-resident yen deposits of foreign governments, foreign central banks and international institutions, and foreign-currency-denominated deposits; and rates have been gradually liberalized on TIRAL-affected instruments (see Chapter 3).

As for the *lending rates* of private financial institutions, the TIRAL prescribed maximum interest rates for loans of under one year to maturity and over ¥1 million made by commercial banks, trust banks, insurance companies and the Norinchukin Bank (the loan rates charged by *sogo* banks, *shinkin* banks and credit co-operatives were circumscribed by their founding laws). This set the upper limits for short-term lending rates for these institutions, although the *de facto* loan-rate ceilings, and the floors, were established according to agreed market practice. Despite the abolition of such anti-competitive market practices in 1975, increased *de facto* flexibility in the setting of loan rates did not materialize until the mid-1980s (see Chapter 3).

Although the private financial institutions' long-term loan rates (that is, of a maturity greater than one year) were not subject to the TIRAL nor determined according to formalized market arrangements, they were nevertheless subject to implicit rules agreed between interested parties, including the official authorities. Accordingly, the pre-1980 *de facto* floors for long-term loan rates were represented by the 'long-term prime rates' (that is, the rates charged to the highest-quality corporate customers) of the long-term credit banks and trust banks. Each institution would set its own prime lending rate at an agreed margin above these rates and changes would be synchronized and be of identical amounts. This system survived intact until the early 1980s since when the long-term prime rates of the long-term credit banks and trust banks have ceased to set the floor for the long-term loan rates of other private banks, and greater flexibility has been introduced into the determination of the latter. Moreover, 'effective' loan rates (nominal rates adjusted for the effects of compensating balances, which are deposited with the lender by the borrower as part of a long-term customer relationship) have converged on nominal loan rates as competitive pressures have forced down the level of compensating balances required either to meet contractual obligations (as in the case of *buzumi* or *ryodate* deposits) or to satisfy customary business relationships.

Another source of influence over lending terms is derived from the market practice of operating on the basis of collateralized transactions. As for most types of financial transaction in Japan, the provision of collateral was required in all lending transactions, with market practice being standardized in 1962. The internationalization of the money and capital markets in recent years, however, has brought about a reduction in the incidence and significance of collateral requirements with uncollateralized transactions, for example, now routinely taking place in the interbank market (see Suzuki, 1987, p. 116).

The final forms of control which impinged upon the private banks' borrowing and lending terms were the restrictions placed on the maturity and minimum size of denomination for certain types of deposit and deposit-like instruments. Maturity controls, for example, applied to time deposits (initially, they had to be of three months, six months, one year or two years' initial term), 'maturity-designated' time deposits (for a period of one year or more and under three years), certificates of deposit (CDs) (initially, for terms of over three months and under six months, although today the terms can vary from two weeks to five years) and money market certificates (MMCs) (initially, they could only be issued with maturities of between one and six months, but today maturities can range from one month to three years, matching those of time deposits). Similarly, minimum sizes of deposit were initially prescribed for time deposits (¥100), 'maturity-designated' time deposits (¥100, with a maximum of ¥3 million applying), CDs (¥500 million) and MMCs (¥50 million). And, finally, to qualify for the payment of 'freely determined' interest rates, large-scale time deposits had, at least initially, to be in excess of ¥1 billion.

NOTES

1. The 1950 Law Concerning Bond Issue by Banks, which permitted ordinary banks to issue financial debentures, was repealed in 1952 on enactment of the Long-Term Credit Bank Law.
2. This is still true today despite the 1981 revision to the law which repealed the sections relating to the operations of savings bank business and which resulted in the renaming of the law as the Law Concerning Joint Operation of Trust Business by Ordinary Banks.
3. The Specialized Foreign Exchange Bank, the Bank of Tokyo, lost its specialist identity (see Hall, 1993, ch. 3) when it merged with the Mitsubishi Bank to form the Tokyo–Mitsubishi Bank on 1 April 1996.
4. That is, special investment trusts, managed only by the trust banks, which represent funds which companies wish to invest in the stock market. Tax incentives induce companies to invest such funds through this medium.
5. For example, since July 1986 the trust banks have been allowed to invest up to 3 per cent (the previous limit was 1 per cent) of their loan assets in foreign bonds and, since August 1986, to invest up to 30 per cent (the previous limit was 25 per cent) of their pension fund assets in foreign-currency-denominated securities.
6. The *sogo* banks also used to specialize in this area but they lost their separate identities on conversion to ordinary banks by the end of 1989 (see Hall, 1993, ch. 3).

REFERENCES

Federation of Bankers' Associations of Japan (1989), *The Banking System in Japan*, Tokyo: FBAJ.

Federation of Bankers' Associations of Japan (1992), *Japanese Banks '92*, Tokyo: FBAJ.

Federation of Bankers' Associations of Japan (1997), *Japanese Banks '97*, Tokyo: FBAJ.

Hall, M.J.B. (1993), *Banking Regulation and Supervision: A Comparative Study of the UK, USA and Japan*, Aldershot, UK and Brookfield, US: Edward Elgar.

Japan Centre for International Finance (JCIF) (1988), 'The past and present of the deregulation and internationalisation of the Tokyo money and capital market', *JCIF Policy Study Series*, No. 10, Tokyo.

Suzuki, Y. (ed.) (1987), *The Japanese Financial System*, Oxford: Clarendon Press.

2. Pressures for reform

PRESSURES WHICH EMERGED DURING THE 1970s AND 1980s

Internal Pressures

In the aftermath of the first oil-price shock of 1973, the Japanese economy underwent important structural change which radically transformed the domestic financial scene. This duly led to internal demands for deregulation at home which would not only improve the efficiency of domestic markets but also end their isolation from the rest of the world.

The structural change alluded to above, which was brought about largely by the impact of higher oil prices on inflation and economic growth – both were adversely affected – resulted in significant changes in the financial positions of the different sectors of the economy. Specifically, the public sector deficit increased, along with the personal sector surplus, while the corporate sector's deficit began to decline. The impact of these changes in the sectoral flow of funds on the financial system was dramatic.

The deterioration in public sector finances,[1] caused by the slowdown in economic activity and a loosening of the fiscal reins, created pressures both for reform of the primary market for government bonds and for expansion of the secondary market. The operating practices in the primary market were put under strain because of the sheer increase in the volume of bonds which the underwriting syndicate (comprising mainly banks but also other financial institutions) was being asked to absorb (see pp. 101–4 and 112 for further details on the operation of the syndicate). Resale in the marketplace was prohibited until 1977 and, in any case, would have resulted in capital losses being incurred because of the low yields paid on the bonds. As the syndicate members were obliged to hold the bonds for a minimum period of one year, after which, in general, the Bank of Japan would purchase them, the burgeoning budget deficits posed funding problems for the banks (being 'overlent', they would have to turn to the Bank of Japan for further advances) and threatened to reduce their profitability by virtue of the enforced increase in the proportion of their investment portfolio held in low-yielding form. Thus, although the operating practices in the primary market had served the purposes of the government well in the past, by minimizing debt-servicing costs, the government began to realize that the post-1974 situation would require modification to existing market procedures. In particular, the funding (that is, cash reserve) burden on the banks, as the main syndicate members, would have to be alleviated by making issues direct to the general public and non-bank financial intermediaries)[2] and/or by allowing banks to sell on to the general public. Both measures would help to reduce the adverse impact on bank profitability which would otherwise result, a goal which would also be served by paying market-related interest rates on the bonds. Indeed, without this the desired secondary market expansion would not occur, as insufficient incentives would be provided to prospective purchasers to guarantee the required non-bank take-up of government stock. We can see, then, that the authorities' desire to finance the burgeoning budget deficits in a non-monetary fashion (control of the money supply came to the fore in 1974) and to protect the banking system from the adverse consequences that would otherwise result, led to a diversification in the types and methods of bond flotation, and this in turn stimulated the development of the secondary market. The concomitant freeing up of long-term yields acted, in turn, to promote expansion in the short-term open markets and to increase pressure on the authorities to relax, if not abolish, interest-rate controls. While the latter, reinforced by extensive administrative guidance, had served the real economy well in the past (for example, by promoting economic growth through industrialization and by stabilizing the financial system), albeit at the expense of a loss of efficiency, a new dawn had arrived. Somewhat belatedly, perhaps, but nevertheless quite unashamedly, officialdom began to champion the cause of efficient markets and institutions, and of equity in regulation, and competition was actively promoted. Moreover, the internationalization of the Japanese financial system was adopted as a clear policy objective.

The needs and demands of the corporate and private sectors were also important in shaping the reform debate. The slowdown in economic activity and general uncertainty following the first oil-price shock caused industry to curtail investment dramatically. This, in turn, substantially reduced their demand for bank credit, a situation in keeping with their desire to reduce dependence on the banking sector for external funding. Indeed, it was this desire which led the corporations to demand greater access to the money and capital markets. This, in turn, would necessitate a widening and deepening of domestic markets and the dismantling of barriers denying entry to overseas markets. Such demands for wider access to alternative sources of funds went hand in hand with a search for higher real returns as corporate financial management gained in sophistication (the so-called *zaiteck* phenomenon). All these demands duly increased the pressure on the government to deregulate domestic markets and interest rates and to internationalize the Japanese financial system.

The personal sector, too, added its weight to demands for reform. Its chief concern was the acceleration in inflation following the oil-price hike and the explosion in monetary growth during 1972 and 1973, which had sharply reduced real rates of return on savings and cut real income growth. This duly led the sector to seek investment outlets offering higher real returns, especially in the light of the absence of any government-financed retirement scheme. Lower product/service charges and greater choice would also have been welcomed. In terms of political muscle, however, it is probably fair to say that the consumer lobby carried little weight at that time.

This was certainly not the case with the banks and other financial institutions, however. The banking lobby, in particular, was in full swing following the fall-off in corporate loan demand and the loss of depositors to institutions (such as the Post Office) and instruments offering higher real returns. Naturally enough, such a state of affairs led banks to demand liberalization of their deposit (and lending) rates, removal of maturity restrictions on their deposits and the power to offer new instruments on which they could pay competitive rates. They also sought the ability to diversify their customer base, which would require, *inter alia*, removal of constraints on domestic activities for some and on foreign activities for all, and additional freedoms to allow them to improve risk management. For the banks, the latter freedom was particularly important because of the maturity mismatch forced upon them by the rigid separation of short-term from long-term finance (at least in respect of borrowing operations). But new hedging and funding opportunities would have been welcomed by all indigenous intermediaries operating in Japan at that time, along with the opportunity to operate overseas in order to diversify away portfolio risk and to maximize risk-adjusted portfolio returns.

By the late 1970s, as a result of a full appreciation of the new economic realities and under growing pressure from all sections of society at home (the pressure from overseas is considered below), the Japanese government had clearly accepted the need for wide-scale deregulation and internationalization. From this time, as is explained below, the process of reform accelerated, a policy by then in keeping with the monetary authorities' wishes. For despite the risk of destabilizing the financial system, particularly in the adjustment phase, the funding problems created by the burgeoning budget deficits, the monetary management problems caused by a more liquid corporate sector and the growth of unregulated non-bank financial intermediaries, together with the need to deepen the foreign exchange market, all necessitated reform.[3] And, on top of these pressures, demands from overseas were reaching a crescendo.

External Pressures

Apart from the 1973–74 oil-price shock which, because of Japan's almost total reliance on imported fuel, did so much to transform the domestic economy and end the isolation of Japan's financial system from the developed world's capital markets, external pressure for reform materialized in the shape of overseas governmental demands for the liberalization and internationalization of the Japanese financial system and for reciprocity in the treatment of overseas financial intermediaries.

The US government was the standard-bearer on both fronts, campaigning vociferously on behalf of the world economy and its own financial institutions, although EC governments – notably West Germany and the United Kingdom[4] – were active on the second front. Leaving aside the issue of reciprocity for the time being, the gist of the US government's argument was that the use of the yen as a reserve currency and in trade and international finance was not commensurate with Japan's position in the global economy (that is, as an important trading nation with huge balance of payments surpluses, and as a large net capital exporter). The hope of the US government was, of course, that if they forced a speedier deregulation of domestic markets on the Japanese government and made them open up their financial system to the outside world, the value of the yen would appreciate, thereby reducing some of their trading surpluses (particularly in manufacturing) with the rest of the world. Unfortunately for the USA, the strength of capital flows won the day as far as the yen was concerned, with large net outflows going to the USA, in part because of the higher interest rates available there.

The demands for reform, arising essentially from trade friction,[5] were formalized in bilateral meetings between the governments of the USA and Japan within the forum of the Joint Japan–US *Ad Hoc* Group on Yen–Dollar Exchange Rate, Financial and Capital Market Issues (henceforth termed the 'Joint Group'), which comprised representatives from the Ministry of Finance of Japan and the US Department of the Treasury. The first evidence of the progress made in these discussions materialized with the publication of the Joint Group's first report in May 1984. This report set out the agreement reached on how Japan should deregulate its financial system and internationalize the yen. The discussion was compartmentalized into the measures required to deregulate Japan's money and capital markets, the requirements needed to ensure 'national treatment reciprocity' for overseas financial intermediaries (that is, the treatment of foreign institutions as domestic intermediaries in respect of their activities in Japan) and the measures to be taken to ensure internationalization of the yen through expansion of the euroyen market. On the first front, the Japanese agreed to remove interest-rate ceilings on 'large' time deposits within three years; on the second, they agreed to allow foreign banks into the trust banking industry; and, on the last, they agreed to relax controls on euroyen lending, eliminate the 'real demand' rule in forward exchange transactions and remove the limits on the banks' 'oversold' spot foreign exchange positions (see Suzuki, 1987, pp. 130–31).

The rationale underlying the Japanese government's general approach to financial deregulation and internationalization of the yen was spelt out in an MoF report which accompanied the publication of the Joint Group report in May 1984. This report, entitled *Present Status and Prospects for the Deregulation of Finance and Internationalization of the Yen*, was followed by a further report, *The Internationalization of the Yen*, which was published in March 1985 and set out the various steps necessary to secure such an objective. And in June 1987 yet another MoF report, *Current Plans for the Liberalization and Internationalization of Japanese Financial and Capital Markets*, was published, setting out the Ministry's latest plans for reform. These comprised: further deregulation of interest rates; expansion of the short-term money market; consolidation and expansion of the futures market; consolidation of the capital market; more freedom and flexibility for financial intermediaries in the conduct of their business; international co-ordination on the supervision of banks and assessment of their capital adequacy; examination of the issues relating to the interpenetration of business by financial intermediaries; and improving the access of foreign financial intermediaries to the securities market.

The reform measures instituted and the drafting of blueprints for reform went some way to placating antagonistic foreign governments in the second half of the 1980s; yet discord remained. This was largely due to the pace, rather than substance, of reform, with concomitant implications for the reciprocity problem. Thus, for example, although foreign banks were admitted to the trust banking industry in 1985, the speed with which foreign firms were being admitted to the Tokyo Stock Exchange ensured consternation on both sides of the Atlantic. Moreover, the US Treasury's national treatment studies served only to highlight the competitive disadvantages faced by foreign firms trying to break into the Japanese marketplace.[6] While acknowledging the formidable cultural and customary barriers facing foreign institutions attempting to establish market share, the US government was keen to ensure that success would not be stymied by regulatory inequities. Accordingly, pressure was brought to bear to remove or reduce tangible barriers to entry and to reduce regulatory disparities by, for example, pushing for a fully developed interbank market (without it, foreign banks, because of their lack of a branch network and hence access to low-cost retail deposits, would be disadvantaged) and for greater access for foreign banks to the Bank of Japan's discount window.

Despite the moves made by the Japanese government to accommodate the demands of foreign governments (the Joint Group was dissolved in April

1988), not everybody in the latter camp was satisfied. In the USA, this dissatisfaction manifested itself in the Riegle–Garn Bill, which threatened retaliation if national treatment reciprocity and effective market access were not perceived to have been given to US institutions operating abroad. Although aborted in October 1990, and in spite of the Federal Reserve's continued opposition to its implementation, the strength of feeling in Congress at the adoption of what was perceived to be deliberate delaying tactics by the Japanese government remained sufficiently strong to ensure that the resurrection of the Bill and its subsequent enaction could not be ruled out. And the vigilance of EC governments and commissioners, especially after the completion of the Single Market in financial services in 1992, continued to ensure that pressure from this side of the globe for national treatment reciprocity (including effective market access) was not relaxed.

THE REFORM PRESSURES OF THE 1990s

Apart from a continuation of the internal and external pressures which emerged during the previous two decades, a number of additional considerations helped to shape the reform debate. Those of major import comprise the rationale behind the 'big bang' programme of reforms (see Chapter 4), the needs of the banking sector, which was experiencing acute difficulties after the bursting of the local asset 'bubble', the need to address apparent weaknesses in external supervision, and the need to address concerns aroused by financial 'scandals'. Each of these is addressed in turn below, but first it is worth noting the continued pressure exerted by the US government and other outside bodies.

Continued External Pressure

Emboldened by the earlier success of the Joint Group initiative, the US government continued to pressurize their Japanese counterparts into yet further liberalization. In December 1994, the Japanese authorities indicated their willingness to meet US demands to open up the management of *public* pension funds to foreign concerns, via investment advisory companies (the private pension fund market had been opened up via the same route in 1990, but foreign firms had met with little success because of business practices based on long-term relationships). At that time the market was the preserve of life companies and trust banks. Then, in January 1995, both sides announced agreement on reforms which would provide foreign firms with greater access to the pension fund, mutual fund, and corporate bond markets. Specifically, the Japanese government pledged to:

- allow foreign investment advisory companies to manage Japanese *public* pension funds through 'limited partnerships' with local trust banks and life companies;
- allow foreign firms to manage *corporate* pension funds through their investment advisory companies;
- ease the restrictions on foreign management of Japanese funds (for example, the 30 per cent limit imposed on equity investment by individual foreign fund managers hired by Japanese funds will be relaxed);
- relax the strict demarcation drawn between investment advisory business and investment trust (that is, mutual funds) business, to make the latter more accessible to foreigners (at that time, investment management operations had to be physically separated from investment trust business, the latter requiring a minimum capital commitment of $3 million);
- consider the introduction of new financial products, such as derivatives;
- examine the operations of the corporate bond market with a view to facilitating greater use by foreigners.

The readiness of the Japanese to accede to the US demands on these fronts can be explained, in part, by their desire to import foreign expertise and to raise the returns on pension fund investments.

In February 1996 the US and Japanese negotiators met again to review the progress made in implementing the January 1995 agreement. The US side were generally pleased at the progress made, although they pressed for further disclosure of information by financial institutions. The Japanese government, in turn, announced plans for the establishment of an asset-backed securities market, the development of which would facilitate the disposal of bad loans by banks. The US side warmly welcomed this development, not least because of the likely business opportunities that would arise for US firms already well versed in such market operations.

Liberalization of the Japanese insurance market proved somewhat more troublesome. Revision to the Japanese Insurance Law in April 1996 abolished, in principle, the strict demarcation hitherto maintained between life and non-life business, including the 'third sector' ('first-sector' business comprised life assurance and endowment policies, 'second-sector' business comprised car and fire insurance policies and 'third-sector' business comprised personal accident, travel and health care policies), although no cross-industry moves (via subsidiaries) had been approved by the MoF by June 1996. The reforms also allowed insurance brokers to participate in the insurance market (for example via the provision of risk management services and advice on which are the best policies to buy, and the direct intermediation of insurance contracts). The problem which exercised the negotiators' minds, however, was how to deregulate the market without damaging the prospects of those foreign firms already active in Japan. As foreigners had been most successful in the 'third sector', the US side wanted a moratorium imposed before the major life companies were allowed into this business. Moreover, they wanted greater foreign access to the car insurance market, with mail order and telephone marketing techniques being allowed. The Japanese, however, wanted to concentrate reform in the early days in the third sector, rather than the first and second sectors which accounted for the bulk of insurance business.

In the event, a compromise was reached whereby, in December 1996, the Japanese government announced that it would delay entry of Japanese life insurance companies into 'third-sector' business until January 1997, with some protection being given to existing foreign operators. Mail order sale of insurance products was sanctioned immediately and deregulation of *non-life* premiums was promised for July 1997. Further liberalization in the industry would take place in the year 2001.

The only other event worth noting on the insurance industry front was the permission given to Lloyd's of London to sell non-life policies in Japan, with effect from 1 April 1997. Prior to this date, their activities would continue to be confined to reinsurance business.

With the switch in focus of the US–Japan trade talks in the middle of 1997 to issues related to Japan's current account surplus – the US team wanted a reduction to be brought about by an appreciation of the yen and an expansion of demand, neither of which were subsequently met to any appreciable degree until the spring of 1998 – the pressure for further financial deregulation came from the World Trade Organization. The 1986–93 Uruguay Round of negotiations had failed to secure a global pact on financial services liberalization but, in July 1997, the Japanese government increased the chances of future success by promising to lift permanently all restraints on foreign companies operating in Japan's financial services market. This would be achieved through, *inter alia*, abolishing the remaining exchange controls and breaking down the 'segmentation' barriers still operating in Japan.

The Rationale for Japan's 'Big Bang'

Despite the liberalizing measures introduced under the Financial System Reform Law of April 1993, which allowed for cross-sectoral entry – albeit through subsidiaries – between ordinary banks, trust banks and securities business (see Chapter 4), the reform which ensued is widely regarded as being 'too little, too late'. Such views have been given added credence by the continuing problems faced by local financial institutions trying to 'resolve' their bad loans in the face of the collapse of Japan's asset 'bubble' (see Yamawaki, 1996) and by the apparent continuing decline in the international competitiveness of Japan's financial intermediaries. Additionally, it was widely felt that not enough had been done to enhance potential benefits for the 'users' of the financial system, to increase the 'efficiency' of financial operations or to 'internationalize' the Japanese financial system. Accordingly, the latest package of proposals is designed to maintain Japan's economic vitality in the twenty-first century by reforming the financial system in a way that will support Japan's economy in the face of a dramatic ageing of the population. Apart from handling such demographic change, the reforms are also designed to accommodate the dual processes of globalization and innovation, and the latest advances in information and telecommunication technologies.

More specifically, the reforms are designed to:

- prevent the hollowing out of Japan's financial markets;[7]
- enhance the international competitiveness of Japan's financial intermediaries;[8]
- enhance the status of the yen as an international currency;
- smooth the flow of capital between Japan and foreign countries;
- facilitate the flow of funds to indigenous growth industries;
- increase 'efficiency' (that is, seek to achieve an optimal allocation of resources via the use, to the fullest extent possible, of the market mechanism – in other words, via the creation of a 'free' marketplace);
- increase the transparency and reliability of markets (that is, create a 'fair' marketplace); and
- maximize 'user' benefits (in the form of investment returns, choice of products, quality of service provision, and so on).

Finally, in order to preserve financial stability in the face of such major reforms, measures were also proposed to promote the sound management of financial institutions and a reduction in settlement risk (for full details see Chapter 4).

The Needs of the Banking Sector

Apart from the fundamental problems afflicting the whole of the Japanese financial system, which 'big bang' is designed, in part, to address, the banking sector has also suffered from a range of debilitating problems which are more specific to its own operations. These problems include the following: continuing weakness in the property market, which hinders bad-debt recovery; continuing weakness in the local stock market, which erodes capital strength, dampens profits recovery and reduces capacity to write off bad debts; a weakening domestic economy, which holds back banks' 'recovery' through its dampening effect on loan demand and profits and its adverse effect on corporate bankruptcies; a national fiscal crisis, which severely limits the government's scope for engineering an economic recovery given the recent easing of monetary policy, which has seen the official discount rate fall to a historic low of 0.5 per cent per annum; an export 'boom', which threatens renewed trade friction with the USA at a time when South East Asian markets are proving difficult because of the currency and financial crises which hit their economies during the latter half of 1997; substantial excess capacity in the finance industry, which, to date, has been slow to diminish, mainly because of the slow pace of financial deregulation and the authorities' 'safety net' policies; very low profitability, recovery from which is threatened by deregulation and the failure to remove the competitive advantages conferred on the postal savings system; and higher deposit insurance levies and contributions to rescue packages (to help fund 'failure resolution' policies), which further weaken balance sheets. These issues are examined in more depth below.

The bad-debt mountain
Since the bursting of the asset price 'bubble' – notably for property and stocks – in the late 1980s to early 1990s, the Japanese banking sector has been languishing under a huge burden of 'bad' debts caused by its direct and indirect (via collateral taken) exposures to said markets. While substantial inroads have been made into provisioning against and writing off the debt mountain, much remains to be done.

Attempts to identify the scale of the problem and to chart the banks' efforts to dispose of their bad debts are hampered by lack of disclosure and frequent changes in the definition of 'bad' loans. For example, the first official estimate (for end March 1992) of the scale of 'non-performing loans' affecting the (21) major banks was not produced until October 1992, banks only being obliged to disclose such figures from end March 1993. Coverage of the data was duly extended to embrace (in principle) all Japanese deposit-taking financial intermediaries – that is, city banks, long-term credit banks, trust banks, regional banks and co-operatives – in September 1995. As for the definition of 'non-performing loans', the early disclosures only included claims (net of the estimated value of collateral backing the loans) against customers in legal bankruptcy and claims on which interest payments were more than six months overdue, due to the suspension of interest payments. This meant 'restructured loans', that is, loans on which interest payments had been cut, and the bad debts of affiliates did not feature in the figures. However, 'restructured loans', defined as loans on which interest rates have been reduced to below the ruling official discount rate, in an effort to reassure

Exhibit 2.1 'Bad' loans of the Japanese banking sector: 1992–97

Date	'Bad' loans outstanding (¥ billion)	Estimate of 'problem loans to be disposed of'[1]
End March 1992	7 000–8 000[2]	–
End March 1993	8 400[2]	–
End March 1994	10 500[2]	–
End September 1994	13 300[2]	–
End March 1995	11 640[2]	–
End September 1995	38 086[3]	18 587[4]
End March 1996	34 799[5,6]	8 305[5]
End September 1996	29 228[7,8]	7 303[7]
End March 1997	27 900[9,10]	4 685[9]
End September 1997	28 078[11,12]	4 348[11]

Notes:

[1] This figure represents an estimate by the Ministry of Finance of the scale of loans for which possible losses have not been provided for nor which are likely to be covered by collateral (i.e. loan losses which are considered 'irrecoverable' and which have not been provided for).

[2] Ministry of Finance estimate of 'non-performing loans' for the 21 largest banks. Figures include claims against customers who went 'bankrupt' and claims on which interest payments were more than six months overdue due to the suspension of interest payments – but *exclude* 'restructured loans' (i.e. those on which interest payments have been cut) and the bad debts of affiliates.

[3] Figures include 'restructured loans' (i.e. loans on which interest rates have been reduced to below the ruling official discount rate) for the first time and now cover all Japanese deposit-taking financial institutions (i.e. city banks, long-term credit banks, trust banks, regional banks and co-operatives).

[4] The figure is *inclusive* of possible losses (estimated at ¥7700 billion) resulting from exposure to the eight *jusen* companies.

[5] The figures *exclude* the Kizu Credit Co-operative (with about ¥1190 billion problem loans), the Fukui Prefecture First Credit Co-operative (¥2.6 billion), the Osaka Credit Co-operative (¥270 billion) and Taiheiyo Bank (¥330 billion).

[6] The figure *excludes* loans to borrowers to which the lending bank(s) is extending help (including forgiving loans) – estimated at ¥3795 billion for all 'major' banks (i.e. excluding regional banks and co-operatives) at end March 1996.

[7] Loans to *jusen* companies are *excluded*, as are the Kizu Credit Co-operative (with approximately ¥1190 billion problem loans), the Osaka Credit Co-operative (¥270 billion), the Kenmindaiwa Credit Co-operative (¥15 billion) and Sanyo Credit Co-operatives (¥17 billion).

[8] The figure *excludes* loans to borrowers to which the lending bank is extending help (including forgiving loans) – estimated at ¥3724 billion for all 'major' banks (i.e. excluding regional banks and co-operatives) at end September 1996.

[9] The figures *exclude* the Hanwa Bank (with around ¥190 billion problem loans), the Sanpuku Credit Co-operative (¥26 billion) and the Hanshin Labour Credit Co-operative (¥3.5 billion).

[10] The figure *excludes* loans to borrowers to which the lending bank(s) is extending help (including forgiving loans) – estimated at ¥3373 billion at end March 1997 for all 'major' banks (i.e. excluding co-operatives but *including* regional banks for the first time).

11 The figures *exclude* the Hokkaido Takushoku Bank, Hanwa Bank, Hanshin Labour Credit Co-operative, Toki Credit Co-operative, Tokai Credit Co-operative, Kitakyushu Credit Co-operative, Kanagawa Credit Co-operative, Tanabe Credit Co-operative and the Choginosaka Credit Co-operative.

12 The figure *excludes* loans to borrowers to which the lending bank(s) is extending help, estimated at ¥3084 billion at end September 1997 for all major banks.

Sources: Ministry of Finance (1995a, 1996a, 1996b, 1997a, 1997c).

(foreign) investors about the health of the banking sector, began to feature in the (collective) data in September 1995, although individual banks were not required to make such public disclosure until end March 1996; and from April 1996, the definition of 'restructured' was widened to include all loans with which borrowers were receiving assistance. Also from April 1996, estimates were provided of the volume of loans outstanding to borrowers to which the lending bank(s) is extending help, including the forgiveness of loans. These changes substantially improved the 'transparency' of reporting, although it wasn't until April 1998 (when new 'rules' came into force requiring banks to assess bad debts more realistically by, for example, including loans on which interest has not been paid for *three* [previously six] months or longer together with a much wider range of 'restructured' loans within the figures reported for non-performing loans, and to set aside reserves for newly-discovered problem loans immediately, that is, without seeking MoF 'clearance') that a more reliable estimate of outstanding problem loans emerged.[9] Undisclosed contingent exposures arising from main bank and *keiretsu* relationships, however, remain a continuing source of concern, as does the decision to allow banks, with effect from end March 1998, to value their securities holdings using either the traditional 'lower of cost or market valuation' convention or 'acquisition cost'. The emergency measure, designed to reduce the pressure on banks' balance sheets by providing them with the means to avoid posting appraisal losses at the end of the financial year because of the fall in stock market prices (the extent of the latent losses, however, must still be revealed in the accounts) has, however, backfired on the authorities. This is because a number of banks have continued to use the 'old' valuation convention, for fear of being accused of attempting to mislead investors, while others have opted to include both methodologies in their published accounts. Finally (the list of 'restructured banks' excluded also differs from year to year), as Exhibit 2.1 indicates, the picture has, in the past, been clouded by the banks' loan exposures to the *jusen* (housing loan) companies, which only dropped out of the figures in September 1996 on resolution of the *jusen* 'crisis' (see below), which involved the affected banks collectively transferring ¥3687 billion to 'special accounts for loan loss write-offs' by end March 1996 and abandoning ¥614 billion of such loans outstanding.

Notwithstanding these difficulties, it was possible to discern a trend decline in banks' (disclosed) bad loans in recent years – see Exhibit 2.1. Based
upon the figures disclosed by city banks, long-term credit banks and trust
banks, bad loans for the industry as a whole appeared to have peaked at end
September 1994 although, as noted earlier, 'restructured' loans did not feature in the data. Since figures have been disclosed for the whole of the
banking industry (that is, since November 1995, following the MoF's detailed examination of banks' bad debts, including restructured loans (see
Exhibit 2.2), during the autumn of 1995), the total of bad loans outstanding
fell from around ¥38 trillion at end September 1995 to just over ¥28 trillion at
end September 1997. This represented a fall from just over 5 per cent of total
loans to under 4 per cent of total loans. Perhaps of more significance are the
figures representing estimates of irrecoverable and unprovided-for loans – the
'problems loans to be disposed of' – which fell from around ¥18.6 trillion to
just over ¥4.3 trillion over the same time period, the fastest annual drop
occurring during the 1995/96 financial year as a result of the resolution of the
jusen crisis (see Exhibit 2.1).

The overall figures, however, masked significant differences between industry types (city banks, long-term credit banks, trust banks, and so on) and,
within each grouping, between individual institutions. When statistics were
first published by industry grouping (for the period ending end September
1995), the overall figure of 5.4 per cent (for the proportion of total loans
classified as 'bad') contrasted with figures of 4.9 per cent, 7.3 per cent, 10.2
per cent, 3.7 per cent, 5.5 per cent and 5 per cent for the city banks, long-term
credit banks, trust banks, regional banks, second-tier regional banks and the
co-operative groupings, respectively (see Exhibit 2.3). Clearly, the trust banks
faced the greatest problems at the time. By end March 1997 the respective
figures for the industry groupings were 3.6 per cent, 5.4 per cent, 6.0 per cent,
2.4 per cent, 3.8 per cent and 4.8 per cent, compared with the overall figure of
3.9 per cent. Clearly, the trust banks had done most, in absolute terms, to
tackle the burden of the debt mountain, although, in relative terms, they
remained the worst performers.

At the individual level, even larger disparities exist. With the approval of
the MoF, Sumitomo Bank become the first Japanese bank ever to report a loss
– of ¥335 billion at end March 1995 – largely because of a substantial
increase in provisions (from ¥500 billion to ¥800 billion) against bad loans.
Such aggressive provisioning was trumped by the Bank of Tokyo–Mitsubishi
(BTM) which announced in September 1997 that it would, in one fell swoop,
dispose of its entire non-performing loan problem by making provisions of
¥1.4 trillion to fully cover its declared bad loans of ¥1.27 trillion. The move
was expected to result in a net loss of ¥750 billion being recorded for fiscal
1997 although, in the event, a pre-tax loss of ¥918 billion (¥524 billion if

Exhibit 2.2 'Bad' loans of Japanese banks by industry grouping: 1995–1997 (¥ billion)

Category of bank	As at end September 1995			As at end September 1996[6]				As at end September 1997			
	'Bankrupt'[1] or 'past due'[2] loans	'Restructured'[3] loans	Total 'bad' loans	Bankrupt loans	Past due loans	Restructured loans	Total bad loans	Bankrupt loans	Past due loans	Restructured loans	Total bad loans
City banks	8 102	5 455	13 557	2 023	5 977	2 951	10 951	2 411	5 693	1 378	9 483
Long-term credit banks	2 116	1 855	3 970	359	1 956	407	2 721	824	1 826	165	2 815
Trust banks	2 797	3 505	6 301	589	2 236	916	3 741	968	2 142	721	3 831
Regional banks	3 348	1 628	4 976	991	1 844	562	3 397	1 272	1 910	333	3 515
Second-tier regional banks	2 202	621	2 822	702	1 186	297	2 185	789	1 069	229	2 087
Co-operatives[4]	6 124	335	6 459	1 735	4 254	244	6 233	2 132	4 049	167	6 348
All banks	24 688[5]	13 398[5]	38 086[5]	6 399[7]	17 453[7]	5 376[7]	29 228[7]	8 396[8]	16 689[8]	2 993[8]	28 078[8]

Notes:

1 Claims against customers who went 'bankrupt' (i.e. who have undergone business failure, including bankruptcy, liquidation, reorganization, etc.).
2 Claims on which interest payments were more than 6 months overdue due to suspension of interest payments.
3 Claims against customers whose interest payments had been reduced to below the official discount rate or deferred.
4 Includes: *shinkin* banks, credit co-operatives, labour credit associations, the Shokochukin Bank, the Norinchukin Bank and credit federations of agricultural co-operatives.
5 Excludes the Cosmo Credit Co-operative (¥380 billion problem loans), Kizu Credit Co-operative (¥1190 billion) and the Hyogo Bank (¥1500 billion).
6 All loans to *jusen* companies are *excluded*. Under the 'resolution' package agreed by the Diet in June 1996, by September 1996 the 'founding' banks had to write off ¥3.5 billion of losses, other banks ¥1.17 trillion and agricultural bodies ¥530 billion.
7 Excludes the Kizu Credit Co-operative (with ¥1190 billion problem loans), the Osaka Credit Co-operative (¥270 billion), the Kenmindaiwa Credit Co-operative (¥15 billion) and the Sanyo Credit Co-operatives (¥17 billion).
8 Excludes the Hokkaido Takushoku Bank, Hanwa Bank, Hanshin Labour Credit Co-operative, Toki Credit Cooperative, Takai Credit Co-operative, Kitakyushu Credit Co-operative, Kanagowa Credit Co-operative, Tanabe Credit Co-operative and the Choginosaka Credit Co-operative.

Sources: MoF (1995a, 1996a, 1996b, 1997c).

Exhibit 2.3   Other balance sheet trends for Japanese banks: total assets, loans and bad loans: 1995–97 (¥ billion)

Category of bank	Total assets				Total loans				Total bad loans			
	End Sept. 1995	End Mar. 1996	End Sept. 1996	End Mar. 1997	End Sept. 1995	End Mar. 1996	End Sept. 1996	End Mar. 1997	End Sept. 1995	End Mar. 1996	End Sept. 1996	End Mar. 1997
City banks	433 213	428 031	445 423	441 879	275 741	278 052	277 055	284 369	13 557	12 418	10 951	10 121
Long-term credit banks	87 329	83 798	85 005	87 261	54 529	52 654	51 462	52 655	3 970	3 433	2 721	2 836
Trust banks	250 755	245 360	284 904	246 134	61 480	61 147	58 285	58 291	6 301	6 017	3 741	3 483
Regional banks	200 223	201 664	199 686	201 041	133 943	137 084	135 061	137 344	4 976	4 227	3 397	3 336
Second-tier regional banks	68 844	70 165	70 357	69 917	51 038	52 594	52 585	52 948	2 822	2 409	2 185	2 012
Co-operatives	263 891	259 279	260 291	260 606	129 106	131 211	129 934	128 536	6 459	6 295	6 233	6 110
All banks	1 304 255	1 288 296	1 345 666	1 306 838	705 838	712 741	704 382	714 142	38 086	34 799	29 288	27 900

Notes:
Data for end September 1995, end September 1996 and end March 1997 exclude certain institutions – see Exhibit 2.1.
Data for end March 1996 exclude the Kizu Co-operative (with ¥190 billion problem loans), the Fukui Prefecture First Credit Co-operative (¥2.6 billion), the Osaka Credit Co-operative (¥270 billion) and the Taiheiyo Bank (¥300 billion).

Sources: MoF (1995a, 1956a, 1996b, 1997a).

34

overseas operations are included) was reported. Similar action was taken by its subsidiary, Nippon Trust Bank, which set aside ¥200 billion to cover all of its non-performing loans although, in this case, a profit for fiscal 1997 was still anticipated because of BTM's willingness to make a special payment of ¥100 billion to Nippon Trust and to purchase its stock. Such action, in turn, provoked Sumitomo Bank to respond by announcing in October 1997 that it, too, would make provisions (of ¥800 billion) in fiscal 1997 to dispose of its problem loans. (In the event, ¥1.04 trillion of provisions were made for fiscal 1997 helping push consolidated [that is, including overseas operations] pre-tax losses up to ¥502.7 billion.) Those with weaker balance sheets will be unable to match such moves, further distancing the 'weak' from the 'strong' and thus polarizing the industry.

Despite the gallant attempts by many institutions to put their bad debt problems behind them, the new disclosure rules introduced this year, the deterioration in the economies of South East Asia and the sharp fall in the local stock market (although the Nikkei 225 index traded around the 18 000 level for the first half of fiscal 1997, it ended the year below the 15 000 level, around which it hovers today) during fiscal 1997 all combined to thwart their good intentions. Thus, despite making collective bad debt disposals of about ¥10.7 trillion and recording a collective pre-tax parent loss of around ¥4.55 trillion, the top 18 banks still face an uphill battle to dispose of their remaining bad debts, now estimated at ¥22 trillion, during the next few years. Of particular concern is their exposure to Asia, with estimates of non-performing loans ranging from ¥3 trillion to ¥6 trillion, up to half of which may necessitate a total write-off. While such numbers pale into insignificance when set aside the corresponding figures for *domestic* bad debt exposures, they represent more than an irritant to those banks which thought they had finally dealt with their bad debt problems. For those with weaker balance sheets, the light at the end of the tunnel, if it ever manifests itself, is not likely to be seen for a number of years yet.

A weak macro-economy

The current weakness of the real economy and general shape of the macro-economy in Japan are major sources of concern for the banking industry. Since bottoming out in October 1993, the economy began slowly to recover (see Appendix, Chart 2.1). However, the Great Hanshin-Awaji earthquake of January 1995, the rapid appreciation of the yen after March 1995 and the slowdown in the US economy threatened to stifle recovery through fiscal 1995. Notwithstanding these adverse developments, however, the official forecast for real GDP growth during fiscal 1995 was put at 1.2 per cent in January 1996 (Ministry of Finance, 1996c), with real growth of 2.5 per cent forecast for fiscal 1996. The government was looking to the private sector, helped by modest tax cuts, to lead the recovery, with the current account surplus forecast to shrink in the wake of the yen's appreciation (Ministry of Finance, 1995b).

In December 1996 (Ministry of Finance, 1996d), and following recorded real growth of 1.2 per cent during fiscal 1995, the forecast ('target'?) for real GDP growth for fiscal 1996 was confirmed at 2.5 per cent. As for fiscal 1997, real GDP growth of 1.9 per cent was forecast, despite plans to raise the rate of consumption tax from 3 per cent to 5 per cent on 1 April 1997, to limit the increase in expenditure on public works programmes to 1.3 per cent, and to end the temporary reductions given in the two previous years in income tax and local inhabitants' tax (Ministry of Finance, 1996e). Again, the government was looking to the private sector to maintain recovery because of the parlous state of the public finances, with public debt outstanding expected to amount to ¥241 trillion by the end of fiscal 1996. (At the end of fiscal 1995 it represented 81.3 per cent of GDP, while the ratio of the budget deficit to GDP stood at 3.9 per cent, both figures well above the EMU 'convergence criteria' of 60 per cent and 3 per cent respectively; see Chart 2.2.) Although a slowdown was anticipated during the first half of fiscal 1997, mainly because of the higher consumption tax rate, a rebound was confidently forecast in the second half, due to the structural economic reforms and deregulation undertaken. A continuing, slow decline in the current account surplus was also anticipated.

In the event, the growth forecasts targets for fiscal 1997 soon began to look wildly optimistic. Moreover, the current account surplus took off. The first signs of trouble appeared with the publication of the Bank of Japan's *tankan* survey of business confidence in June 1997. This indicated that, although manufacturing industry had not been badly hit by the rise in consumption tax, any recovery would most likely be export driven, following the depreciation of the yen. Figures published later that month confirmed that the current account surplus had taken off, reaching 2.5 per cent of GDP (see Chart 2.3). More worryingly, the trade surplus with the USA rose to a two-year high of $5.2 billion, raising the spectre of a renewed trade war with that country, despite the fact that the current account surplus was the natural corollary to the huge capital account deficit, which the US authorities positively welcomed.

The gloom finally descended in October 1997 with the release of the latest *tankan* business survey and confirmation of September's preliminary figure for second-quarter GDP showing a fall of 2.9 per cent (equivalent to an annualized contraction of 11.6 per cent). The combined evidence suggested that the economy was teetering on the brink of recession, with car manufacturers slashing output to reduce stockpiles, consumer expenditure failing to recover following consumers' attempts to beat the programmed consumption tax hike by bringing forward purchases to the first quarter of 1997, corporate sales and profits forecasts being revised downwards, and unemployment (already at a postwar high; see Chart 2.4) and corporate collapses rising (see Chart 2.5).[10] Moreover, manufacturers had become markedly less optimistic about the future in September, matching the increased pessimism amongst non-manufacturers. The only bright spots were a recorded increase in retail sales of 2.3 per cent between July and August, and a further jump in the trade surplus, reaching ¥1655 billion in September (up 37 per cent on the previous year). The latter source of comfort, however, served only to accelerate fears about a resumption of trade conflict with the USA, something which would prove most damaging to exporters and the economy given the regional downturn in activity in South East Asia (which takes over 40 per cent of Japan's exports) following the various currency crises which afflicted economies in that area.

Data released before the end of 1997 confirmed the seriousness of the situation. New car registrations fell by 23.5 per cent in November, on a year-on-year basis. Imports fell by 4.2 per cent during the same month, the first decline for 43 months. Export growth slowed to 6.4 per cent overall on a month-by-month basis, with exports to Asia falling by 1.9 per cent. (A trade *deficit* with the rest of Asia was recorded for January 1998.) And the recorded fall in GDP for the six months to September (compared with the previous half-year) of 1.4 per cent elicited an acknowledgement from the Economic Planning Agency that the economy was at a 'standstill'. Forecasts for real GDP growth during fiscal 1997 were duly revised downwards from 1.9 per cent to 0.1 per cent (a figure subsequently undershot), with growth of 1.9 per cent forecast for fiscal 1998 (Ministry of Finance, 1997b).

Given the government's fiscal crisis, which had prompted the announcement of a plan to introduce an emergency package of spending cuts[11] starting in April 1998 as a move towards reducing the budget deficit to 3 per cent of GDP by the year 2003 (as required by the Fiscal Reform Law of 1997), and the lack of scope for monetary relaxation – the official discount rate stood at a historical low of 0.5 per cent (see Chart 2.6) – their room for manoeuvre was extremely limited. Structural reform and deregulation might deliver positive economic stimuli in the medium to longer term but, in the short term, were likely to prove neutral or even impact negatively on the real economy. Much-needed tax reform, embracing cuts in corporation tax, capital gains tax, securities transactions tax, land holdings tax, and regional taxes on fixed assets and land sales, might eventually prove successful in stimulating turnover and recovery in those sectors of the economy but, in the *short term*, would only exacerbate the government's fiscal problems.

Being so firmly 'boxed in', the government, at least initially, failed to come up with a solution for kick-starting the economy, only holding out the prospect for further deregulation (for example, to promote the securitization of real-estate loans) and tax reform in the future.[12] Under pressure from the markets, the US government and Asian leaders to abandon fiscal rectitude in the short run, however, the government finally unveiled plans to boost the economy via fiscal means on 16 December 1997. The proposals, including those measures concerned with stabilizing the financial sector (see Chapter 5), were formally adopted by the Liberal Democratic Party (LDP) two days later (and were subsequently approved by the Diet in January 1998).

As far as the fiscal system was concerned, the LDP proposed a total of ¥860 billion of tax cuts to boost the economy. These comprised: a three percentage point cut in corporate tax, to take effect in fiscal 1998 (bringing the basic rate down to 34.5 per cent and the overall rate, including local tax, to 46.36 per cent); a phasing out of the securities transactions tax (it would be halved, to 0.1 per cent, during 1998 and abolished by the end of 1999); and cuts in land and property taxes (for example, the tax on owning land would be suspended). Such cuts would be offset by an increase in tobacco tax, however; and anticipated cuts in capital allowances were expected to render the move on the corporate tax front revenue-neutral.

Although welcoming the government's (belated) acceptance of the need for an immediate fiscal boost to the economy, the market was disappointed at the limited scale of the cuts and their direction. After all, the fiscal stimulus only represented about 0.2 per cent of GDP, and would fail to offset the effect of public expenditure cuts planned for fiscal 1998.[13] Moreover, the tax cuts were targeted at the corporate sector rather than the consumer, whose spending 'strike', due to concerns abut employment prospects and future pension provision, is the major cause of concern.

Disappointment, however, soon gave way to mild euphoria when, the following day, the prime minister performed a remarkable U-turn and announced a one-off ¥2000 billion worth of *income* tax cuts for fiscal 1998 (it was approved by the Diet at the end of January 1998). Although again moderate in scale, the significance of the move lay in demonstrating the prime minister's recognition of the seriousness of the Japanese economy's plight and the danger to the world's economy of continuing governmental inaction. Having swallowed one bitter pill, the government may now find it easier to grasp the nettle and provide a bigger fiscal stimulus if that proves necessary, a view endorsed by the unveiling of a ¥16.65 trillion stimulus package towards the end of April 1998.

The package, which included ¥12 trillion of new government expenditure and ¥4 trillion of additional (lump sum) income tax cuts for 1998/99 (for full details see Economic Planning Agency, 1998) and which necessitated revisions to the Fiscal Structural Reform Law of November 1997 to accommodate the budgetary and funding implications, was widely criticized, however, for failing to embrace permanent tax cuts (by which was meant long-term *structural* reform of the tax system) and for directing too much (¥7.7 trillion) of the additional expenditure at relatively unproductive, yet politically rewarding, public works projects. While the Economic Planning Agency forecast that the package would add about two percentage points to GDP over the ensuing twelve months, thereby allowing for the attainment of the government's 'forecast' of 1.9 per cent growth in real GDP during fiscal 1998, most outside commentators took a much more conservative view, in anticipation of a more modest stimulus to the real economy.

Excess capacity and low profitability

Excess capacity and low profitability, the former indeed exacerbating the latter, have been long-standing problems afflicting the Japanese banking (and financial) sector. Until recently, however, the promotion of indirect finance over direct finance, the operation of price cartels, the segmentation 'rules' used to secure functional separation (see Hall, 1993, ch. 6) and buoyant local property and stock markets have allowed banks to get by on very fine operating margins (see Chart 2.7). Deregulation and the bursting of the local asset bubble, with concomitant effects on trading profits and bad debts, have since contrived severely to dent banks' profits, leading to pressure to cut operating costs. Typically, such 'restructurings' involve slimming down the branch network, paring down overseas operations and cutting staff costs. Whilst some have eschewed balance sheet size for return on equity and risk-adjusted return on assets as their strategic objectives, even fewer have yet to get to grips with their perilously high cost-to-income ratios.

For those institutions deemed beyond redemption, there is still an apparent reluctance[14] to allow their exit from the industry – see next section. 'Mergers' with stronger institutions would still appear to be the favoured option, although the stronger banks' increasing resistance to official suasion ('arm-twisting') on this front, the weakening of *keiretsu* relationships, the gradual abandonment of the 'convoy' system (Yamawaki, 1996) and the introduction of 'prompt corrective action' (PCA – see below) are likely to herald a 'tougher' line being taken in the future. 'Forbearance' may yet give way to resolution via liquidation, as called for under PCA (see Chapter 4).

Continuing weakness in the domestic property and stock markets

As noted earlier, the continuing malaise in these local markets poses a number of problems for Japanese banks. Weak property prices, in both the residential and commercial sectors of the market (nationwide, commercial property prices and residential land prices fell by 6.1 per cent and 1.4 per cent respectively during 1997; see Chart 2.8), have both depressed earnings and substantially weakened balance sheets as a result of banks' direct and indirect (via collateral) exposures to such markets. Anticipation of some recovery in prices, perhaps induced by official efforts, such as those made in March and October 1997,[15] to stimulate the property sector, has also slowed down the disposal of associated bad debts and militated against the development of the securitization of property-backed loans.

The poor performance of the local stock market since the late 1980s – for much of October 1997, the Nikkei 225 index was languishing at around the 17 000 mark, less than half of the historic peak of just under 40 000 recorded at the end of 1989 (see Chart 2.9) – has also served to depress earnings and weaken balance sheets, not least because of the erosion caused to latent gains on securities holdings which, under the Bank for International Settlements' (BIS) 'rules', count as 'Tier 2' capital (see Hall, 1993, ch. 8).[16,17] The weakening in *keiretsu* relationships and the need to bolster declared earnings has led many institutions to sell into any market strengthening, thereby retarding further recovery of a market still largely supported by foreign demand.

Following the collapse of the Nikkei 225 to around the 16 300 level at the end of October 1997, as part of the worldwide 'mini-crash' triggered, apparently, by nervousness about future corporate earnings and weaknesses in the economies of South East Asian countries, it is unclear what the future holds in store. (The Nikkei 225 average finished the year below 15 000.) With the threat of an imminent domestic recession and increased nervousness from overseas investors, a prolonged bear market is a distinct possibility. And if the 'internationalization' planned by the authorities is indeed delivered by the Japanese 'big bang', there is always the prospect that price–earnings ratios in Japan will finally converge to the levels prevailing in Western markets. Japanese banks would then be unwise to look to a recovery in the local stock market as the means of salvation. Indeed, further damage from this quarter is likely to result in the short to medium term, with the government's ability to hold up prices through the exertion of moral suasion – on both banks and governmental investment institutions – severely circumscribed compared with earlier moves on this front (although the government announced in March 1998 that it was considering allowing trust banks to invest postal savings and insurance funds in the local stock market).[18]

Threats posed by deregulation
Although creating significant new opportunities, especially in the securities and insurance areas following the proposed acceleration in cross-sectoral entry under the Financial System Reform Law of April 1993 – see Chapter 4 – deregulation is very much a double-edged sword for the Japanese banks. Many of the potential benefits from opening up the insurance market, for example, are only available in the medium to longer term whilst, of course, their own markets are being opened up to intense competition at an earlier

date. Moreover, the 'internationalization' package of measures and pressure from the US government will ensure that competition with foreign operators, with a long history of involvement in the operation of mutual funds, funds management, securitization, mergers and acquisitions ('M&A') activities, and so on, also intensifies. And on top of this, the pace of disintermediation, which was reflected in a record ¥8800 billion of yen bond issues by Japanese corporations during fiscal 1997, is set to accelate under 'big bang', with fee income also coming under pressure because of the abolition of the foreign exchange bank system.

While most expect the stronger city banks, as beneficiaries of economies of scale and scope, to be the ultimate *domestic* winners, under a universal banking umbrella[19] (with smaller regional banks, broking houses – Sanyo Securities filed for bankruptcy in November 1997, followed by Yamaichi Securities later that month and then by Maruso Securities in December – and (life) insurance companies being the major losers), there is a growing belief that the real threat to domestic operators will come from overseas. Although market shares in financial services taken by the overseas sector in Japan have, hitherto, been paltry, this may be about to change. The growing opportunities available to them in the funds management business (especially pensions funds),[20] the incipient market for securitized assets[21] and the prospect of greater investment business (including 'M&A')[22] activity suggest that foreign operators, with their greater adaptability, focus and expertise, may yet become a powerful force in Japan. This view would be reinforced if domestic customers abandon indigenous firms in the wake of continuing revelations concerning the ineptitude of and dubious business practices adopted by domestic operators. Mindful of this, a number of Japanese banks have recently agreed tie-ups[23] with overseas operators, raising the possibility that an outright purchase of a Japanese firm by an overseas predator may not be that far off.[24]

Another defensive strategy, but this time aimed primarily at warding off the domestic competition, is to seek out appropriate merger partners. Amongst major banks, Dai-Ichi Bank's merger with Nippon Kangyo Bank (to form the Dai-Ichi Kangyo Bank), Mitsui Bank's merger with Taiyo Kobe Bank (to form the Sakura Bank), Kyowa Bank's merger with Saitama Bank (to form the Asahi Bank) and Mitsubishi Bank's merger with the Bank of Tokyo (to form the Tokyo–Mitsubishi Bank) are all examples of attempts to consolidate in advance of the imminent intensification in competition. And developments in the *shinkin* and regional bank sectors[25] confirm that such defensive strategies are not confined to the 'major bank' sector.

Failure resolution policies and the impost on the banks

As if the catalogue of woes paraded above were not enough to contend with, the stronger banks have also had to shoulder much of the burden associated with the 'resolution' of problem banks and their affiliates. This has involved them in being coerced into rescuing struggling institutions through merger or participation in an industry 'lifeboat', in incurring the bulk of the costs involved in solving the *jusen* crisis and, via increased contributions to the deposit insurance fund, in underwriting the soundness of the banking system. (Each of these issues is explored further in Chapter 5.)

The Need to Address Weaknesses in External Supervision

Currently, banking supervision is shared between the central bank (the Bank of Japan) and the Ministry of Finance (MoF), although the latter is the main supervisory agency (Hall, 1993, ch. 6, pp. 149–53). The normal gamut of prudential devices is employed, that is, licensing, examination, monitoring, management interviews, capital adequacy assessment, liquidity adequacy assessment, exposure limits, deposit insurance, and so on (Hall, 1993, ch. 7). In addition, exhaustive moral suasion ('administrative guidance', as it is called in Japan) is exercised by the MoF to ensure compliance with policy 'guidelines'. (The practice of issuing 'notices' will, however, largely end in June 1998.)

Despite this impressive array, at least on paper, of supervisory tools, however, questions must be asked in the light of the difficulties banks have found themselves in in recent years. Of course, the primary blame must lie with the managements which allowed the unfortunate situation to develop, but external supervisors also have questions to answer. How did banks manage to build up such large exposures to the local stock and property markets, given the operation of exposure limits and guidelines? Were the authorities aware of the scale of these exposures? Is the number (and experience) of bank examiners sufficient to allow for a thorough and frequent investigation of all banks' operations? Should not the authorities have acted sooner to address the problems afflicting the banking sector? Were the authorities right to have extended the official 'safety net' in the fashion chosen (that is, to guarantee *all* deposits and to preserve the top 20 banks until at least the end of March 2001)? Should the banks have been asked to shoulder such a heavy burden in the failure resolution policies adopted by the authorities? Is external supervision sufficiently rigorous or intrusive enough? Does not the practice of '*amakudari*' (that is, the subsequent employment of MoF officials by the finance industry) weaken the credibility of official supervisory policy and risk undermining its effectiveness? (These and other related issues are addressed in Hall, 1998a and Yamawaki, 1996. The authorities' reaction to this implied criticism is covered in Chapter 5.)

Financial Scandals

The last source of pressure for reform came from a desire to clean up the financial system in the wake of evidence of wide-scale, if not endemic, corruption and wrongdoing within the financial sector.

The first 'post-Recruit scandals' – the bribery and corruption scandals of 1988 which eventually brought down the then Prime Minister Nakasoni – afflicted the banking sector, with the Daiichi Sogo Bank, Sumitomo Bank and Mitsui Trust and Banking featuring prominently in the headlines. The first-mentioned got into trouble because of serious breaches of the MoF's loan exposure rules relating to loans to single customers, and the running of the bank was eventually – in 1988 – taken over by the MoF because of the loss of confidence in the senior management of the bank. The other two banks' claims to infamy resulted from their links with the notorious Mr Kotani, a stock market speculator indicted on charges of stock manipulation. Sumitomo Bank was also involved with the Itoman scandal because of the size of the loan exposure incurred in respect of the trading company.

These incidents were soon followed by others, calling into question the good names of other banks. For example, the Industrial Bank of Japan (IBJ), the largest long-term credit bank, was berated for lending up to ¥240 billion to an Osaka restaurateur and stock speculator Ms Inoue, who was eventually indicted for breach of trust, forgery and fraud in 1991. The small Osaka-based credit co-operative Toyo Shinkin Bank was also found to be closely involved in the affair, having issued Ms. Inoue with ¥342 billion worth of forged CDs, which were then used as collateral for loans from the IBJ and 11 other banks. The issuing of forged CDs was subsequently shown to have been a more widespread phenomenon, with Fuji Bank, Tokai Bank and Kyowa Saitama Bank all eventually being implicated.

Nor were the scandals confined to the banking sector. In 1991, for example, 21 brokerage firms, including the 'big four', admitted the illegal practice (it also results in tax evasion) of compensating favoured corporate clients for stock trading losses (up to ¥173 billion was involved), while some of them were also accused of stock price manipulation, making illegal loans and having close ties with organized crime syndicates. Although some company presidents duly departed – though rarely from their respective boards! – in recognition of the responsibilities they bore, the dubious and illegal practices apparently continued unabated in many firms, as demonstrated below. Relationships with the criminal fraternity were not severed – payments were still made to the *sokaiya*, or corporate racketeers, to induce them to refrain from interrupting shareholders' meetings or otherwise embarrassing the incumbent board members – and the illegal compensation of favoured clients for trading losses persisted.

The first firm evidence of continuing links between financial institutions and the *sokaiya* appeared in March 1997 when Nomura Securities, the largest brokerage firm in Japan, admitted such relationships (as well as compensating favoured clients for trading losses). The president and 15 board members subsequently resigned over the affair, with three later being arrested following a Securities and Exchange Surveillance Commission (SESC) inquiry. (A former vice-president and a former managing director were subsequently – in January 1998 – arrested on bribery charges concerned with attempts to secure bond-underwriting contracts.) The consequences for the company were dire. Apart from a generalized loss of confidence in the firm, a host of local companies severed ties with it, and the MoF, on the recommendation of the SESC, decided on the following punitive action:

(i)   to suspend the firm's proprietary trading in stocks (including futures and options) for a period running from 6 August 1997 to 31 December 1997;
(ii)   to suspend all stock trading by the firm for a period running from 6 August 1997 to 12 August 1997;
(iii)   to suspend the firm's brokerage operation in the First Corporate Division of the main office from 6 August 1997 to 5 December 1997;
(iv)   to suspend the firm's brokerage operations in the main office (except in the First Corporate Division) from 6 August 1997 to 5 September 1997; and
(v)   to prohibit the firm from underwriting or making a bid for Japanese public bonds during the period running from 6 September 1997 to 31 December 1997.

In addition, Nomura was asked to draw up an 'implementation plan' designed to clarify managerial responsibilities within the firm, reinforce internal controls, improve compliance with laws and regulations, improve internal operating procedures, and ensure all relationships with *sokaiya* and any other anti-social elements are terminated for good.

Nomura was far from being the only guilty party as far as relationships with the *sokaiya* were concerned, however. Following determined efforts by the SESC to identify other transgressors, the following firms were subsequently implicated: the Dai-Ichi Kangyo Bank (also accused of breaking the Banking Law by seeking to circumvent the MoF's on-site inspection, for which it was subsequently fined a nominal sum – as in the Nomura case, board resignations, the arrest of senior executives (a former chairman committed suicide), temporary suspension of business operations and administrative action all ensued); Daiwa Securities (board resignations and suspension of business operations ensued); Nikko Securities (a managerial reshuffle and

MoF-imposed supervision of business operations ensued); and Yamaichi Securities (board resignations, arrests of senior executives and MoF-imposed suspension of business operations duly ensued before the firm finally closed its doors in November 1997). Like Nomura, those broking houses implicated suffered severely from the financial penalties imposed and the loss of corporate clients as a result of their involvement, factors which contributed to the poor results posted for fiscal 1997. [Although Nomura returned to the black, posting net profits of ¥22.9 billion, Daiwa and Nikko securities reported net losses of ¥58 billion and ¥47.1 billion for fiscal 1996 and 1997 respectively].

Moving away from *sokaiya*-related scandals and the illegal compensation of favoured clients for trading losses (Yamaichi Securities were involved with both, hiding the losses (at least ¥260 billion worth) off balance sheet through a series of so-called *tobashi* deals, which involved moving the 'losses' from one account to another, frequently ending with the losses being parked offshore), other notorious cases involved the violation of US laws by Japanese firms and an attempted rigging of the world's copper market. Both the Asahi Bank and, more seriously, Daiwa Bank were implicated in the former; whilst the Sumitomo Corporation was accused of the latter charge.

The case against Asahi Bank, and its New York branch, was that it misused confidential supervisory information, made false statements to Federal Bank supervisors and obstructed a Federal Reserve investigation. The bank was duly fined $5 million in February 1997 for its misconduct.

The Daiwa Bank affair was altogether more serious. It arose out of the bank's eventual admission, in September 1995, that it had lost over $1.1 billion in trading US Treasury bonds over an 11–year period. The bank claimed that the losses were first discovered in July 1995 and that the delay – until 18 September 1995 – in informing regulators in the USA and Japan was due to a desire to await the outcome of a detailed internal investigation. The US authorities alleged that they were deliberately misled during inspection of the bank's New York offices in the early 1990s; and that in November 1993 they had been told, wrongly as it turned out, that the bank's senior trader in New York, Mr Iguchi, was no longer responsible for both trading and settlement.

On 18 September 1995 Mr Iguchi was charged with fraud and the forging of trading slips to cover up his bond-trading losses. On 3 October the bank was ordered by the Federal Reserve to curtail most of its New York operations. On 9 October, the bank's top officials, including the president, the deputy president and a managing director (the chairman vowed he would leave in March 1996) resigned, with the bank admitting that its US trust banking arm had also lost $97 million on bond trades in the 1980s and that these, too, had been hidden for several years! Intriguingly, the bank also claimed that it had informed the MoF of its losses *six weeks* before telling the US authorities. The latter revelation forced from the MoF an admission, previously denied, that it knew about the bank's losses well before (that is, on 8 August) it chose to notify the US authorities (on 18 September). Not surprisingly, the US authorities were far from pleased at having been misled by both the bank and the Japanese authorities – the Finance Minister formally apologized to the US Treasury Secretary for the MoF's own failings in October 1995 – and, in November 1995, Daiwa Bank was ordered to close its US operations by 2 February 1996. At the same time, the US Justice Department announced that criminal charges would be brought against the bank, for misleading bank regulators and obstructing justice (via an attempted cover-up), and the general manager of its New York office. The outcome of this criminal action, which followed Mr Iguchi's earlier admission of guilt to charges of fraud, was that, on 28 February 1996, Daiwa Bank pleaded guilty to the criminal charges levelled against it and agreed to pay a fine of $340 million.

Apart from being ejected from the USA, Daiwa Bank also suffered punishment at home, with institutional investors – such as the Ministry of Posts and Telecommunications, the Postal Life Insurance Bureau and the Pension Fund Association – refraining from placing funds for management with the bank, and the Japanese authorities imposing their own penalties. The latter also took action to restore domestic and international confidence in Japanese financial oversight via efforts to enhance information disclosure with overseas financial regulators, and improved supervision and inspection of financial firms' overseas offices.

Another scandal worthy of mention is the so-called 'Sumitomo affair'. This involved Sumitomo's senior trader, Mr Hamanaka, in concealing $2.6 billion worth of losses on copper futures trades and necessitated a co-ordinated effort around the world, involving central banks and regulators, to prevent a collapse of the copper market. The familiar story of inadequate internal controls and ignored warning signs duly emerged, as did allegations of a 'cover-up' by senior staff of Sumitomo. The announcement of the losses, in June 1996, was followed by the arrest of Hamanaka in October 1996. In March 1998 he was sentenced to eight years in jail for fraud and forgery. Once again, the competence and integrity of corporate management in Japan was called into question, as was the adequacy of external supervision. (Sumitomo Corporation eventually agreed to pay $133 million to settle claims arising from the work of regulators in the USA ($125 million) and the UK ($8 million) and to set aside $25 million for the compensation of injured parties.)

As if this catalogue of crime, dishonesty and incompetence were not enough, the whiff of scandal became yet more odorous in 1998. Before the end of January, Japan's Finance Minister, Mr Hiroshi Mitsuzuka,[26] had been forced to resign to shoulder responsibility for the arrest of two MoF officials[27] from the bank inspection division, who had allegedly received bribes, in the form of lavish entertainment, in return for providing banks[28] with advance warnings of impending inspections during the period 1994–96. Mr Takeshi Komura, another of MoF's senior officials, also decided to go. This MoF-induced scandal was, in turn, preceded by yet further revelations of wrongdoing at Nomura Securities, this time concerning allegations, which resulted in the arrest of two former company executives (plus a former MoF official), that Nomura[29] had bribed officials, via the provision of lavish entertainment, at Japan's Highway Public Corporation to provide them with information which would help them secure contracts for the underwriting of eurobonds issued to finance road construction.

Nor did the rot stop here. The Bank of Japan become yet another victim of the scourge of corruption following the arrest, in March, of the head of its Capital Markets Division for allegedly passing on market-sensitive information (about forthcoming money market operations) to banks[30] in exchange for lavish entertainment.[31] This event duly prompted the resignation later that month of Mr Yasuo Matsushita, the Bank's Governor, who was replaced by Mr Masaru Hayami, a former Bank official.[32] Others featuring in the limelight, but for the wrong reasons, included the MoF (again),[33] Nikko Securities[34] and the Vice-Minister of Finance for International Affairs, Mr Eisuke Sakakibara.[35]

Above all, what these (and other) events demonstrated was an apparent industry-wide lack of integrity and skill within the management ranks of the Japanese financial services sector, and glaring deficiencies in the supervisory authorities' inspection and surveillance functions. Restoration of confidence, both at home and abroad, in the activities of financial firms and external supervisors alike demanded a clean-up of the industry, more transparency in reporting and a thorough overhaul of supervisory practice. Failure to deliver on any of these fronts would have disastrous consequences for the future success of the financial services sector in Japan.

APPENDIX

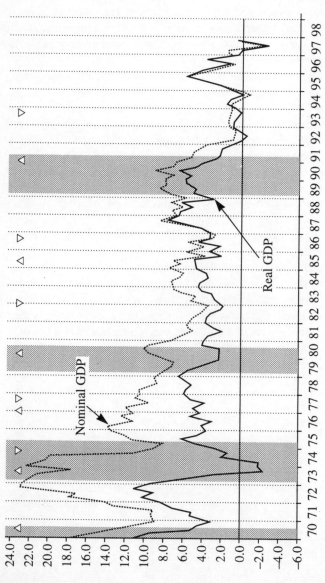

Source: BoJ, 1998.

Chart 2.1 GDP growth rate: 1970–98 (percentage change from previous period, seasonally adjusted at annual rate, three-quarter moving average)

48

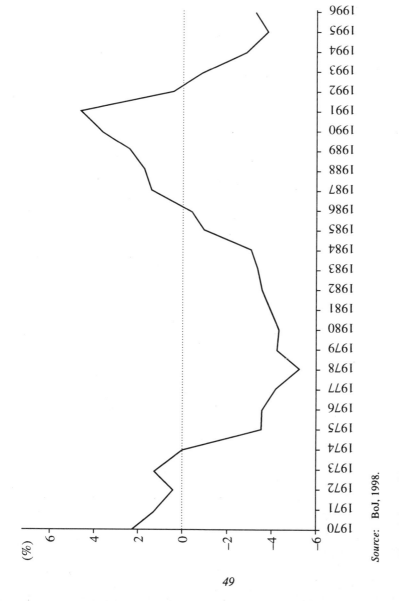

Source: BoJ, 1998.

Chart 2.2 Public sector debt ratio: 1970–96 (annual)

49

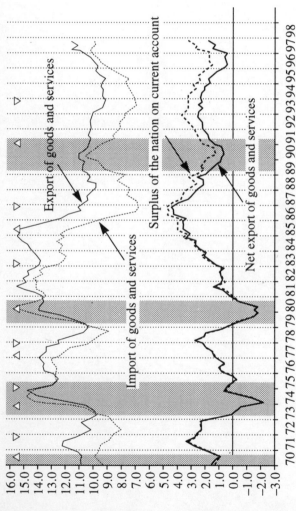

Note: Difference between surplus of the nation on current account and net exports of goods and services = Factor income received from abroad – Factor income paid abroad.

Source: BoJ, 1998.

Chart 2.3   Export and import of goods and services: 1970–98 (quarterly) (per cent of nominal GDP)

50

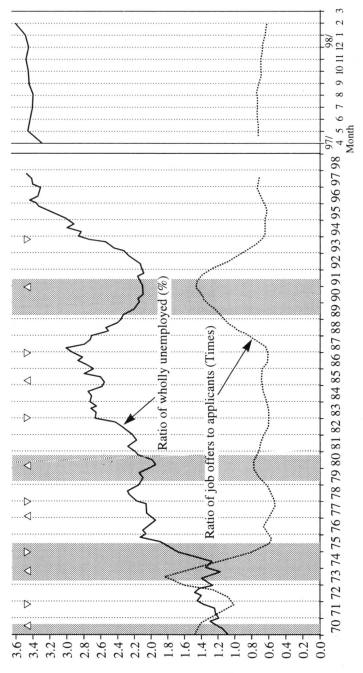

Source: BoJ, 1998.

Chart 2.4   Unemployment ratio: 1970–98 (monthly)

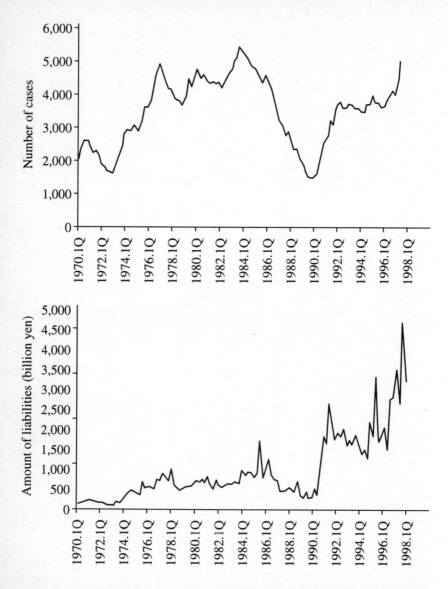

Sources: Federation of Bankers' Associations of Japan, 'Suspension of Business Transaction with Banks'; Tokyo Shoko Research Ltd., *Tosan Geppo* (Monthly Review of Corporate Bankruptcies).

Source: BoJ, 1998.

Chart 2.5   Corporate bankruptcies: 1970–98 (quarterly)

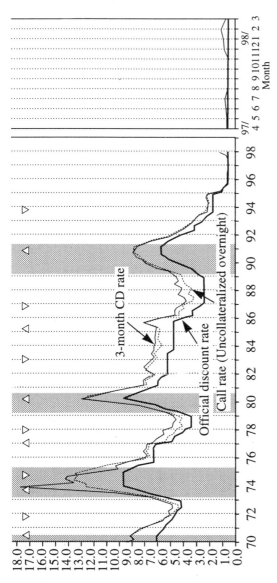

Notes:

1. Official discount rate: quarterly data are arithmetic averages of end of month figures.
2. 3-month CD rate: 3-month repurchase agreement prior to 2Q 79 (end of month); after 3Q 79, new issue basis by all banks (monthly average); data for Dec 96 based on city, long-term credit, and trust banks (monthly average).
3. Call rate: collateralized overnight rate prior to 4Q 86.

Source: BoJ, 1998.

Chart 2.6   Short-term interest rates: 1970–98 (monthly) (per cent per annum)

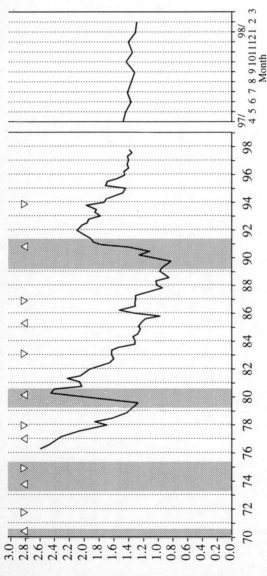

Notes:
Lending margin = Average contracted lending rates (new loans and discounts of member banks of Bankers' Association of Japan) – Average cost of funding.
Average cost of funding: weighted average of funding costs at member banks of Bankers' Association of Japan.

Source: BoJ, 1998.

Chart 2.7 Lending margin (average contracted lending rate on new loans and discounts minus average cost of funding): 1970–98 (monthly) (per cent)

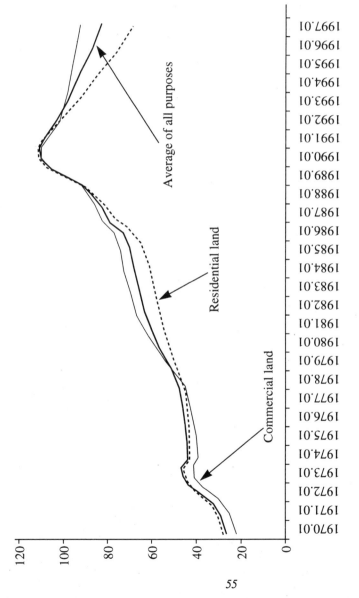

Note: Figure for March 1990 = 100.

Source: BoJ, 1998.

Chart 2.8 *Land price indices of urban areas: 1970–97 (half-yearly)*

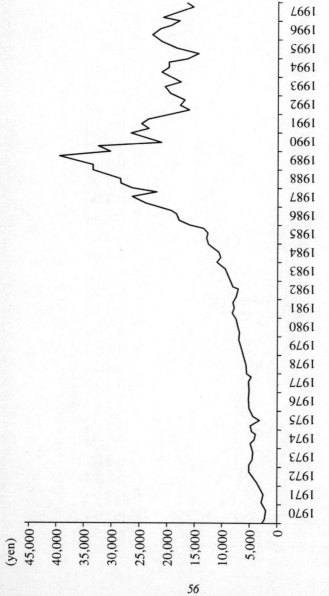

Source: BoJ, 1998.

Chart 2.9 Nikkei stock average (TSE 225 issues): 1970–98 (quarterly)

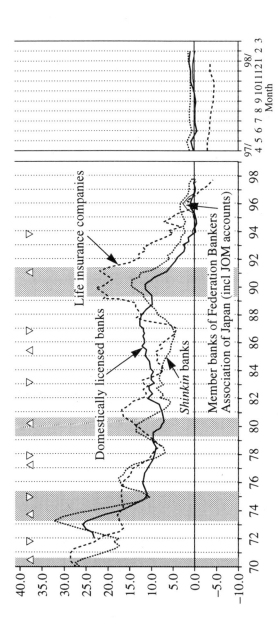

Notes:

1. Domestically licensed banks: banking accounts of domestically licensed banks + trust accounts of domestically licensed banks. Prior to 1Q 77, banking accounts of member banks of Federation of Bankers' Association of Japan are banking accounts of former member banks of Federation of Bankers' Association of member banks of Federation of Bankers' Association of sogo banks. Prior to 3Q 93, banking accounts of member banks of Federation of Bankers' Association of Japan (domestic accounts) + trust accounts of member banks of Federation of Bankers' Association of Japan.

2. The data for domestically licensed banks and life insurers and *shinkin* banks are averages of end of month figures; for member banks of Federation of Bankers' Association of Japan (including JOM accounts), averages of monthly averages.

3. Prior to 4Q 91, 27 companies basis; after 1Q 92, all insurance basis. (Source: Life Insurance Association of Japan.)

Source: BoJ, 1998.

Chart 2.10 Loans and discounts outstanding by type of financial institution: 1970–98 (monthly) (percentage change from a year earlier)

NOTES

1. By 1986 Japan had, at 50 per cent, the highest ratio of all the major economies for long-term government debt as a percentage of GDP.
2. Although this does not generate more cash reserves for the banks as a group, it does alleviate cash reserve pressure as compared with the situation where direct sales to the banks are made.
3. This need was first recognized when a flexible exchange-rate regime was introduced in 1973, for it then became clear that a deeper foreign exchange market would be required if the authorities were to be allowed the option of transacting in the foreign exchange markets to moderate exchange-rate volatility. The incompatibility of an efficient foreign exchange market and underdeveloped and highly regulated money and capital markets also became apparent at this time.
4. In the late 1980s, Japanese banks' ambitions to become gilt-edged market makers were stalled pending agreement on the number (and timing) of British firms to be admitted to the Tokyo Stock Exchange.
5. The central banks' desire to diversify reserve asset holdings was, however, distinct from this issue although it would ideally require the establishment of a fully fledged Treasury bill market in Japan.
6. As far as the Japanese banks are concerned, their clients' allegiance, partly because of the prevalence of 'main bank' relationships, is legendary, as are their funding advantages arising from access to low-cost deposits (because of deposit-rate controls) and low-cost capital (because of the relatively high valuation of their shares on the local stock market compared with other countries). Traditionally, low capital requirements, again by international standards, and the passivity of local stockholders are also believed to have contributed to the Japanese banks' success in gaining market share overseas and in retaining it at home.
7. Of particular concern were Japan's securities markets. For example, since its inauguration in 1992, the Tokyo Stock Exchange's (TSE) electronic *settlement* system only accounts for 30 per cent of trades, with 'T+1' settlement apparently still some years away. Similarly, *trading* is very 'low-tech', with the top 150 stocks still traded by open outcry (and even the remainder are only nominally screen-traded, since they have to be executed via manual input by operators at the head office of the TSE, i.e. bids and offers cannot be posted directly on the system via terminals in the brokers' own offices). These and other problems* have resulted in two-thirds of trading volume in Nikkei 225 stock futures being conducted outside Japan, with a high proportion of trades in the major Japanese stocks also taking place overseas (London's SEAQ International, for example, accounts for about 30 per cent of total turnover in such stocks). The total value of share transactions which took place in Tokyo during the whole of 1995 was equivalent to $889 billion, compared with $1.134 trillion in London and $3.083 trillion in New York. As for derivatives, as of the end of March 1995 the net value for the notional principal for Tokyo's transactions was $5.099 trillion, compared with transactions of $10.382 trillion and $8.147 trillion in London and New York respectively. Foreign company listings on the TSE are also much lower than in London and New York.

    International comparisons of average daily turnover in foreign exchange also demonstrate how far Tokyo lags behind. For example, during April 1995 average daily turnover in Tokyo was $161 billion, compared with $464 billion and $244 billion for London and New York respectively.

    * That is, burdensome regulations and taxes (a securities transactions tax of 0.21 per cent and an interest-income withholding tax on savings of 20 per cent are levied) and high trading (fees and commissions, the latter amounting to 1 per cent for individuals, are payable) and operating (e.g. renting office space) costs.
8. Again, focusing on securities operations, by October 1997 overseas players had overtaken domestic securities companies in the share of TSE trades accounted for (although the situation might be reversed in the future once the impact of the announcement of the local

broking houses' involvement in payments to corporate racketeers – the *sokaiya* – begins to wane). Figures reported in November 1997 showed that the shares taken by the two US investment banks Merrill Lynch (8 per cent) and Morgan Stanley (7.5 per cent) surpassed those taken by local operators, with Nomura Securities and Daiwa Securities only accounting for 5.43 per cent and 5.2 per cent respectively. Overall, in October 1997 foreign brokers accounted for 38.7 per cent of TSE trades, with the 'big four' local brokerage houses only accounting for 18.4 per cent. This was the second month in succession that the foreign brokers' market share had exceeded that of the 'big four', a situation which prompted the latter to suspend the disclosure of their market shares of TSE trades.

9. Worryingly, figures released by the MoF in January 1998 suggested that, using a broader definition for 'non-performing', the Japanese banking sector's 'bad' debts might be as high as ¥77 trillion (equivalent to over 12 per cent of loans outstanding), as compared with the previous official estimate of ¥28 trillion. Several factors, however, caution against taking these figures at face value (see Hall, 1998b), notwithstanding the increase in the figures for collective bad debts reported in May 1998.

10. The level and rate of increase in corporate bankruptcies, due to the weak economy, moribund stock and property markets, the gradual weakening in *keiretsu* relationships (involving the disposal of cross-shareholdings) and the banks' tightening of lending (including demands for increased collateral) are now a serious cause for concern. The earlier collapses of property developers, such as EIE International (in 1993), Moruto Komuten (February 1996) and Sueno Kosan (November 1996), and non-bank finance companies, such as Equion Corp (February 1996) and Aichi (February 1996), have recently been followed by a spate of further collapses of non-bank financial intermediaries (e.g. Shinkyoto Shimpan, Nichiei Finance, All Corp., Koei Corporation, Apollo Leasing and Daiichi Corporation) and corporate enterprises (e.g. Tada, Tokai Kogyo, Nitto Kogyo, Daito Kogyo and Toshuku). And recent 'restructurings' by construction companies Sato Kogyo, Tobishama, Aoki and Fujita may presage further trouble.

    During fiscal 1997, a total of 17 490 companies collapsed with combined liabilities of ¥14 520 billion, an increase of over 50 per cent on the previous year.

11. The proposed cuts embraced the following: general expenditures to be cut by 0.5 per cent (¥200 billion) in fiscal 1998; defence spending to be held at zero or negative annual growth in the three years from April 1998 (¥920 billion to be cut over the five years from April 1997 to March 2002); public works programmes to be cut by 7 per cent for fiscal 1998 and by 15 per cent in the three years beginning April 1998; the increase in social security spending to be held at ¥300 billion (¥800 billion forecast); agricultural outlays to be restrained (¥6100 billion package of assistance, programmed to end in April 2000 will now be spread out until 2002); overseas aid budget to be cut by ¥100 billion during fiscal 1998; help for small businesses to be held for three years to a maximum of the assistance given in fiscal 1997.

12. Apart from the measures designed to boost the property market (see note 15 below), the ruling Liberal Democratic Party (LDP) proposed for consideration, in an announcement made on 21 October 1997, the following: tax reform (the LDP would seek the abolition of the securities transactions tax, a cut in corporate tax and a cut in capital gains tax – currently levied on individuals at rates of between 26 and 52 per cent); further deregulation (i.e. of the price of telephone calls, of trucking fees and of foreign ownership of broadcasting and telecommunications); and a minor fiscal stimulus (via enactment of a supplementary budget to assist farmers, and the bringing forward to fiscal 1997 of the public works programme of fiscal 1998, with payment being delayed until 1998). This was followed by an announcement on 15 November 1997 of additional proposals – including the introduction of a UK-style 'private finance initiative' and cuts in postal and Internet charges – for stimulating the economy which, together with the October proposals, were expected to inject ¥10 000 billion into the economy during fiscal 1998. And then, on 18 November 1997, the Economic Planning Agency confirmed earlier proposals aimed at boosting the local property market, reaffirmed the government's commitment to its 'big bang' programme and other deregulation measures, and announced new measures to help small and medium-sized enterprises starved of bank finance (up to ¥23 000 billion

might be made available during fiscal 1997 and 1998 from governmental intermediaries) and to promote the 'globalization' of Japanese industry.

13. These were subsequently confirmed in the draft budget for fiscal 1998, approved by the Cabinet on 25 December 1997. Under the government's plans: public expenditure is to be cut by the largest ever amount (i.e. by ¥570.5 billion, reducing it to ¥44 540 billion), bringing it 1.3 per cent below this year's target; public works expenditure is to be cut by 7.8 per cent to ¥8990 billion; defence spending is to be cut (for the first time in 40 years) by 0.2 per cent to ¥4940 billion; and overseas development aid is to be cut by 10.7 per cent to ¥974 billion. The planned changes will raise the overall budget by 0.4 per cent to ¥77 670 billion, and will result in the fiscal deficit reaching 5.5 per cent of GDP. (The Fiscal Reform Bill, passed on 28 November 1997, aims to reduce the budget deficit to below 3 per cent of GDP by the year 2003.)

14. Indeed, the authorities formally vowed to preserve the top 20 banks (although one, the Hokkaido Takushoku Bank, was subsequently allowed to fail) and to protect *all* deposits, notwithstanding the limited *de jure* protection available under existing deposit insurance arrangements, until the end of March 2001.

15. The package announced on 31 March 1997 was designed to encourage the development of a market in real-estate collateral, thereby assisting the banks in the disposal of their bad debts, and to promote urban development. Specifically, the government promised to take measures to improve the profitability of real estate held as collateral, to promote the securitization of collateralized real estate, to establish a database for real estate held as collateral and to make public the latest appraisal values of the collateral.

The measures aimed at improving the profitability of real-estate collateral embraced the following: government purchases of ¥380 billion worth of city area sites from the Housing Loan Administration Corporation, the Resolution and Collection Bank and the Co-operative Credit Purchasing Company (to be funded by the Japan Development Bank, municipal bonds and other subsidies), the land to be used for parks, sports grounds, old people's homes and other public facilities; sanctioning of the establishment of investment trusts, allowing investors to buy and sell portions of property developments in small lots; allowing the integration of fragmented small lots of land into larger sites in parallel with an easing of zoning restrictions on development; facilitating the building of high-quality residences in urban areas by non-governmental developers.

As for the promotion of the securitization of real-estate collateral, the following were promised: amendment to the securities law to allow banks and securities firms to deal in securitized property loans; new legislation allowing for the establishment of special-purpose companies to assume foreclosed property and issue asset-backed bonds; reform of the business and tax regulations affecting such companies (the existing rule banning the resale of asset-backed securities within two years would be abolished and the current situation, whereby land acquisition and registration tax have to be paid as if the land itself was being bought, would be reviewed); measures designed to increase the liquidity of beneficiary rights issued by trust banks (under current rules, trust banks cannot offer beneficiary rights to the public), such as designating trust certificates on real-estate business loans as 'securities' under the Securities and Exchange Law, and reform of the tax treatment of transactions in small-sized trust certificates on real estate held as collateral; removal of the ban on interest-payment guarantees by non-life insurance companies (to allow for the provision of a new form of credit guarantee); authorization of the securitization of ¥500 billion worth of bad debts originated by the former *jusen*, starting in May 1997; enhancement of investor protection and tougher disclosure requirements in respect of the securitization of foreclosed commercial real estate; and revision of the Foreign Exchange Law to allow for more overseas investment.

The proposed stimulus package (it had to be put to the Diet for ratification before 12 December) announced on 21 October 1997 was part of a broader package of emergency measures designed to kick-start the stagnating economy. Those measures concerned with boosting the property sector embraced the following: land tax reform (the government promised to try to freeze or abolish the land holdings tax (currently levied at the rate of 0.15 per cent), and to review regional taxes imposed on fixed assets (currently levied at the rate of 1.4 per cent) and land sales); an easing of the rules on creating companies to securitize real-estate loans; a broadening of the availability of tax credits for the purchase of residential housing; and an easing of zoning restrictions on development. As can be seen, much of the package is represented by those measures promised in March, with few additional ideas emerging.

16. The difficulties in raising 'Tier 1' capital, via rights issues or retained earnings, and the prospect of life assurance companies reducing their subordinated loans, another source of 'Tier 2' capital for the banks, have raised the spectre of a severe 'capital crunch' enveloping the Japanese banking sector, a development which would exacerbate the widening 'credit crunch' (see Chart 2.10). To counter this, banks such as Sumitomo Bank and the Industrial Bank of Japan have recently raised funds overseas through the issue of dollar-denominated, non-cumulative, perpetual preferred stock by US subsidiaries (which counts as 'Tier 1' capital under the Basle capital accord). A premium of over 300 basis points over LIBOR (London Inter-Bank Offered Rate) was necessary, however, to stimulate demand.

17. The erosion of latent gains on securities holdings, which, at end September 1997, amounted to about 50 per cent of the banking sector's bad debts (of ¥28 trillion), also reduces the banks' capacity to write off bad debts.

18. Rather, the authorities have recently switched tack and sought to curtail selling pressure by restricting the short selling of shares. Moreover, the Securities and Exchange Surveillance Commission is examining allegations that 'speculators' had deliberately fed false rumours to the market in order to reap financial gains from short selling. The Securities and Exchange Law is to be amended to include a provision that will result in profits gained from market manipulation being forfeited; and the penalties levied on miscreants by self-regulatory organizations will be raised as a deterrent.

19. Made possible by removal of the prohibition on the formation of holding companies under the reform of the Anti-Monopoly Law – see Chapter 4.

20. For example, in April 1996, the rules governing the operations of investment advisory companies (including foreigners) was changed to allow 'independent' investment advisory companies to manage up to 50 per cent (the previous figure was 33⅓ per cent) of private sector employee pension funds. And from March 1999 the restriction will be lifted completely. The major beneficiaries of this liberalization are likely to be foreign operators, as the main domestic players, the life assurance companies, announced in April 1996 that they were cutting the guaranteed return they offered to investors from 4.5 per cent to 2.5 per cent because of the financial difficulties they were experiencing at that time. Also, it was announced in September 1997 that, from November 1997, the pension regulations would be changed yet again to allow investment advisory companies access to corporate pension money (¥15 000 billion worth) held on so-called 'tax-qualified' pensions.

These new moves, together with deregulation of the major public sector pension fund, the Pension Welfare Service Public Corporation (Nempuku) – which is now allowed to commit all of its funds (approx. ¥20 000 billion) to investment advisers if it so chooses (about half of its funds were allocated to foreign managers in 1997) – and the drift away from the large domestic broking houses in the wake of the *sokaiya* scandal by other domestic investors, have stimulated considerable interest in the West. Following earlier moves by the likes of Goldman Sachs and Mercury Asset Management, Commerzbank of Germany announced in September 1997 that it was to establish an investment trust fund management operation in Tokyo early in 1998. (In 1998 it also bought seats on the Tokyo and Osaka Stock Exchanges.) And the same month, the Dutch bank ABN Amro, already the largest overseas commercial bank operator in Japan, announced that it was to develop further its asset management and investment banking business, involving the establishment of a new equity operation – via its broking arm ABN Amro Securities (Japan) – to take advantage of developments in the securitization field.

21. To date, Sanwa Bank (May 1997), the Bank of Tokyo–Mitsubishi (June 1997), Yokohama Bank (July 1997), Sumitomo Bank (July and September 1997), Hokkaido Takushoku Bank (August 1997), Sakura Bank (August 1997), and Fuji Bank (March 1998) have all either engaged in securitization, typically disposing of property-related non-performing loans, or announced plans to do so in the near future.

22.   The traditional impediments to hostile takeovers in Japan embrace the following: (i) stifling regulation, which allowed the inefficient to survive; (ii) the *keiretsu* relationships, which resulted in large cross-holdings being firmly held by friendly companies; and (iii) little pressure being exerted on executives and directors to maximize shareholder value, investors being more concerned with prospective capital gains than dividends. This situation, however, is now slowly changing. The old 'convoy system', which involved the strong companies in nurturing the weak in the interests of collective strength, is slowly disintegrating, with the result that weak companies are no longer assured of support from stronger corporate relatives, their main banks (Sakura Bank, for example, refused to assist Apollo Leasing in July 1997) or government (Hanwa Bank, for example, was closed down in November 1996). The *keiretsu* system, too, is crumbling under the pressures of deregulation and competition and the need to shore up earnings through the realization of capital gains on securities holdings. And, finally, given the moribund state of the local stock market, investors are slowly realizing the error of their ways in focusing solely on prospective capital gains. The pressure to deliver dividend growth and the sanctioning of holding company structures, which, if 'consolidated taxation' is granted, will facilitate the disposal of unprofitable business, should serve to stimulate M&A activity.

23.   Recent strategic alliances embrace the following: Citibank's link with the Japanese Post Office which gives the former access to the latter's huge ATM network early in 1998; Bankers Trust's business tie-up and equity exchange with Nippon Credit Bank (announced in April 1997); Barclays Bank's alliance with Hokkaido Takushoku, involving the development of joint asset management and investment banking services in Japan (June 1997); Sumitomo Life Insurance's (the third largest Japanese life assurer) linkage with the US fund management group Franklin/Templeton jointly to develop international equity investment (July 1997); GE Capital's (the consumer finance subsidiary of the General Electric Group in the USA) link-up with Sakura Bank to promote the sale of credit cards and other consumer finance products in Japan (July 1997), and with Toho Mutual, the Japanese life assurance group, to market Western-style insurance products to Japanese clients (February 1998); Sumitomo Trust and Banking's agreement with Gartmore Investment Japan to strengthen the former's asset management operations in Europe (July 1997); Swiss Bank Corporation's link-up with the Long-Term Credit Bank of Japan, involving a small exchange of shares and the creation of joint investment banking and asset management businesses and the setting up of a new private banking operation in Japan (July 1997); Citibank's agreement with Sumitomo Trust Bank to develop joint investment bank products to be sold through the latter's branch network (September 1997); Bankers Trust's alliance with Daiwa Securities to develop the latter's fund management operations in the USA (October 1997); Dresdner Bank's joint venture with Meiji Life (Japan's fourth largest life assurance group) to offer asset management services to Japanese customers (March 1998); and Daiwa Securities' joint venture with Donaldson Lufkin and Jenrette of the USA to offer US investment opportunities to individual Japanese investors (March 1998). Moreover, Fidelity, the US fund management group, began selling mutual fund products through a branch of the Long-Term Credit Bank (branches of Sumitomo Bank and Sanwa Bank will be used in the future) in December 1997, a move likely to be followed by the US fund management group Invesco and others.

24.   If Bankers Trust of the USA ever exercises its call options on Nippon Credit Bank, as acquired under an agreement announced in October 1997, it would lead to the former becoming one of the largest shareholders in the latter. The arrangement is instructive in that it demonstrates an increased willingness on the part of Japanese institutions to entertain foreign ownership, a trend confirmed by the June 1998 announcement that the US financial services group Travelers is to take a 25 per cent equity state in Nikko Securities, a development which might yet result in outright foreign ownership. (Although Merrill Lynch turned down the opportunity to acquire Yamaichi Securities outright, it announced its intention to hire former staff and acquire some of Yamaichi's branches in order to set up a fully fledged, independent retail brokerage operation in Japan in December 1997. Its plans were confirmed in February 1998, with Merrill Lynch Japan Securities due to begin operations in June 1998 or thereabouts.)

25. Amongst the *shinkin* banks, the proposed merger of the Hanna Shinkin Bank and the Fuji Shinkin Bank was announced in January 1997; while the Osaka Shinkin Bank and the Sanwa Shinkin Bank merged, retaining the former's name, in October 1997. With respect to regional banks, the Hokkaido Takushoku Bank, the weakest city bank, and the Hokkaido Bank, a leading regional bank, announced in April 1997 that they were to merge to form a 'super-regional bank', although the formal merger was put on hold in July for a period of at least six months while discussions took place about how to deal with their bad debts and how to restructure their operations. The collapse of Hokkaido Takushoku Bank in November 1997, however, finally put paid to the proposed merger. And in October 1997, two small Osaka-based regional banks, the Naniwa Bank and the Fukutoku Bank, announced their intention to merge by October 1998.

26. He was replaced by Mr Hikaru Matsunaga, a former Minister of International Trade and Industry and, at the time, the Chairman of the budget committee in the lower house, who pledged to restore public confidence in the Ministry of Finance by ensuring that disciplinary action would be taken against anyone found guilty of wrongdoing. He also set up a new internal inspection group to stamp out collusion with financial institutions and other forms of corruption amongst the Ministry's bureaucrats. (Over 1000 MoF staff, employed in the banking, securities, inspection and international finance departments, were subsequently subjected to 'vetting' in respect of their informal contacts with banks and broking houses established over the previous five years. As a result, 112 were disciplined, including the Director Generals of the Banking and Securities Bureaus, both of whom duly resigned.)

27. They subsequently committed suicide, as did another official not under suspicion.

28. Those initially implicated embraced Asahi Bank, Dai-Ichi Kangyo Bank, Sanwa Bank and the now-defunct Hokkaido Takushoku Bank; but, in February, Sumitomo Bank and the Bank of Tokyo–Mitsubishi were added to the list of suspects.

29. The Industrial Bank of Japan became embroiled in the affair in February 1998 following a police raid on its headquarters and the arrest of the former accounting director. A Finance Ministry official and two employees from the Corporation subsequently committed suicide, apparently because of the affair. And, later that month, three more banks (the Long-Term Credit Bank, Fiji Bank and the brokerage unit of Sakura Bank) and two securities firms (Daiwa Securities and Nikko Securities), were also similarly accused of providing lavish entertainment in order to win bond-underwriting contracts.

30. That is, the Industrial Bank of Japan, Sanwa Bank, the Bank of Tokyo–Mitsubishi, Fuji Bank, Sumitomo Bank and Sakura Bank.

31. In response to allegations made in the press earlier, the Bank had quizzed over 600 staff about possible improper relationships with financial institutions. Ninety-eight officials were subsequently disciplined, including three senior executives. The Executive Director leading the in-house probe, although not under suspicion himself, also committed suicide later.

32. Although he had worked at the Bank between 1947 and 1978, rising to become Director for International Affairs, Mr Hayami was chosen from outside the ranks of serving MoF and BoJ officers to assuage the general public's disdain for the authorities' handling of the post-'bubble' economy and its involvement in corrupt and unethical behaviour. The Deputy Chairman of the BoJ, Mr Toshihiko Fukui, was also replaced, with effect from 1 April 1998, by Mr. Sakuya Fujiwara, a stern critic of the MoF and the BoJ; and the second Deputy Chairman to be appointed on 1 April was named as Mr Yutaka Yamaguchi, currently in charge of policy planning.

33. Both because of its original failure to acknowledge that it knew of (at least some of) Yamaichi Securities' hidden losses before the firm collapsed, and because of the arrest, in March 1998, of two of its senior officials – a deputy section chief at the Securities Bureau and an inspector at the watchdog body, the SESC – on suspicion of taking bribes from banks and broking houses (i.e. Nomura Securities, Nikko Securities and Sumitomo Bank) in exchange for approving the use of new financial products.

34. Apart from its part in the bribery of MoF officials – see note 33 above – the firm was accused of making illegal payments (arising from discretionary trading) to the former

LDP member Mr Shokei Arai, who committed suicide before his case could be brought before the courts.
35. Mr. Sakakibara had been absolved from any wrongdoing – he is alleged to have assisted a friend in financial difficulties in the early 1990s, when he was head of the MoF bureau in the Tokai area of Tokyo, by persuading Daiwa Securities to make good investment losses incurred by his friend – in an earlier MoF investigation but, in order to prove that government officials are 'whiter than white', the case is to be re-examined.

REFERENCES

Bank of Japan (1998), *Main Economic Indicators of Japan*, Economic Statistics Division, Research and Statistics Department, April.

Economic Planning Agency (1998), *Summary of Comprehensive Economic Measures* (preliminary translation), Tokyo, 24 April.

Hall, M.J.B. (1993), *Banking Regulation and Supervision: A Comparative Study of the UK, USA and Japan*, Aldershot, UK and Brookfield, US: Edward Elgar.

Hall, M.J.B. (1998a), 'Financial reform in Japan: redefining the role of the Ministry of Finance', *Journal of International Banking Law*, **13**(5), 171–6.

Hall, M.J.B. (1998b), 'What is the truth about the scale of Japanese banks' bad debts?', mimeo, Economics Department, Loughborough University, January.

Ministry of Finance (1995a), *Non-Performing Loans, etc., of Japanese Deposit-Taking Financial Institutions (as of the end of September 1995)*, Tokyo, December.

Ministry of Finance (1995b), *Highlights of the Draft Budget for Fiscal Year 1996*, unofficial translation, Tokyo, December.

Ministry of Finance (1996a), *Non-Performing Loans, etc., of Japanese Deposit-Taking Financial Institutions (as of the end of September 1996)*, Tokyo, December.

Ministry of Finance (1996b), *Non-Performing Loans, etc., of Japanese Deposit-Taking Financial Institutions (as of the end of March 1996)*, Tokyo, July.

Ministry of Finance (1996c), *Economic Outlook and Basic Policy Stance on Economic Management for FY 1996*, provisional translation of Cabinet decisions reached on 22 January 1996, Tokyo, January.

Ministry of Finance (1996d), *Economic Outlook and Basic Policy Stance on Economic Management for FY 1997*, provisional translation of Cabinet decisions reached on 19 December 1996, Tokyo, December.

Ministry of Finance (1996e), *Highlights of the Draft Budget for Fiscal Year 1997*, unofficial translation, Tokyo, December.

Ministry of Finance (1997a), *Non-Performing Loans, etc., of Japanese Deposit-Taking Financial Institutions (as of end of March 1997)*, Tokyo, July.

Ministry of Finance (1997b), *Highlights of the Draft Budget for Fiscal Year 1998*, unofficial translation, Tokyo, December.

Ministry of Finance (1997c), *Non-Performing Loans, etc. of Japanese Deposit-Taking Financial Institutions (as at end of September 1997)*, Tokyo, December.

Suzuki, Y. (1987), *The Japanese Financial System*, Oxford: Clarendon Press.

Yamawaki, T. (1996), 'The forbearance policy: what went wrong with Japanese financial regulation?', *Loughborough University Banking Centre Paper*, no. 106/96, November.

PART 2

Financial Reform

3. Financial deregulation: 1975–97

The deregulation implemented during this period can be conveniently categorized under four headings: the internationalization of the yen; the liberalization of interest rates; the deepening of domestic financial markets; and the promotion of cross-sectoral entry under the Financial System Reform Act of 1993. Each of these topics will now be considered in turn.

INTERNATIONALIZATION OF THE YEN

'Internationalization of the yen' refers to the official measures taken to widen the international use of the yen in a variety of capacities, such as in international trade, international financial transactions and the holding of yen-denominated assets as official reserves by foreign governments. (Data relating to these developments are given in Exhibit 3.1.) The various post-1978 liberalizing measures which contributed to the internationalization of the yen are presented, in chronological order of appearance, in Exhibit 3.2. As can be seen, the measures comprise three groups: (i) those associated with the liberalization of the euroyen market (including the establishment of a Tokyo offshore market); (ii) those associated with the liberalization of the yen-dominated[1] foreign bond market in Japan; and (iii) those associated with a deepening and internationalization of the foreign exchange market.

Liberalization, in fact, pre-dated these initiatives, a major turning point arriving in February 1973 with the floating of the yen. This was followed by some piecemeal relaxation of exchange controls (for example, in April 1978 non-corporate residents were allowed to hold foreign currency deposits with Japanese banks up to a limit of ¥3 million) and then, in March 1979, foreign governments and qualifying[2] international organizations were added to the list of overseas bodies – previously comprising only the international financial institutions – eligible to issue euroyen bonds. The amendment to the Foreign Exchange and Foreign Trade Control Law of 1947 in December 1980, however, set the scene for a dramatic acceleration in the pace of the yen's internationalization in the early to middle part of the 1980s.

Under the exchange control amendment, the philosophy underlying control was turned on its head. That is, in principle, cross-border transactions

Exhibit 3.1   Internationalization of the yen: 1980–95*

A. Yen's use in financial transactions

Currency shares of euromarket transactions (%)

	End 86	End 87	End 88	End 89	End 90	End 91	End 92	End 93	End 94	End 95
	Cross-border positions of banks (assets)									
Yen	5.3	6.9	7.1	6.7	6.7	5.9	4.4	4.4	4.9	6.1
US dollar	65.1	58.1	59.0	57.5	52.8	51.6	53.3	53.3	51.2	49.2
DM	13.0	14.0	13.0	13.5	14.1	13.6	15.0	15.3	16.0	15.8
	Outstanding of bond issues									
Yen	9.5	12.2	12.1	10.5	11.4	12.2	12.3	13.8	15.9	15.8
US dollar	5.17	43.8	43.9	45.3	41.3	39.1	40.3	38.4	35.6	34.2
DM	9.8	9.9	9.4	9.7	10.0	9.6	10.0	10.2	10.8	12.2

Note: Adjusted for exchange-rate effects.

Source: BIS, 'International Banking and Financial Market Developments'.

B. Yen's use in Japan's current transactions

Shares of yen-denominated transactions in Japan's exports and imports (%)

	1983	1984	1985	1986	1987	1988	1989	1990	1991	1992	1993	1994	1995
Exports (in value)	34.5	33.7	35.7	35.5	34.7	34.3	34.7	37.5	39.4	40.1	39.9	39.7	36.0
Imports (in value)	3.0	NA	7.3	9.7	11.6	13.3	14.1	14.5	15.6	17.0	20.9	19.2	22.7

Note: 1992 through 1995 data cover only September in each year.

Source: Ministry of Trade and Industry, Japan.

C. Yen's use in trade of selected industrial countries

Currency denomination of trade invoicing: 1980, 1988 and 1993 (%)

Exports	1980			1988			1993		
	National currency	Japanese yen	Other	National currency	Japanese yen	Other	National currency	Japanese yen	Other
France	62.5	–	37.5	58.5	0.5	41.0	52.9	1.0	46.1
Germany	82.3	–	17.7	81.5	0.5	18.0	78.5	0.4	21.1
Italy	36.0	–	64.0	38.0	–	62.0	–	–	–
Japan	29.4	29.4	70.6	34.3	34.3	65.7	39.9	39.9	60.1
UK	76.0	–	24.0	57.0	–	43.0	–	–	–
USA	97.0	–	3.0	96.0	1.0	3.0	–	–	–

Imports	1980			1988			1993		
	National currency	Japanese yen	Other	National currency	Japanese yen	Other	National currency	Japanese yen	Other
France	33.1	1.0	65.9	48.9	1.3	49.8	46.1	1.4	52.5
Germany	43.0	–	57.0	52.6	2.5	44.9	53.2	2.1	44.7
Italy	18.0	–	82.0	27.0	–	73.0	–	–	–
Japan	2.4	2.4	97.6	13.3	13.3	86.7	20.9	20.9	79.1
UK	38.0	–	62.0	40.0	2.0	58.0	–	–	–
USA	85.0	1.0	14.0	85.0	3.0	12.0	–	–	–

Sources: Page (1991); Black (1990); Alterman (1989); the Ministries of Finance of France, Germany, Italy and Japan; US Commerce Department, Bureau of Labor Statistics.

Exhibit 3.1 (continued)

D. Yen's use in official transactions

Shares of yen-denominated assets in official reserves (%)

	End 87	End 88	End 89	End 90	End 91	End 92	End 93	End 94	End 95
Yen	7.5	7.1	7.3	8.2	8.7	7.8	8.0	8.2	7.1
US dollar	67.8	55.3	51.9	50.3	50.9	55.1	56.2	55.9	56.4
DM	14.4	14.5	18.0	17.4	15.7	13.5	14.1	14.3	13.7

Source: IMF, Annual Reports.

* Taken from Japan Centre for International Finance (1997).

Exhibit 3.2   *Internationalization of the yen: the programme of deregulation*
              post-1978

Liberalization measure	Date effective
Foreign governments and international organizations authorized to issue euroyen bonds	1 March 1979
Liberalization of exchange controls under an amendment to the Foreign Exchange and Foreign Trade Control Law of 1947	1 December 1980
Ban on short-term euroyen lending to non-residents lifted	1 June 1983
'Real demand' rule abolished	1 April 1984
Guidelines on issue of euroyen bonds by residents relaxed	1 April 1984
Standard for issuing *shibosai* bonds relaxed	1 April 1984
Rules concerning the issue of *samurai* bonds relaxed	1 April 1984
Ban on issue of external bonds with long-term forward exchange contracts lifted	1 April 1984
Ban on issue of dollar-denominated yen-linked bonds lifted	1 April 1984
Non-prudential limits on overseas yen lending from Japan abolished	1 April 1984
Ban on short-term euroyen lending to Japanese residents lifted	1 June 1984
Restrictions on conversion of foreign currency into yen abolished	1 June 1984
Short-term euroyen loans to non-residents liberalized	1 June 1984
Investment in Japanese real estate by non-residents liberalized	1 July 1984
Rules concerning issuing of *samurai* bonds relaxed	1 July 1984
Issuing of euroyen bonds by foreign private corporations, state and local governments, and government agencies authorized	1 December 1984

Exhibit 3.2   (continued)

Liberalization measure	Date effective
Rules concerning non-resident euroyen bond issues relaxed	1 December 1984
Lead management of euroyen bond issues liberalized	1 December 1984
Standard for issuing of *samurai* bonds by private companies relaxed	1 December 1984
Issuing of euroyen CDs (up to six months' maturity) authorized for overseas branches of Japanese banks and foreign banks	1 December 1984
Medium-term and long-term euroyen lending to non-residents sanctioned	1 April 1985
Regulations preventing currency swaps lifted	1 April 1985
Standard for issue of *samurai* bonds by private companies relaxed	1 April 1985
Standard for eligible private sector issuers of non-resident euroyen bonds relaxed	1 April 1985
20 per cent withholding tax payable by non-residents on Japanese euroyen bonds abolished	1 April 1985
'Dual-currency' euroyen bond issues sanctioned	1 June 1985
Criteria for resident euroyen convertible debenture issues relaxed	1 July 1985
Criteria for resident euroyen bond (straight and with warrants) issues relaxed	1 October 1985
Abolition of the 'no return rule' for *samurai* bond issuers	1 February 1986
Floating-rate euroyen notes and currency conversion euroyen bond issues sanctioned	1 April 1986
Standard for issue of *samurai* bonds by private companies relaxed	1 April 1986
Rating system introduced for issuers of *shibosai* bonds	1 April 1986

Exhibit 3.2   *(continued)*

Liberalization measure	Date effective
Standard for eligible private sector issuers of non-resident euroyen bonds changed	1 April 1986
The period during which 'flow-back' of resident euroyen bond issues into Japan is barred was cut from 180 to 90 days	1 April 1986
Foreign banks authorized to issue euroyen bonds	1 June 1986
Relaxation of the 'one-third rule' for *shibosai* bond issuers	1 November 1986
Operations on the Tokyo offshore market commenced	1 December 1986
Restrictions on the issue of euroyen bonds with a four-year maturity lifted	1 June 1987
Criteria for resident euroyen bond issues relaxed	1 July 1987
The euroyen CP market was established	November 1987
Issuance of domestic CP by foreign firms (*samurai* CP) sanctioned	1 January 1988
Maximum maturity of euroyen CDs extended (from one to two years)	1 April 1988
Criteria for issuance of euroyen CP relaxed	1 December 1988
Medium-term and long-term euroyen lending to residents sanctioned	May 1989
Four-year minimum maturity threshold for non-Japanese issues of euroyen bonds relaxed (to three years)	June 1989
Liberalization of rules relating to residents' overseas deposits	July 1989
Relaxation of restriction on overseas deposit accounts	July 1990
Samurai bond market opened up to issuers with an investment grade credit rating	1 July 1992
Criteria for resident euroyen bond (convertible, straight and with warrants) issues relaxed	1 July 1992

Exhibit 3.2   (continued)

Liberalization measure	Date effective
Foreign governments and institutions without a credit rating allowed to issue euroyen bonds	July 1993
Criteria for resident issues of foreign currency-denominated bonds relaxed	July 1993
'Blanket approvals', lasting for a year, available to non-resident issuers of yen-denominated bonds inside and outside Japan, and to resident issuers of yen-denominated bonds outside Japan	1 April 1995
'Lock-up' period in respect of non-resident issues of euroyen bonds abolished	2 August 1995
Relaxation of eligibility criteria for use of shelf registration system	Fiscal 1995
Abolition of restrictions imposed on non-resident issues of euroyen commercial paper	Fiscal 1995
'Issuance eligibility criteria' for bond issues in Japan by non-residents and resident issues of euroyen bonds outside Japan abolished in their entirety	1 January 1996
Further relaxation of foreign exchange controls, including an easing of restrictions on resident holdings of foreign currency deposits abroad	February 1996
'Lock-up' period in respect of resident issues of euroyen bonds reduced from 90 to 40 days (the latter period now also applying to dual-currency bonds)	1 April 1996
Foreign commercial banks allowed to issue *samurai* bonds for the first time	April 1997

Sources: JCIF (1988), pp. 37–60; Osugi (1990), pp. 10–17; Suzuki (1987), pp. 124–7; FBAJ (1992), p. 12; FBAJ (1996), p. 12; press reports.

were made completely free unless specifically disallowed, although there is a proviso allowing for their reintroduction under broadly defined emergency conditions. This policy change both recognized and further encouraged the rapid growth of cross-border flows of funds. Prior to the amendment, such cross-border flows manifested themselves largely in the growth of 'impact loans' (that is, foreign currency loans made by foreign banks resident in Japan which were not tied to any particular use)[3] to Japanese residents. After December 1980, however, the scale and diversity of cross-border flows expanded enormously as a result of the growth in yen-denominated loans by Japanese residents to non-residents,[4] in resident holdings of foreign currency[5] and in non-resident issues of yen-denominated bonds in Japan.[6] Japanese companies were also given more freedom to borrow abroad.

Despite the amendment and further subsequent easing in the exchange control regulations (see Exhibit 3.2), the position reached at the end of 1990 was still such that Japanese residents could not open portfolio investment accounts overseas nor avoid channelling funds for overseas investment through authorized financial companies in Japan. While these arrangements allow the MoF to oversee all such transactions, they do, nevertheless, undermine the spirit of the new approach adopted towards the use of exchange controls.

Liberalization of the Euroyen Market

The euroyen markets are the markets on which yen-denominated financial assets are traded outside Japan. The biggest euroyen market is based in London, other important centres being located in Singapore, Hong Kong and New York. Trading is conducted through the medium of eurocurrency instruments (euroyen deposits, euroyen CDs, euroyen CP and euroyen loans) and euroyen bonds. The Japanese banks have the largest share in euroyen transactions; the remainder are accounted for by foreign banks, foreign monetary authorities and other non-financial institutions.

The markets flourished in the early 1980s because of the relative advantages they enjoyed *vis-à-vis* domestic markets. For example, euroyen transactions have always been free from domestic controls in the shape of interest-rate controls and legal reserve requirements and from the practices that prevail in domestic markets, such as the collateral requirements. But gradual relaxation of restrictions on euroyen trading and the abolition of the withholding tax on interest income received by non-resident holders of euroyen bonds served to accelerate the rate of growth towards the middle of the decade. This deregulation can be traced in Exhibit 3.2.

As far as the *non-resident issue of euroyen bonds* is concerned, the first major development occurred in March 1979, when foreign governments and international organizations with a good previous trade record in issuing yen-denominated foreign bonds in Japan were added to the list of institutions eligible to make such issues. Since the inauguration of the market in 1977 and prior to March 1979 the only eligible issuers had been the international financial institutions (the European Investment Bank made the first issue). The range of eligible issuers was further expanded in December 1984 when foreign private corporations, state and local governments, and government agencies were added to the list. At the same time, the guidelines relating to non-resident euroyen bond issues were relaxed, in line with the May 1984 Joint Group report, together with the standard determining the eligibility of the issuer. For public sector issuers, those with a credit rating of 'A' or above from Standard & Poors or Moody's were eligible; for private sector issuers, a minimum of an 'A' rating from either of the two aforementioned credit rating agencies plus fulfilment of the *samurai* market criteria (see below) was required. The standard for private sector issuers (or guarantors) was further relaxed in April 1985, to a minimum credit rating of 'A'. One year later, the criteria for determining the eligibility of private sector issuers were further changed (relaxed?) by making eligibility depend solely on achieving a minimum credit rating of 'A' from any one of five rating agencies; two[7] foreign (Standard & Poors and Moody's) and three domestic (the Nippon Investors' Service, the Japan Credit Rating Agency and the Japan Bond Research Institute).[8] Accordingly, non-resident private sector firms (or their guarantors) with a minimum credit rating of 'A' were unconditionally eligible to make euroyen bond issues, just like non-resident public sector bodies. Further liberalization of the issuance eligibility criteria occurred in July 1993 when foreign governments and institutions without a credit rating were allowed to issue euroyen bonds. And finally, in January 1996, the criteria were abolished in their entirety in respect of non-resident euroyen bond issues in Japan. (This also applies to *resident* issues of euroyen bonds *outside* Japan.)

Other deregulatory moves of note on this front embraced the sanctioning of a diversification in products[9] and of foreign bank issues of euroyen bonds[10] (June 1986) (permission for which had previously been withheld because of the implied infringement of the principle of separation of long-term from short-term finance), the introduction of a system of 'blanket approvals' (April 1995), abolition of the so-called 'lock-up' period (August 1995), during which time the sale of euroyen bonds to Japanese residents is prohibited,[12] and relaxation of the eligibility criteria for use of the shelf registration system.[13]

Turning to *resident issues of euroyen bonds,* the first deregulatory move made was the relaxation in April 1984 of the guidelines governing their issue. Accordingly, collateral and disclosure requirements were modified, although this failed to elicit any issues. The exemption from withholding tax on interest income granted to non-resident holders of Japanese euroyen bond issues in April 1985 under the Special Taxation Measures Law, however, duly stimulated demand.

Further measures to stimulate supply were forthcoming in July 1985 when the criteria of issue for resident euroyen convertible debentures were relaxed. This was followed in October 1985 by a relaxation in the criteria for resident euroyen bond issues in the form of straight corporate bonds and bonds with warrants. Then, in February 1987, the criteria determining the eligibility of prospective resident issuers of euroyen bonds were further relaxed by introducing the credit rating system that applied in the domestic (unsecured) corporate bond market. The new system took effect from 1 July 1987 and meant that all Japanese companies rated 'AA' and above and those rated 'A' with net assets of over ¥55 billion could unconditionally issue straight euroyen bonds by public offer in the euromarkets. Additionally, those Japanese companies with net assets in excess of ¥150 billion, and to which the warrant of straight bonds is applicable, could unconditionally issue straight euroyen bonds by public offer. For all other prospective resident euroyen bond issuers, size-related requirements had first to be satisfied (see JCIF, 1988, p. 82 for details). With effect from 1 July 1992, the criteria for resident euroyen bond issues were further relaxed. Henceforth, the minimum rating requirement for a company to issue yen-denominated convertible bonds was 'BBB'; and Japanese companies with a credit rating of 'A' or better became eligible to issue straight and with-warrants euroyen bonds. Net asset requirements were also eased for other prospective issuers. Finally, with effect from 1 January 1996, the issuance eligibility criteria for resident issues of euroyen bonds outside Japan were completely abolished.

Apart from the relaxation of the issuance criteria, liberalization also occurred through the sanctioning of a more diverse set of products and through a relaxation in the restrictions limiting 'flow-back' into Japan. On the former front, the issuance of dual-currency bonds was recognized in June 1985, with the recognition of floating-rate note issues and currency conversion bond issues following in April 1986. And on the latter front, the 'lock-up' period was cut from 180 days to 90 days in April 1986, and then to 40 days (applicable, henceforth, to both straight and dual-currency bonds) in April 1996. Moreover, as noted above in respect of *non-resident* issues, the system of 'blanket approvals' introduced in April 1995 was also applied to resident issues of euroyen bonds outside Japan, as did the relaxation of the eligibility criteria for use of the shelf registration system introduced during fiscal 1995.

Switching attention towards the trade in *eurocurrency instruments*, it can be seen from Exhibit 3.2 that measures were also taken on this front to stimulate activity. For example: the ban on short-term euroyen (bank) lending to non-residents was lifted in June 1983; the non-prudential limits on overseas yen lending were abolished in April 1984; the ban on short-term euroyen lending to Japanese residents was lifted in June 1984; the issue (by non-resident banks including banking affiliates of Japanese financial institutions and foreign branches of Japanese banks) of euroyen CDs (with a maturity of up to six months) was authorized in December 1984; medium- and long-term euroyen lending to non-residents was authorized in April 1985; and the euroyen CP market was established in 1987 (issues confined to non-residents), with restrictions on (non-resident) issues being abolished during fiscal 1995. Restrictions on medium-term and long-term euroyen lending to Japanese residents remained (at least until May 1989), however, because of fears that liberalization would put unsustainable pressure on Japan's domestic long-term prime rate, thereby complicating monetary and exchange rate management.

Following this liberalization a relatively free market in yen-denominated eurocurrency instruments developed.[14] Euroyen deposits made by non-residents were completely free of control, although, in respect of residents' transactions, some controls did apply. Thus, while interbank transactions were free in principle, administrative guidance prohibited medium- or long-term euroyen borrowing by domestic branches. Moreover, foreign deposits by non-bank residents were also prohibited in principle (that is, they required prior approval). As far as euroyen lending was concerned, loans to non-residents were free of controls for those institutions not required to provide notification, although voluntary restraint was expected to be exercised in respect of medium- and long-term loans to foreign branches of domestic corporations. As regards euroyen lending to Japanese residents (impact loans), however, only the short-term loans were regulation-free; the medium- and long-term loans were subject to advice concerning voluntary restraint until May 1989. Similarly, while yen remittances from domestic to foreign offices were completely liberalized, only the short-term ones moving in the other direction were so treated, the others being subject to advice concerning voluntary restraint. Finally, as regards euroyen CD issues, they were free of controls for those institutions not required to provide notification so long as they had an original maturity of less than six months. Sales to residents, however, were prohibited

The third general area of liberalization which was used to stimulate activity in the euroyen market was the establishment in December 1986 of a *Tokyo offshore market*.[15] By functioning as the centre for the world's transactions in yen, the offshore market should promote both the expansion in euroyen transactions and the internationalization of the yen.

The difference between the offshore market and the euroyen market is that only the latter is open to residents, thereby achieving isolation of the former from domestic banks. Thus, within the offshore market, authorized foreign exchange banks mediate between non-residents through transactions in any currency. Securities trading, however, is not authorized for fear of breaching the principle of separation of domestic and offshore markets.

To date, the market's growth has been unspectacular (outstanding claims stood at around $400 billion by the end of 1988). This is because of the market's comparative lack of appeal *vis-à-vis* the offshore centres of London, New York, Singapore and Hong Kong. For although transactions are free of interest-rate controls, reserve ratio requirements, deposit insurance requirements and withholding taxes, as in other offshore centres, the participants' inability to trade securities (only loans and deposits are authorized) and liability to corporate and local taxes and stamp duty, among other things, render participation relatively unattractive. (Economist Publications, 1986, ch. 2; for a more detailed analysis see Hanzawa, 1991.)

Liberalization of the Market in Foreign Yen-Denominated Bond

Yen-denominated foreign bonds may be divided into two distinct categories: those issued by public offer (*samurai* bonds) and those issued by private placement (*shibosai* bonds). The reform of each market will be considered in turn.

As can be seen from Exhibit 3.2, the first amendment to the issuance rules established in February 1981[16] for the *samurai* bond market was carried out in April 1984. The range of eligible issuers was expanded – henceforth, to include those with an 'AA' credit rating (the old minimum rating requirement was 'AAA') in respect of first-time public offer of international organization bonds and public bonds – and the maximum amount per issue stipulated for international organizations was increased.[17]

Further relaxation in the rules of issuance occurred later in the year. In July, eligibility for the first-time public offer of international organization bonds and public bonds was extended to embrace those with a minimum credit rating of 'A'; the per-unit issue amount was further increased and ceilings for the finest issues were also scrapped; and issuing plans were made more elastic, from adjustments every quarter to every month. And then, in December, the standard determining the eligibility of private sector issuers was changed yet again, the standard used in the domestic market for unsecured straight corporate bonds being applied. Yet further revisions of this standard were carried out in April 1985 and April 1986 to match the revisions made to the standard applying to Japanese companies in the domestic straight corporate bond market. Accordingly, after April 1986, all overseas companies (or guarantors) with a credit rating[18] of 'A' or above ('BBB' if their issues carried a government guarantee) were unconditionally eligible to issue *samurai* bonds in Japan.[19] The eligibility standards applying to new issuers[20] in both the public and private *samurai* bond markets thereby became harmonized, depending on a uniform rating system. Then, with effect from July 1992, access to the *samurai* bond market was extended to all foreign borrowers or organizations with an investment grade credit rating. And finally, as for *resident* issues of euroyen bonds outside Japan, the issuance eligibility criteria were abolished completely in January 1996.

Apart from the relaxation of issuance rules, liberalization of the *samurai* bond market also took place through official recognition of a more diversified set of financial products (for example, dual-currency bond issues were authorized in November 1985) and through the introduction of a system of 'blanket approvals' and relaxation of the eligibility criteria for use of the shelf registration system (see above). Moreover, in April 1997, foreign commercial banks were allowed to issue *samurai* bonds for the first time,[21] Citicorp duly availing itself of the new opportunity that same month.

In the *shibosai* bond market, a standard determining the eligibility of issuers did not surface until July 1983. This was duly relaxed in April 1984, and then in April 1986 a formal rating system was introduced. Under this system, issuers (confined to international organizations, states, provincial governments and other government agencies) are restricted in the amount that they can raise according to their credit rating: the higher it is, the higher the permitted ceiling on issue amount. All issues, however, are subject to the same maturity restriction – a minimum of five years.

As well as the relaxation in the standard determining the eligibility of issuers, which culminated in the abolition of the standard in January 1996, liberalization also manifested itself in other areas. For example, in February 1986 the so-called 'no-return rule' was abolished. This rule had been used to prohibit issuers of *samurai* bonds in Japan from also making *shibosai* issues. The rule was dropped following protests from former *samurai* bond issuers who were keen to tap the *shibosai* market.

Another example was the relaxation of the 'one-third rule' for *shibosai* bond issuers in November 1986. Under this rule, the amount of funds raised from *shibosai* issues could not exceed one-third of the amount raised from *samurai* bond issues. Again, following protests, the rule was relaxed by allowing *samurai* bond issuers to include their foreign-currency-denominated bond issues within the calculations, thereby reducing the severity of the restriction.

Although these changes, together with the liberalization of the *samurai* bond market discussed above, certainly expanded the capacity of the yen-denominated foreign bond market in Japan, it became relatively unattractive to issuers, as compared with the euroyen bond market, once deregulation of the latter market had begun in earnest. Accordingly, the market began to decline in 1986 both by number and volume of issuance, although the popularity of *shibosai* issues in the first half of 1986, following the relaxation of issuing guidelines, ensured that this segment of the market actually grew during the calendar year. Future growth, however, could not be relied upon and by the end of the first quarter of 1987 the share of euroyen bonds in international bond issues had risen to 14 per cent (from 1 per cent in 1984).

The principal factors militating against the growth of the *samurai* market in the mid-1980s were identical to those holding back development of the straight bond market: lack of competition amongst underwriters (that is, Japanese brokers), which allowed issuance fees and other charges to be held at extortionately high levels; the involvement of trustee banks as guarantors of the bonds, which pushed up issuance fees; the failure of the pricing mechanism to reflect differences in credit ratings, which drove issuers with high credit ratings to the euroyen market and induced retail customers to favour high-coupon (that is, with a low credit rating) bonds; and the cumbersome issuance process which involved securing MoF approval for each issue. Although the last-mentioned problem was dealt with by the introduction of the blanket approvals system in April 1995 and the subsequent relaxation in the eligibility criteria for use of the shelf registration system, and prices now more accurately reflect differences in credit ratings, the other problems remain. Notwithstanding this, however, the liberalization carried out in recent years, including the repeal of the issuance eligibility criteria, the introduction of dual-currency and reverse dual bonds, and the admission of developing countries and their financial institutions to the market, has led to a resurgence in activity. Accordingly, over ¥2.1 trillion of new issues were made in 1996 and, by June 1997, over ¥3.8 trillion of new issues had successfully been sold, taking total claims outstanding to around ¥1200 trillion. The growing use of *samurai* bonds as asset-backed securities and the emergence of non-bank financial institution issuers under the government's 'big bang' proposals should help to maintain momentum. Future development, however, will be heavily influenced by Japan's interest-rate policy, exchange-rate stability (especially between the yen and the US dollar and between the yen and the Australian dollar) and further product diversification.

Internationalization and Deepening of the Foreign Exchange Market

The final group of measures covered in Exhibit 3.2 relates to the government's attempt to internationalize and deepen Japan's foreign exchange market in order to promote and sustain the internationalization of the yen.

The first post-exchange-control-liberalization measure of note was the abolition of the 'real (or actual) demand' rule in April 1984. The control was designed to prevent exchange-rate volatility due to speculation by ensuring that there always existed an actual underlying transaction whenever an authorized foreign exchange bank engaged in a forward exchange transaction.

The need to expand risk-hedging opportunities for economic agents in the wake of the dramatic expansion in foreign transactions, however, spelt the end for this restriction.

The abolition of the yen conversion limits in June 1984 was the other significant development. Designed to prevent exchange-rate instability arising from a sudden influx of short-term capital, it involved the establishment of ceilings on the amount of yen which banks could secure through conversions of foreign currency.[22] Following the Joint Group's recommendation that it be scrapped as part of the effort to internationalize the foreign exchange market, the authorities duly obliged.

The only other measures taken, apart from the occasional easing of restrictions imposed on residents' holdings of foreign currency deposits overseas, related to the types of foreign exchange transaction sanctioned. In July 1984, for example, 'direct' (by-passing the foreign exchange brokers) foreign exchange dealing between banks was permitted except for yen/dollar transactions; and in February 1985 even this exclusion was removed. (For more recent developments see Nakaishi, 1991.)

LIBERALIZATION OF INTEREST RATES

Deposit-Rate Deregulation

In accordance with the so-called 'Action Programme', the MoF began deregulating deposit interest rates in October 1985. The initial move involved allowing banks to pay whatever rates they liked on *time deposits* of an initial term to maturity of between three months and two years which had a minimum denomination of ¥1 billion. The minimum deposit amount for the qualifying time deposits on which freely determined rates could be paid was then gradually reduced during the ensuing 18-month period (see Exhibit 3.3), with the cut-off point being down to ¥100 million by April 1987. Then, in October 1987, *all* 'large' (over ¥100 million) time deposits with a minimum initial term to maturity of one month were freed from interest-rate controls.

These moves, however, still left 'small' time deposits and all demand deposits subject to regulation,[23] although rates in the bond *gensaki* market (see below) and the CD market remained free from control (as they had been since the markets' inception), together with the rates applying in the interbank market (which were liberalized in 1979).[24] The authorities, though, soon reaffirmed their regulatory zeal with a progressive lowering of the qualifying threshold for the payment of freely determined rates, which came down to ¥3 million in November 1991 (for 'super' time deposits). This was followed by complete liberalization of all time-deposit rates in June 1993, with the inter-

Exhibit 3.3   Liberalization of time-deposit rates in Japan

Date introduced	Liberalization measure
October 1985	Time deposits in excess of ¥1 billion and with initial term of between three months and two years were freed of interest-rate controls.
April 1986	The minimum-sized time deposit of the above type, freed from interest-rate controls, was reduced to ¥500 million.
September 1986	The minimum size of time deposit of the above type on which interest-rate controls ceased to apply was changed again, to ¥300 million.
April 1987	The qualifying level for the payment of 'freely determined' interest rates was reduced, yet again, to ¥100 million for time deposits of the above type.
October 1987	The interest rates on *all* 'large' (i.e. over ¥100 million) deposits with a minimum initial term of one month were liberalized.
April 1988	The qualifying threshold for the payment of 'freely determined' rates on large time deposits was cut to ¥50 million.
November 1988	The qualifying threshold for the payment of 'freely determined' rates on large time deposits was cut to ¥30 million.
April 1989	The qualifying threshold for the payment of 'freely determined' rates on large time deposits was cut to ¥20 million.
October 1989	The qualifying threshold for the payment of 'freely determined' rates on large time deposits was cut to ¥10 million.
November 1991	The initial term to maturity of large time deposits qualifying for the payment of freely determined interest rates was extended from two years to three years (i.e. interest rates on time deposits of over ¥10 million and of an initial term of between one month and three years were liberalized). Interest rates on time deposits of over ¥3 million and of an initial term of between three months and three years (so-called 'super' time deposits) were liberalized.
June 1993	All time-deposit rates liberalized.

Source: Federation of Bankers' Associations of Japan (1996), p. 10.

est rates on demand deposits (excluding current accounts) being liberalized in October 1994.

Apart from the deregulation of interest rates on 'large' time deposits, the Japanese authorities also sought to increase the range of interest-rate-control-free deposit-type instruments available in the marketplace. Indeed, the sanctioning of issues of non-negotiable money market certificates (MMCs) (in essence, time deposits) in March 1985 was the first official step taken to liberalize 'large' deposit rates since the agreement reached in 1984 by the Joint Group on how Japanese financial markets were to be deregulated and internationalized. At the beginning, however, restrictions were applied on the minimum denomination, the initial term and the maximum interest rate payable. Moreover, banks were limited in the amount of funds they could take through this medium. Gradually, however, these restrictions were relaxed (see Exhibit 3.4), with the result that by October 1987 the banks' funding limits had been removed, the minimum denomination was down to ¥10 million and the initial term could run from one month to two years. Interest ceilings remained in place until November 1990, however, although the minimum size of 'deposits' qualifying for the liberalized rate was reduced further in subsequent years, falling to ¥1 million in April 1990 and to ¥500 000 during 1991. The minimum denomination constraint, moreover, was abolished during 1992, paving the way for full liberalization of interest rates on small-lot deposits by end June 1993.

Such deregulatory moves meant that by the end of September 1990 the share of city bank deposits taken on a deregulated interest-rate basis had risen to 65 per cent of total deposits as compared with 16 per cent at the end of March 1986. And for credit unions, the growth was even more remarkable – from 2 per cent to 44 per cent during the same period. The figures explain why, even without the deregulation of non-time deposits, the funding costs of Japanese deposit-taking intermediaries have risen so dramatically in recent years.

Two factors which significantly affected the pace of deposit-rate liberalization were the attitude of the Ministry of Posts and Telecommunications and the nature of the fiscal system which provided individuals with a limited range of opportunities for tax-free saving. Moreover, as is explained below, these factors were interrelated.

Under the fiscal system prevailing until April 1988, an individual saver could obtain exemption from tax of up to ¥14 million of savings. These exemptions applied to 'small-lot' deposits with the banking system under the so-called *maruyu* system (up to a maximum of ¥3 million of deposits), to deposits with the Postal Savings Service managed by the Ministry of Posts and Telecommunications (MPT) (up to a maximum of ¥3 million of deposits, the same as the limit imposed on such holdings), to investment in government

Exhibit 3.4   *Relaxation of controls on money market certificates*

Date new control applied	Minimum denomination (¥ million)	Initial term	Interest-rate ceiling	Funding limit[a]
			Nature of controls	
March 1985		1–6 months		75% of net worth 150% of net worth
October 1985	50	1–6 months	CD rate minus 0.75%	
April 1986		1–12 months		200% of net worth
September 1986	30	1–12 months		250% of net worth
April 1987	20	1 month– 2 years	CD rate minus 0.75% for maturities up to 1 year. CD rate minus 0.5% for maturities of over l year	300% of net worth
October 1987	10	1 month– 2 years	As above	No limit
June 1989	3	1 month– 2 years	As above	
October 1989		1 month– 3 years	As above	
April 1990	1	1 month– 3 years	As above	
November 1990			Ceiling removed	
April 1991	0.5			
June 1992	Minimum requirement abolished			

Note: [a]   Applied to Japanese banks.

Sources: Japan Centre for International Finance (1988), Table 2–15, p. 33 (as adapted and updated); Federation of Bankers' Associations of Japan (1996), p. 10.

bonds under the so-called *marutoko* system (again, up to a maximum of ¥3 million of investments), and to 'property accumulation savings' (up to a maximum of ¥5 million). Such tax exemptions were very much seen by investors as a *quid pro quo* for the suppressed deposit and investment yields which they were forced to accept and, as a result, any liberalization scheme was always likely to be preceded by tax reform (that is, a reduction or removal of tax relief) if post-tax yields were not to increase too dramatically.

Tax reform of this nature, however, was more widely supported by the banking industry than the MPT as, despite the apparent competitive neutrality achieved under the above arrangements, wide-scale abuse of the ¥3 million limit on individual deposit holdings with the Postal Savings Service ensured that *de facto* the banks were at a competitive disadvantage.

In the event, the system of tax exemptions was revised in April 1988, the first two exemptions listed above being removed from all except the aged (65 plus), widows and the physically handicapped. The exemption on investment in government bonds was retained, however, as was the last-mentioned exemption, with pension contributions qualifying alongside housing investment for the first time.

To soften the blow for the Postal Savings Service which, at that time, accounted for about one-third of all personal savings in Japan and constituted the largest financial institution in the world, new freedoms were extended to it. These embraced the ability to sell government bonds over the counter (up to a maximum of ¥5 million per customer), to extend loans to customers using such bonds as collateral (loans on the security of 'time', 'collection' or *teigaku* (see below) deposits were sanctioned in 1973), and to manage directly a proportion of the funds invested with it.

The last-mentioned freedom is significant because prior to May 1987 the Postal Savings Bureau had to hand over all its receipts to the Trust Fund Bureau at the MoF which, in turn, used the proceeds for infrastructural investment. Under the agreement which accompanied the tax reform, the MoF's Trust Fund Bureau would pay ¥2000 billion into a Postal Savings Financial Deregulation Fund in fiscal 1987 against the funds deposited with it by the Postal Savings Bureau. Half of this was to be used to underwrite newly issued government bonds and half was to be available for self-management by the Postal Savings Bureau, although, at least initially, investment was to be restricted to government and municipal bonds, public corporate bonds, short-term deposits at financial institutions, 'principal-guaranteed' money trusts and designated corporate and foreign bonds. The plan also called for further annual additions (increasing by ¥500 billion each year) to the fund until 1991, at which time it was estimated that around 10 per cent (that is, ¥15 000 billion) of the Postal Savings Bureau's funds would be under internal management.

The new investment freedom accorded the Postal Savings Bureau was certainly welcomed by the MPT which for a long time had argued that liberalization of its own investment yield should precede or, failing that, accompany 'deposit-rate' liberalization. The above move, together with the payment of a market-related 'redeposit rate' by the Trust Fund Bureau in 1987 on the balances turned over to it for investment by the Postal Savings Bureau, was thus conducive to securing the MPT's support for full deposit-rate liberalization. Nevertheless, the latter's preferred solution was for gradual reform, with market-rate-linked 'deposit' products being introduced prior to full 'small-lot' interest-rate liberalization. The approach adopted by the MPT inevitably slowed the pace of reform, with the banks being reluctant to move without the Postal Savings Bureau's concurrent movement on the rates and terms applicable to its own deposit instruments.

Consideration of the latter conveniently leads into a discussion of the competitive balance prevailing at that time between the commercial banks and the Postal Savings Service. In 1987 the Postal Savings Service offered six kinds of deposit to the general public: ordinary deposits; collection ('instalment') deposits; *teigaku* deposit certificates ('fixed-amount' deposits); time ('fixed-term') deposits; housing instalment deposits; and education instalment deposits (Postal Savings Bureau, 1987). Of these instruments, the 'fixed-amount' deposits were by far the most significant, accounting for 90 per cent of all postal savings at the end of March 1985. They are unique to the Postal Savings Service and may be withdrawn without prior notice and without penalty after six months on deposit. Moreover, they can remain on deposit for up to ten years, with interest being compounded twice a year. Holdings of housing instalment deposits and educational instalment deposits entitle the holder to privileged-rate loans from the Housing Finance Corporation and People's Finance Corporation, respectively.

Compared with its commercial bank competitors, the Postal Savings Bureau could thus offer (government-guaranteed) 'deposits' of a longer term (ordinary private banks were restricted to maturities of up to two years[25] at that time and long-term credit banks to maturities of five years maximum); and the yields on instruments of a comparable term were generally more competitive by virtue of the policy adopted on compounding of interest (banks only compound once a year) and their freedom from the restrictions imposed under the TIRAL (Temporary Interest Rate Adjustment Law – see below), reserve ratio requirements and deposit insurance requirements. On the other hand, the investment restrictions noted above reduced the Postal Savings Bureau's relative competitiveness, although the full gamut of prudential controls (see below) was also avoided.

The determination of deposit rates on postal savings was conducted in a different manner to that used in respect of private deposit rates. In place of the TIRAL regulations was a system involving the Cabinet, the MPT and the Postal Services Advisory Council, a body comprising a mix of academics, postal savings depositors, postal life insurance policy-holders and postal annuities owners. In accordance with the Postal Savings Law, the interest rates on postal savings were determined by Cabinet on the basis of a report submitted by the Minister of Posts and Telecommunications who, in turn, consults the Postal Services Advisory Council. In this way, a two-tier system of deposit rates arises which, on occasions, can complicate monetary management of the economy. As a result, the MoF has been keen to ensure a degree of conformity in the private and postal deposit-rate structures by securing a tripartite agreement between itself, the MPT and the Cabinet Secretariat. First established in 1981, this tripartite agreement remains in place today. Notwithstanding this, however, there have been occasions (such as in the winter of 1983) when the spirit if not the letter of the agreement has not been adhered to, with the MPT widely viewed as the offending party. With the Postal Savings Bureau operating as a non-profit-making body, such obstinacy served to accentuate the competitive imbalances in the run-up to full deposit-rate liberalization and beyond. In December 1992, however, agreement was reached between the MoF and the MPT on procedures for determining the interest rates to be paid on *teigaku* deposit certificates. Henceforth, greater account had to be taken of the general trend in deposit rates paid by depository institutions, and destabilizing directional changes in deposit flows had to be avoided.

Loan-Rate Deregulation

Like their deposit interest rates, the *short-term* loan rates of private financial institutions are regulated in accordance with the Temporary Interest Rate Adjustment Law of 1947 (see below). Under this law, lending-rate ceilings are established for all commercial banks, trust banks, insurance companies and the Norinchukin Bank. For the *sogo* banks, *shinkin* banks and credit co-operatives, the maximum loan rates are set in accordance with the relevant laws – that is, the *Sogo* Bank Law, the *Shinkin* Bank Law and the Law for Small Business Co-operatives – which empower the Minister of Finance to set the ceilings.

In principle, private financial institutions are free to determine their short-term (less than one year) lending rates within the legal ceilings, but in practice their actual room for manoeuvre has been circumscribed by agreed market practice. In the case of the banks, for example, the actual maximum short-term loan rates charged were linked to the official discount rate in June 1958 in accordance with the agreed policy of the Federation of Bankers' Associations of Japan (FBAJ). And in March 1959, again under an FBAJ agreement, a standard rate (*hyojun kinri*) system was adopted whereby the standard rate (known as the 'short-term prime rate'), which applied to loans and discounts of bills of the highest creditworthiness, moved by exactly the same amount as the official discount rate. This, of course, set the *de facto* floor for short-term lending rates, with lending rates being set at levels between this and the agreed ceiling largely according to the perceived creditworthiness of the borrower and the closeness of other business relationships with the bank.

These arrangements, however, were called into question in 1975. Under the Anti-Trust Laws they were clearly anti-competitive and were duly abolished in April of that year. After that the Governor of the BoJ requested that banks follow changes in the official discount rate, usually by the same absolute amount, and the banks, accordingly, moved both their prime rates and their actual loan-rate ceilings in line with the discount rate, with certain banks leading the way under the so-called 'leading bank' system.

This arrangement survived until the mid-1980s but, with the rapid increase in the growth in the share of funds procured by banks through floating-rate deposit instruments after interest-rate liberalization, pressure inevitably built up to link loan rates to a prime rate reflecting more closely the actual costs of raising funds. Such a new formula was formally adopted in January 1989, whereby the prime rate is determined by adding a certain 'spread' (or margin) to a base rate which represents a weighted average of various types of interest rates, regulated and deregulated. Thus, today, short-term prime rates are no longer closely linked to the discount rate, although legal ceilings still apply, but at levels which are not constraining. And the growing use of 'spread' banking will further sever the traditional linkage. This will have knock-on effects for the long-term prime lending rate, traditionally determined by adding a certain spread to the five-year funding costs of long-term credit banks and trust banks.

THE DEEPENING OF DOMESTIC FINANCIAL MARKETS

The Money Market

A substantial degree of deepening of the Japanese money market was achieved during the 1980s by liberalizing operations on existing markets, creating new markets and securing closer integration with overseas markets. These policies will now be addressed by analysing developments in the interbank and open markets in turn.

As noted earlier in this chapter, the *interbank market* (which currently boasts claims outstanding in excess of ¥50 trillion), the bulk of transactions in which had to pass through one of the six money-broking firms (the *tanshi*) until December 1990, comprises the call money market, the bill discount market and the 'Tokyo-dollar call money market'. The call money market is where financial institutions engage in the borrowing and lending of very short-term funds between themselves. Although, in principle, call transactions have to be conducted through call money market dealers, some take place directly between institutions. Traditionally, only those financial institutions which had accounts at the Bank of Japan were allowed to borrow in the

Exhibit 3.5   Liberalization of the Japanese money market: the programme
of financial deregulation in the interbank market

Date action taken	Developments in the call money market	Developments in the bill discount market
June 1978	Rate quotations made flexible	Deregulation of resale and of rates on bills of more than 1 month's outstanding maturity
October 1978	Introduction of free-rate 7-day calls	
November 1978		Introduction of free-rate 1-month bills; rates on 'over-3-months ends' bills and 'over-4-months ends' bills liberalized
April 1979	Rate quotation system scrapped and all rates liberalized Unconditional calls changed into virtual 'next-day' calls (the former variety ceasing to exist) Introduction of 2–6-day calls	
October 1979		Rate quotation for 'over 2-months-ends' bills scrapped: all rates liberalized
October 1980		Settlement terms changed from the 'over-month-end' method to one computed by the number of months after the day of response
November 1980	'Straddling' (i.e. the listing of both borrowing and lending as outstanding at the same time) by lenders (e.g. regional banks, trust banks, etc.) recognized The four major securities companies authorized to borrow call money	'Straddling' of bills bought by lenders and call money recognized
April 1981	City banks allowed to make call loans	

Exhibit 3.5 (continued)

Date action taken	Developments in the call money market	Developments in the bill discount market
December 1981	Eight more securities companies allowed to borrow call money Borrowing limits for 'large' securities companies increased	
April 1982		Dealing by money market dealers authorized
February 1983	Two more securities companies allowed to borrow call money	
March 1985		City banks allowed to purchase bills
May 1985		Securities houses allowed to invest in the bill market
June 1985		Introduction of 5–6-month bills
July 1985	Unsecured transactions in overnight calls and 7–day calls began	
August 1985	Introduction of 2–3-week calls	
September 1985	Unsecured transactions in 2–3-week calls allowed	
August 1986	Introduction of unsecured 'weekend' calls	
July 1987	Start of unsecured transactions in 2–6-day calls	
November 1988	Unsecured transactions in calls of up to 6 months allowed	Range of acceptable maturities expanded to include instruments with maturities down to 1 week Abolition of quotation system
April 1989	Unsecured transactions in calls of up to 1 year allowed	Dealings in bills of up to 1 year to maturity allowed
November 1990	Abolition of quotation system and introduction of offer–bid system in unsecured call money market	

Sources: Adapted from JCIF (1988), Table 2.6, pp. 14–16; Osugi (1990), p. 40.

call money market, all transactions took place on a secured basis (for details of acceptable collateral, see JCIF, 1988, p. 18), and rates were fixed under the 'quotation' system.[26]

The process of liberalization (see Exhibit 3.5) began in June 1978 when the Bank of Japan, under pressure from the city banks, introduced greater flexibility into the setting of call rates. It did this by offering guidance to the call dealers as to when and by how much rates should be charged, thereby introducing a greater element of flexibility into the quotation system. After liberalization, rate changes occurred every day to reflect even minor changes in demand and supply conditions and in expectations. This move was followed, in October 1978, by the introduction of seven-day transactions (prior to this, transactions were for settlement on the same day ('same-day' transactions), or on the following day ('unconditional' transactions)) which were to be conducted on a 'free-rate' basis. And the process of rate liberalization culminated in the scrapping of the rate-quotation system in April 1979, after which, in theory at least, all transactions were to be conducted on a free-rate basis. Since November 1995, the Federation of Bankers' Associations of Japan has published, on a daily basis, a yen TIBOR (Tokyo Inter-Bank Offered Rate) which acts as a reference rate for Japanese money markets. The yen TIBOR, which is published at noon each day, reflects prevailing rates on the unsecured call market by taking account of the rates offered by 18 'reference' banks (including city banks, trust banks and long-term credit banks).

Apart from these rate-liberalization measures, the authorities also sought to promote the development of the call market by expanding the range of transactions that can take place in the market and the number of eligible participants.

The first policy resulted in the introduction of two–six-day calls in April 1979 and two–three-week calls in August 1985, together with the introduction of unsecured trading ('intermediary calls').[27] Initially (July 1985) confined to overnight calls and seven-day calls, unsecured trading spread to two–three-week calls in September 1985 and to two–six-day calls in July 1987. Unsecured transactions in 'weekend' calls were also introduced in August 1986.

Expansion in the numbers eligible to participate in the market was achieved by first allowing city banks to make call loans (April 1981) and then by re-admitting securities companies – the four major ones in November 1980, followed by eight middle-ranking ones in December 1981 and a further two in January 1983 – to the call market as borrowers (they were excluded following the crisis in the securities industry in 1966).

Liberalization of the bill discount market can also be traced using Exhibit 3.5. As far as the deregulation of interest rates is concerned, the initial move was made in June 1978 when the rates on bills with an outstanding maturity of over one month were liberalized. This was followed by the liberalization of rates on 'over-three-months-ends' bills[28] and 'over-four-months-ends' bills in November 1978 and of rates on 'over-two-months-ends' bills in October 1979. As one-month[29] bills had been traded on a 'free-rate' basis since their introduction (in November 1978), this meant that by October 1979 all bill rates had been liberalized.

As well as the deregulation of interest rates, liberalization of the bill discount market was also concerned with expanding the range of transactions undertaken. Thus, the resale of bills of over one month's outstanding maturity was liberalized[30] (in June 1978) and the maturity of bills traded was diversified (five- and six-month bills were introduced in June 1985). The latter move was made to accommodate demands for longer-term trading and to facilitate interest-rate arbitrage between the interbank and open markets by creating instruments of the same maturities as are available there (that is, in the CD, BA and euroyen markets). The range of bills eligible for discount in the market has also been enlarged through time,[31] as has the ranks of eligible participants; money market dealers were admitted in April 1982 and city banks, as purchasers, in March 1985.

Deepening of the Tokyo-dollar call money market, the third constituent of the interbank market, has been achieved through deregulation of transactions in foreign currencies, removal of the restriction on the maturity of transactions (a limit of six months applied prior to December 1980) and a rapid expansion in the number of participants active in the market (authorized foreign exchange banks – domestic and resident foreign – and brokers are eligible).

The Tokyo-dollar call market, or the short-term foreign currency market in which financial institutions borrow and lend on an unsecured basis amongst themselves, was established in April 1972 to smooth out the short-term surpluses and deficits in foreign currency which arose. Since the December 1980 amendment to the Foreign Exchange and Foreign Trade Control Act, however, which deregulated foreign-currency-denominated transactions, the market has functioned as a convenient place in which to invest surplus foreign currency balances or raise short-term foreign currency loans, thereby deepening the local foreign exchange market. Although, as implied by the name, almost all transactions are denominated in US dollars, there is no restriction on the type of foreign currency which may be transacted.

Moving to an assessment of developments in the *open money markets,* it is convenient to start by looking at the liberalization of the (negotiable) CD market. As can be seen from Exhibit 3.6, the first development following inauguration of the market in May 1979 was an increase in the ceiling placed on the amounts which (deposit-taking) financial institutions could raise from CD issues in April 1980, although it did not take effect until April 1981. The

Exhibit 3.6 *Liberalization of the Japanese money market: the programme*
of financial deregulation in the open market

Date action taken	Developments in the CD market	Developments in the bond *gensaki* market	Other developments
October 1978		Ceiling on *gensaki* selling by city banks expanded (from ¥5bn to ¥20bn)	
May 1979	Negotiable CD (free-rate) market established Minimum unit size of issue set at ¥500m; ceiling on issuance (effective January to March 1980) set at 25% of net worth (10% of yen-denominated loan and securities accounts for foreign banks, which were also given a mininum issue limit of ¥3bn); term of CDs to be over 3 months and under 6 months Money market dealers started trading in CDs	Non-resident participation (through securities companies) allowed	
April 1980	Ceiling on issuance increased (effective April 1981 to January 1983) to 50% of net worth (20% of yen-denominated loan and securities accounts for foreign banks)	Ceiling on *gensaki* selling by city banks abolished	
April 1981		City banks authorized to buy *gensaki*	
February 1983	Ceiling on issuance expanded (effective January to March 1984) to 75% of net worth (30% of yen-denominated loan and securities accounts for foreign banks, with a minimum issue limit of ¥5bn)		

Exhibit 3.6 *(continued)*

Date action taken	Developments in the CD market	Developments in the bond *gensaki* market	Other developments
January 1984	Minimum unit of issue reduced from ¥500m to ¥300m Ceiling on issuance increased (effective April to June1985) to 100% of net worth[a] (50% of yen-denominated loan and securities accounts for foreign banks, with a minimum issue limit of ¥8bn)		
April 1984	Domestic trade in CDs and CDs issued abroad pe rmitted		
June 1984			Yen conversion limits scrapped
April 1985	Minimum unit of issue reduced from ¥300m to ¥100m Minimum term of issues reduced from 3 months to 1 month		
June 1985	Securities companies allowed to trade in CD market		Yen-denominated bankers' acceptance (yen BA) market created
October 1985	Ceiling on issuance expanded to 150% of net worth plus 25% of uncommitted MMCs to take effect immediately (75% of yen-denominated loan and securities accounts for foreign banks, with a minimum issue limit of ¥12bn)		
February 1986			First 'Treasury bills' (TBs) (of 6 months' maturity with a minimum denomination of ¥100m) issued
February 1986			Securities companies authorized to operate in the secondary yen BA market

Exhibit 3.6   (continued)

Date action taken	Developments in the CD market	Developments in the bond *gensaki* market	Other developments
April 1986	Maximum term of issues increased to 1 year Ceiling on issuance expanded, with immediate effect, to 200% of net worth plus 25% of uncommitted MMCs (100% of yen-denominated loans and securities accounts for foreign banks, with a minimum issue limit of ¥20bn)		
September 1986	Ceiling on issuance expanded, with immediate effect, to 250% of net worth		
April 1987	Ceiling on issuance expanded with immediate effect to 300% of net worth (but all limits scrapped for foreign banks) Minimum size of issue cut from ¥100m to ¥50m		
May 1987			Minimum denomination for BAs halved to ¥50m; maximum maturity extended to 1 year (from 6 months)
August 1987			Minimum denomination for TBs halved to ¥50m
October 1987	Ceiling on issuance scrapped (took effect immediately)		
November 1987			CP market established
April 1988	Issues with maturities of between 2 weeks and 2 years sanctioned		
September 1989			3-month TBs introduced

Exhibit 3.6   (continued)

Date action taken	Developments in the CD market	Developments in the bond *gensaki* market	Other developments
February 1990			CP issuance by securities companies permitted
April 1990			Minimum denomination for TBs cut to ¥10m
April 1991			Minimum net asset requirement (¥33bn) for prospective issuers of CP abolished
June 1993			CP issuance by non-bank financial institutions permitted
April 1994			CP issuance by insurance companies permitted
October 1995	Maximum term of issues extended to 5 years		CP issues of less than 2 weeks sanctioned
January 1996			Abolition of restrictions imposed on payment of interest by banks (and securities companies) against cash collateral posted by borrowers of bonds led to the development of a market in cash-secured bond borrowing transactions
April 1996			Bond repo market launched (evolved from the stock lending market – the *taishaku* market – which is free from transactions tax, unlike the *gensaki* market)

Note: [a]   From July to September 1985 the ceiling on issuance was expanded, yet again, to include 25 per cent of uncommitted MMCs.

Sources: Adapted from JCIF (1988), Table 2.6, pp. 14–16; Federation of Bankers' Associations of Japan (1996), p. 10; press reports.

ceiling was raised from 25 per cent of net worth for Japanese banks (10 per cent of yen-denominated loan and securities accounts for foreign banks) to 50 per cent of net worth (20 per cent of yen-denominated loan and securities accounts for foreign banks). The ceiling on issuance was gradually extended through further increases in January 1983, January 1984, October 1985, April 1986, September 1986 and April 1987 (see Exhibit 3.6 for details), with the limit finally being removed in October 1987 (April 1987 for foreign bank issuers).

Apart from the gradual relaxation in issuance limits, the terms of issue were also deregulated. Thus, for example, the stipulation of May 1979 that the maturity of CDs must be over three months and under six months was relaxed in April 1985, when the minimum term was reduced to one month from three. In a similar vein, the maximum term was increased to one year in April 1986. In April 1988 issues with maturities of between two weeks and two years were sanctioned. And finally, in October 1995, the maximum term was extended to five years. Restrictions on the minimum unit size of issue were also relaxed. Set at ¥500 million in May 1978, it came down to ¥300 million in January 1984. It was cut again in April 1985 to ¥100 million, reaching the current level of ¥50 million in April 1987.

The only other major developments in the CD market were the admission of securities companies as traders in June 1985 (prior to this date, trading had been confined to money market dealers, financial institutions and their affiliates) and the start of *gensaki* trading in CDs in 1980.

As for the bond *gensaki* market, the first major development following the market's inauguration in 1949 was the expansion of the ceiling on *gensaki* selling (that is, borrowing) by city banks from ¥5 billion to ¥20 billion, authorized in October 1978. This decision was made in the light of the growth of the market and the large-scale flotation of government bonds and was followed by the abolition of the ceiling in April 1990.

Under guidance issued by the MoF[32] all corporations are eligible to engage in transactions[33] in the bond *gensaki* market although, in practice, the participants have comprised securities companies, financial institutions (public and private) and other corporate entities. Non-resident participation was first authorized in May 1979 and city banks were authorized to act as buyers (that is, lenders) in April 1981. Non-financial corporations were traditionally the largest lenders, with securities companies being the largest borrowers. These decisions were taken in the light of the decline in lending activity which followed the establishment of the open market in CDs in May 1979 and the stultifying effect of the securities transactions tax which is levied on sellers. The liberalization of capital transactions under the 1980 amendment to the foreign exchange law led to further growth in the market share of non-residents.

Developments in the open market outside these two markets centred, in the main, on the creation and subsequent evolution of new money markets (see Exhibit 3.6). Thus a yen-denominated bankers' acceptance (yen BA) market was created in June 1985; Treasury bills (TBs) were first issued in February 1986; a commercial paper (CP) market was established in November 1987; and a market in cash-secured bond-borrowing transactions sprang up in January 1996, duly leading to a proper (that is, free of transactions tax) bond repo market in April 1996.

The creation of the yen BA market was a direct outcome of the US–Japan 'yen–dollar' deliberations and was designed to broaden and deepen the short-term money market in Japan and to contribute towards the internationalization of the yen. Prior to June 1985 the yen BA was virtually non-existent because of the development of the short-term money market around the interbank market and because of the very low level of yen-denominated trade financing.

The market is open to financial institutions and corporate entities, resident and non-resident, although, for the time being at least, the original sale of eligible[34] bills is limited to the authorized foreign exchange banks which underwrite the bills.[35] Those authorized to deal in the secondary market, however, comprise financial intermediaries, money market dealers, affiliates of financial institutions and (since April 1986) securities companies. To date, the market's development has been stymied by the imposition of stamp duty on sales (although this was reduced in October 1987) and cumbersome rules on secondary market trading. And the costs of borrowers and net returns to lenders have not been sufficiently attractive to stimulate interest.

Treasury bill (TB) issues started in 1986 in the form of issues of six-month maturity discount bonds. TBs (or, more precisely, short-term government bonds) differ from other short-term (with a maturity of about 60 days) government securities, such as foreign exchange fund bills, in that they cannot be under-written by the Bank of Japan[36] and are issued through a competitive price-bidding system to institutional investors (individuals cannot buy them). Although the minimum unit size of issue has been progressively reduced in recent years – from ¥100 million to ¥50 million in April 1987 and then to ¥10 million in April 1990 – and the minimum term reduced to three months in September 1989, a fully fledged TB market, as the British and Americans know it, was still some way off in 1990.[37] This militated against further use of the yen as a reserve currency and the development of efficient money market operations in short-term government securities as the main instrument of monetary policy. In this manner, the internationalization of the yen and of Japanese financial markets was impeded. By end January 1997, however, TBs accounted for 17.5 per cent of the ¥71 trillion of open money market claims outstanding, with the bulk of trading occurring in *gensaki* form (MoF, 1997). (CDs accounted for 47.4 per cent, CP for 14.6 per cent, and the bond *gensaki* market for 18.8 per cent.)

The next open money market to be established in Japan was the commercial paper (CP) market in November 1987. The delay in its introduction stemmed, in part, from the banking industry's opposition on the grounds that it would violate the principle of collateral in markets, to the detriment of the investor and, possibly, the wider financial system, and retard the development of the bill markets (the induced disintermediation was not mentioned). The arguments in favour, such as lower cost and more flexible funding, espoused by the industrial sector, eventually won the day, however, and the market has proved very successful.[38]

A rating system was introduced in December 1988 to determine the eligibility of issuers. To qualify, firms had to have over ¥33 billion in net assets and their debt had to be rated in the top two rating classes. Today, the borrowers in the CP market are highly rated corporations, securities companies, insurance companies, non-bank financial intermediaries and even foreign investment banks (Merrill Lynch launched a ¥100 billion issue in March 1998), while the lenders (that is, the purchasers) are institutional investors. Sales are handled by banks and securities companies (resident foreign and domestic), as companies are not allowed to issue CP direct to institutional investors, and issues are generally guaranteed. The minimum issue size is ¥100 million and maturities can extend up to nine months.

The last open money market in Japan – the market in cash-secured bond-borrowing transactions – emerged in January 1996 following the MoFs elimination of the restrictions imposed on the payment of interest by banks (and securities companies) against cash collateral posted by borrowers of bonds. The setting of the rate at the secured overnight call rate minus 1 per cent had, in effect, stymied development of the market (which now performs the same functions as the repo market) because borrowers had to shoulder the 1 per cent interest burden.

The Capital Market

The deepening of the capital market in Japan has been achieved through liberalization of the bond market, internationalization of the stock and bond markets and the introduction of futures markets for bond and other trades. Much remains to be done, however, if the private bond market (that is, the market in industrial bonds – *shasai* – issued by non-financial, private companies) is to realize its full potential.

As far as the liberalization of the public bond market is concerned, the reform programme is almost entirely associated with the development of the government bond market (see Exhibit 3.7). In terms of issuing (primary market) activities, the government has contributed to the deepening of the market by broadening the range of bond types on offer, by diversifying their maturities and by diversifying selling methods. Thus, for, example, 'deficit bonds'[39] (alternatively termed 'special government bonds'), which are issued each fiscal year to make up for any shortfall in the general account, were introduced in 1975 for the first time to complement the other two types of government bond available: construction bonds and refunding bonds. The former of these two are used to finance public works projects, in accordance with Article 4 of the Public Finance Law; and the latter, in accordance with the Law Concerning Special Account of Government Bonds Consolidation Fund, to redeem earlier bond issues. Government bonds may also be differentiated by the form in which the yield is offered; fixed-rate coupon, floating-rate and discount bonds are all available today.

Diversification by maturity began in earnest in the mid-1970s. As can be seen from Exhibit 3.7, five-year discount bonds supplemented the usual ten-year interest-bearing bond issues in 1977 and this was soon followed by the introduction of medium-term (two-, three- and four-year) interest-bearing bonds before the end of 1980. These medium-term bond issues were, in turn, followed by issues of very long-term bonds (that is, with maturities of 15 years upwards) in 1983, further filling in the spectrum of maturities.

Finally, in respect of marketing tactics, new methods of issue were experimented with towards the end of the 1970s. Thus, for example, medium-term government coupon bonds were sold through public auction rather than through indirect public subscription, where a syndicate for the subscription is formed to guarantee uptake of the full issue in the event of undersubscription by the general public, the method traditionally used to sell long-term government coupon bonds. Similarly, private placement gave way to public issue, initially by indirect public subscription but later by auction, in respect of the sale of very long-term bonds in 1986 and, in 1987, the first (partial) public auction of ten-year coupon bonds was carried out. The first full public auction occurred in 1989.

As for developments in the secondary government bond market, the impetus for change came from governmental recognition in the mid-1970s that the likely scale of future budget deficits necessitated alleviation of the burden borne by the members of the underwriting syndicate and most especially the city banks (see below). Accordingly, measures were taken to promote the wider circulation of government bonds. This involved, at first, relaxation of the restrictions on the sale by syndicate members of bonds to the general public but then spread to authorization of banks' retail sale of newly issued bonds and, eventually, of their dealing in existing bonds.

The relaxation of the restrictions on the syndicate members' sale of government bonds is traced in Exhibit 3.7. As can be seen, liberalization started with deficit bonds, spread to construction bonds and then to bonds listed on the stock exchange. In respect of bank product accounts, all time restrictions

Exhibit 3.7   *Liberalization of the public bond market: the programme of deregulation*

Date effective	Liberalization measure
1975	Government issue of 'deficit bonds' begins
January 1977	Government issue of 5-year discount bonds begins
April 1977	The selling of 'deficit' bonds 1 year after issuance by the members of the underwriting syndicate recognized
October 1977	The selling of 'construction' bonds 1 year after issuance by the members of the underwriting syndicate recognized
June 1978	Government issue (by public auction) of 3-year interest-bearing bonds begins
June 1979	Government issue of 2-year interest-bearing bonds begins
May 1980	The selling of government bonds listed on the stock exchange 7–9 months after issuance by the members of the underwriting syndicate permitted
June 1980	Government issue of 4-year interest-bearing bonds begins
April 1981	Minimum period before syndicate members could sell government bonds listed on the stock market reduced to the beginning of the month following a 3-month period after issue (i.e. about 100 days)
February 1983	Government issue of very long-term (i.e. with a maturity exceeding 10 years) interest-bearing bonds begins with the issue (by private placement) of 15-year floating-rate bonds
April 1983	Banks and other financial institutions begin to engage in retail sale of newly issued, long-term interest-bearing government bonds
August 1983	Government issue (by private placement) of 20-year fixed-rate bonds begins
October 1983	Retail sale of newly issued, medium-term and discount government bonds begun by banks and other financial institutions

Exhibit 3.7   (continued)

Date effective	Liberalization measure
June 1984	Banks permitted to deal in (existing) government bonds with a remaining term of under 2 years in the secondary market
October 1984	3 US banks allowed to start dealing in government bonds
June 1985	In respect of bank product accounts, sales of government bonds listed on the stock exchange permitted at the beginning of the second month after issuance (i.e. after about 40 days). Restrictions on which government bonds banks could deal in lifted. More banks authorized to deal
October 1985	Bond futures market established in Tokyo
April 1986	In respect of bank product accounts, minimum holding period of government bonds listed on the stock exchange reduced, allowing sales at the beginning of the first month after issuance (i.e. after about 10 days). In respect of bank investment accounts, sales permitted at the beginning of the second month after issuance (i.e. after about 40 days)
June 1986	More banks added to the list of authorized dealers in government bonds. Full dealing permitted to those authorized in June 1985
October 1986	20-year interest-bearing government bonds sold by public issue (using syndicate underwriting method)
December 1986	*Zenshinren* bank allowed to engage in retail sales of government bonds
January 1987	Post offices allowed to engage in retail sales of government bonds (effective April 1988)
April 1987	Agricultural co-operatives authorized to engage in retail sales of government bonds
June 1987	In respect of bank product accounts, all time restrictions on the sale of government bonds listed on the stock exchange scrapped. In respect of bank investment accounts, sales permitted at the beginning of the first month

Exhibit 3.7 (continued)

Date effective	Liberalization measure
	after issuance (i.e. after about 10 days). Life assurance companies authorized to engage in retail sales of government bonds (with effect from October 1987). Foreign banks, *sogo* banks and *shinkin* banks allowed to deal in government bonds
September 1987	Public auction system for sale of 20-year interest-bearing government bonds introduced
October 1987	Part of a 10-year interest-bearing government bond issue sold by auction
July 1988	20-year government bond futures contract launched (complements 10-year contract launched in October 1985)
April 1989	Auction system for the sale of long-term (i.e. with a maturity of 10 years) interest-bearing bonds introduced
June 1989	Futures and options trading (e.g. in interest, currency, etc.) began on the Tokyo International Financial Futures Exchange
May 1990	Options on 10-year government bond futures introduced
February 1996	5-year government bond futures contract launched

Sources: Adapted from JCIF (1988); press reports.

on selling were eventually scrapped in June 1987 although, for bank investment accounts, the minimum period banks had to wait before selling remained at around ten days after June 1987.

The first retail sales of newly issued government bonds (*madohan*) by banks and other financial institutions were made in April 1983, in accordance with the guidelines established by the MoF in March 1982 within its document entitled *On the Securities Business of Banks and Others*. Retail sales of medium-term bonds followed in October 1983 after the issuance of new guidelines in May 1983 incorporated in an MoF document entitled *On the Securities Business of Financial Institutions*. Other institutions later authorized to engage in the retail sale of government bonds include the *Zenshinren* bank (received authorization in December 1986), post offices (permission granted in January 1987 but not effective until April 1988), agriculture co-operatives (authorized in April 1987) and life assurance companies (granted permission in June 1987, with effect from October 1987).

Bank dealing in existing public bonds began in June 1984 although, at least initially, only in bonds with a remaining term of under two years. This restriction was lifted in June 1985 for those banks authorized in June 1984, and in June 1986 for those authorized in June 1985. Those banks acquiring authorization at this stage comprised the city banks, the long-term credit banks, the trust banks, ten regional banks and the Norinchukin Bank. This list, however, was gradually extended to include foreign banks (three US banks received authorization in October 1984 and more were authorized in June 1987), more regional banks (a further 50 received authorization in June 1985), *sogo* banks (over 40 were authorized in June 1986 and more in June 1987) and *shinkin* banks (which received authorization in June 1987).

Apart from these liberalizing measures, the development of the government bond market has also been enhanced by the creation of a bond futures market in October 1985, the creation of a financial futures exchange in April 1989, on which both options and futures are traded, and the adoption of more flexibility in the setting of issue terms (they are now revised every month).

The incentive to set up futures markets came from recognition of the need to create additional hedging opportunities for securities holders (for further details, see Suzuki, 1987, p. 140) and of the danger that the development of the domestic capital market would be adversely affected if Japan did not move to match the international competition in the global financial marketplace. The authorization granted to certain foreign securities companies resident in Japan to act as participants in the (government) bond futures market, alongside the member companies of the Tokyo Stock Exchange, a number of domestic non-member securities companies and the other financial institutions[40] licensed to deal in public bonds, was a further testament to the authorities' desire to broaden, deepen and internationalize the domestic bond market.

As for the increased flexibility in issue terms (that is, yields to subscribers) evident in today's government bond market, it is clear that this is both a result and cause of the market's consolidation. Increased flexibility was made possible (and necessitated) by relaxation of the restrictions on resale. In turn, it stimulated further demand, thereby broadening and deepening the market.

The success of all these measures to enhance the development of the government bond market can be gauged by referring to the data for trading volumes. In fiscal 1996, for example, of the ¥3190 trillion worth of trades (includes buying and selling) in yen bonds, 94 per cent was accounted for by transactions in government bonds (MoF, 1997). This compares with just 2.3 per cent in fiscal 1975. Moreover, trading in government bond futures during fiscal 1996 amounted to ¥2517 trillion.

The final set of measures concerned with the internationalization and deepening of the Japanese capital market comprise those associated with the deregulation of the yen-denominated foreign bond market and the euroyen bond market, the internationalization of the yen and the authorization of foreign companies to operate in domestic financial markets. All these issues have already been covered in some depth but, in connection with the development of the local stock market, it is worth re-emphasizing the growth of the foreign presence in Japan.

The rise in foreign stock listings, the growth in the number of overseas companies with securities-dealing licences and the admission of foreign companies to the Tokyo Stock Exchange, whether under foreign governmental pressure or not, are arguably as important for the development of the local stock market as was the admission of foreigners into trust banking, funds management and investment advisory activities for the development of those 'industries'. Concerted efforts to improve transparency (over-the-counter transactions in listed stocks are prohibited in principle) and to eliminate malpractice, notwithstanding the scandals of the late 1980s and early 1990s,[41] through, for example, the toughening of insider-dealing legislation, should also eventually bear fruit once the belief in the integrity of the market has been re-established.[42] The ability to engage in stock futures (and options) trading, first undertaken on the Osaka Securities Exchange in June 1987 (although stock index trading did not take place until 1988), is another positive feature contributing to the deepening of the local market.

The segment of the capital market with a less-than-auspicious track record is the local (straight) corporate bond market. Thus, while the volume and value of convertible (into stocks of the issuing company at a stated time in the future) and 'with-warrants' (providing holders with the right to purchase a given amount of stock at a fixed price at a stated date(s) in the future) bond issues soared during the latter half of the 1980s,[43] in line with the local stock market, the market in straight corporate bonds languished.

Apart from the competitive advantage or disadvantage deriving from gyrations of the stock market, the reasons behind the market's relatively poor performance have long been recognized: the inflexibility, compared with either the eurobond market or the domestic convertible debenture market,[44] of the criteria determining the eligibility of issuers, of the collateral requirements,[45] of the terms of issue, and of issuing procedures. To date, however, reform of practices in the domestic primary market has been slow to materialize and of limited impact.

The reform that has been undertaken began with relaxation of the 'collateral rule' which required issuers of general industrial bonds[46] to put up collateral[47] to cover the payments of interest and principal. Initiated in January 1983, the process of deregulation involved relaxation of the criteria determining eligibility for issues of unsecured domestic bonds. The reforms implemented in April 1984, October 1985 and February 1987 meant that by the last date the number of companies eligible to issue unsecured straight bonds by public offering had increased from two in March 1979 to 180.

Under the regime in force in February 1987, all companies rated 'AA' and above (or their equivalents) by recognized rating agencies, and those rated 'A' with net assets in excess of ¥55 billion, could issue unsecured straight corporate debentures by public offering. Additionally, companies with net assets in excess of ¥150 billion and which had been authorized to make 'with-warrant' issues were also eligible to issue unsecured straight corporate debentures by public offering. And finally, companies not satisfying these requirements but with net assets of at least ¥55 billion were still eligible to make such issues if they met certain financial requirements (the requirements were tougher for firms with net assets of under ¥100 billion – for further details, see JCIF, 1988, p. 82). The switch from using minimum-net-worth criteria to credit ratings to determine the eligibility of issuers was carried a step further in July 1987 when a *bona fide* rating system was introduced for bond issuance.

Reforms designed to increase competition in the new issuing market and to increase flexibility in issuing conditions (that is, coupon, issue price, maturity, issuing amount, issuing period and so on) centred on curtailment of the system of rotating underwriting mandates whereby the 'big four' securities houses took it in turns to act as underwriters to bond issues, negotiating on the issuer's behalf the issuing conditions with the issuers 'commissioned bank' (see below). From May 1987, issuing companies were encouraged to solicit competitive bids from a range of securities companies and to choose a lead manager on the basis of its evaluation of the companies' proposals in respect of issuing conditions. Subsequent to this, the actual issuing conditions would then be confirmed following discussions between the issuing company and the lead manager. The lead manager would then be held responsible for arranging a syndicate of managers and underwriters, determining the allocations within the syndicate, and helping to ensure the success of the issue by acting as a market maker in both the primary and secondary markets.

The improvement in flexibility in issuing conditions secured through this route was complemented by the authorities' decision to relax the restrictions on the maturity of issues and to sanction floating-rate note (FRN) issues. Accordingly, the traditional range of maturities – 6, 7, 10, 12 and 15 years – was extended to include shorter maturities (four years and less)[48] and FRN issues were sanctioned, all before the end of 1989.

Attempts were also made to boost the private placement *(shibosai)* market which, prior to July 1987, suffered from restrictions on the size of issue (it could not exceed the minimum issuing amount of bonds sold by public offering – ¥2 billion); the range of issuers (companies that had previously issued bonds by public offering were not eligible to make private placements under the so-called 'no-return' rule), the range of purchasers (only institutional investors, totalling not more than 49 in number, could make purchases and, for issues of over ¥1 billion, confirmation of investment purposes had to be filed with the head of the Securities Bureau of the MoF); and on resale (the extent of it was limited, and the Securities Bureau had to be informed of such occurrences). Following concerted pressure from the corporate sector the market was reformed with effect from July 1987 by abolishing the 'no-return' rule, raising the limits on individual issues to ¥10 billion and liberalizing the resale of bonds for issues of over ¥2 billion (banks, securities companies and, later, insurance companies were authorized to operate in this fashion).

The remaining reforms undertaken in the 1980s related to attempts to simplify issuing procedures. Traditionally, issuers had to wait for up to 30 days from the date of registration before they were allowed to proceed with their issues, but this waiting time was reduced to 15 days in April 1987. Shelf registration, along the lines operating in the US market, duly followed in 1989. The costs associated with the perpetuation of the 'commissioned bank' arrangement, whereby issuers are legally required under Article 304 of the Commercial Code to commission a bank to arrange collateral and to deal with many aspects of bond placement, remained in place, however, as did the ceiling on corporate bond issues (which limited firms' borrowing to twice their net asset value).

In the spring of 1992 signals emanating from the government suggested that it was in favour of abolishing the 'commissioned bank' system, allowing companies to issue bonds with maturities of one and two years, eliminating the limits on corporate bond issuance and broadening the range of companies allowed to raise funds through the domestic bond market. In the event, the only measures to appear before the promulgation of the 'big bang' initiative were a sanctioning of five-year issues (in April 1993), a relaxation of the eligibility criteria for use of the shelf registration system (in fiscal 1995) and further relaxation of the issuance eligibility criteria. The last-mentioned development saw, with effect from 1 April 1993, the minimum standard for prospective issuers of unsecured corporate bonds (straight and with-warrants) being lowered from a minimum credit-rating requirement of 'A' to one of 'BBB'. Moreover, with effect from October 1993, the net asset requirements were abolished in respect of the issuance of straight bonds or with-warrants bonds with a minimum rating of 'A'. And finally, in January 1996, the issuance eligibility criteria were abolished in their entirety.

THE PROMOTION OF CROSS-SECTORAL ENTRY UNDER THE FINANCIAL SYSTEM REFORM ACT OF 1993

Apart from the admission of foreign entities into trust banking, funds management and investment advisory business (see below) and the elimination of MoF-imposed regulations on the opening of new bank offices and the launch of new deposit products (in June and October 1995 respectively), the only other pre-'big bang' reform of note relates to the breakdown of barriers segmenting banking from securities and insurance business in Japan.

The Regulation of Japanese Commercial Banks' Domestic Securities Activities

As noted in Chapter 1, the separation of 'banking' from other types of business was historically secured through the joint use of legislative provisions and 'administrative guidance' (that is, moral suasion). The major components of the statutory framework governing the domestic operations of Japanese commercial banks were the Banking Law of 1981, Article 65 of the Securities and Exchange Law of 1948 and the Anti-Monopoly Law of 1947.

The Banking Law of 1981
Under Article 2 (Clause 2), banking business for an ordinary bank is defined as 'the taking of deposits or instalment savings, along with the lending of funds or the discounting of bills, and/or the handling of funds transfer'. Article 3 goes on to establish that the taking of deposits or instalment savings is the exclusive prerogative of banks, thereby denying securities companies access to the deposit-taking business.

Permissible (that is, ancillary or securities) non-banking business activities for ordinary banks are set out in Articles 10 (ancillary) and 11 (securities), and Article 12 prohibits engagement in any other lines of non-banking business. However, this does not preclude other forms of non-banking business – the so-called 'peripheral' business activities – being offered through domestic affiliates although, should this option be chosen, the banks become subject to strict rules concerning the capital subscription rate – 100 per cent in cases where the affiliate acts as the institution's agent or engages in 'non-essential' segments of the institution's business, and no more than 5 per cent in cases where the affiliate engages in business corresponding to ancillary or peripheral business. Moreover, the types of business permitted to affiliates with close staffing or funding ties with the institution are limited to those specified by notification of the Director General of the Banking Bureau at the Ministry of Finance (MoF) (see Chart 3.1).

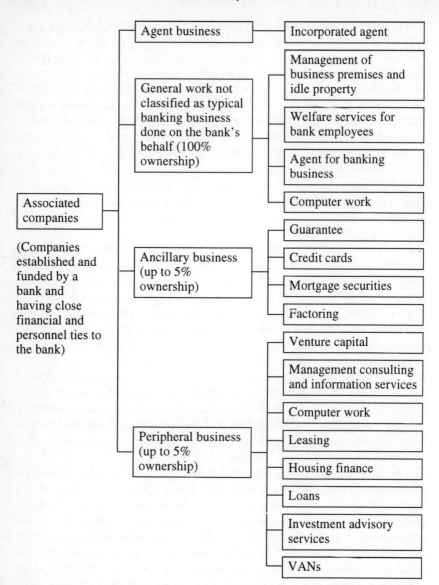

Source:　FBAJ (1989), Fig. 3.6, p. 73.

Chart 3.1　Classification of Japanese banks' associated companies

The ancillary business permitted under Article 10 (clause 2) comprises the following: the guarantee of liabilities and acceptance of bills; the purchase and sale of securities, dealing in major index securities futures, in securities options and in foreign securities futures (but only for investment purposes or on receipt of a written request for a customer); the lending of securities; the underwriting of government bonds, local government bonds and government-guaranteed bonds (but not for subsequent sale) and placement of bonds underwritten; the acquisition and ceding of monetary claims, as designated by ordinance of the MoF; the provision of subscription agency services for local government bonds, corporate bonds, and other securities; the provision of agency services for banks and other entities engaged in financial business; the handling of money transactions on behalf of national and local government bodies and corporations; the safekeeping of securities, precious metals, and other items; the changing of money; and dealing in financial futures on a custodial basis (FBAJ, 1989, pp. 43–4). Additionally, ancillary business is supposed to be of a similar nature to bank business, should not exceed bank business in volume terms and should be conducted on proper business lines, that is, it should generate income.

Permissible securities activities listed in Article 11 comprise various operations in connection with government and other bonds, including underwriting and offering for subscription and sale. Notwithstanding this, banks must still obtain permission from the MoF to engage in such securities activities, in accordance with Article 65 of the Securities and Exchange Law. Further securities activities are sanctioned as ancillary business under Article 10 of the 1981 Banking Law, as has just been noted.

Trust business is permitted under the Concurrent Trust Business Law of 1981 and may also be conducted through affiliates.

The Securities and Exchange Law of 1948

Under Article 65, banks (and trust companies and certain other forms of financial institutions, such as insurance companies) are prohibited from engaging in any form of securities business[49] except in cases where: (i) a bank purchases or sells securities on the written order and for the account of its customers; or (ii) a bank purchases and sells securities for its own investment purposes in accordance with the provisions of other laws or for the account of a trust or pursuant to a trust agreement; or (iii) a bank engages in securities transactions with respect to national government bonds, local government bonds or government-guaranteed bonds. (Special approval has to be obtained from the MoF to engage in these activities, however.)

The separation of securities and banking business effected by Article 65 applies not only to the banking and securities companies themselves but also to their Japanese subsidiaries. The law does not apply to Japanese companies' overseas operations, however.

The Anti-Monopoly Law of 1947 (as amended in 1977)

In spite of the provisions of the Banking Law and the Securities and Exchange Law, ordinary Japanese banks can, of course, diversify into securities business indirectly through their own and their subsidiaries' and affiliates' investments in Japanese securities companies. While Article 11 of the Anti-Monopoly Law limits such equity stakes to 5 per cent, multiple holdings within a banking group would allow for much larger exposures to be built up – if not effective control to be secured. In recognition of this danger, somewhat belatedly, some might argue, the MoF moved in May 1988 to limit the extent of such ties by instructing banks to limit *group* holdings of securities houses' equity to less than 50 per cent of the total outstanding.

Implementation and interpretation of the legal provisions

As is evident from Chart 3.1 securities business does not feature among the lines of business which ordinary banks are allowed to offer through affiliates with close staffing or funding ties. This means that, *de facto,* banks' securities opportunities arise, in the main, from the exclusions to the general prohibition incorporated in Article 65 of the Securities and Exchange Law. Thus, ordinary banks *can*, in law: buy and sell securities domestically on the written order and for the account of their customers; buy and sell securities domestically for the account of a trust or pursuant to a trust agreement; buy and sell securities domestically for their own investment purposes and, with MoF approval, engage in a wider range of securities activities abroad (see below); and, again with MoF approval, engage domestically in securities operations with respect to public bonds.

The last two categories are significant as they indicate the extent to which banks are dependent upon the whims of the MoF in respect of their securities operations. Moreover, extensive MoF *administrative guidance* has also to be adhered to. As far as *domestic* securities operations are concerned, ordinary banks were prohibited until 1983 from engaging in *any* securities activities other than the underwriting of public bonds – all banks belonged to the government bond underwriting syndicate – and the buying and selling of securities for investment purposes, despite the additional concessions available under Article 65. Since them however, the MoF has taken a more liberal line and gradually relaxed the constraints imposed on banks' domestic securities activities. For example, in April 1983, banks were permitted to sell long-term[50] public bonds which they had underwritten to the general public[51, 52] and, in June 1984, general dealing in public bonds was permitted.[53] These two moves necessitated amendments to the Banking and Securities and Exchange Laws but, in line with Article 65 of the latter, prior authorization was still required from the MoF

More recently, opportunities have arisen for the banks in the commercial paper[54] and government bond options and futures markets.[55] They are also permitted to engage in housing-loan mortgage trust activities (that is, operations in mortgage-backed securities)[56] and, subject to obtaining a discretionary fund-management licence, in the management of new money destined for certain kinds of pension funds. Finally, apart from their trust business activities, they also engage in investment advisory activities according to the Investment Advisory Law of 1986 and can act as intermediaries for the private placement of public or private bonds. The advisory services, however, are usually provided through affiliations with securities investment advisory companies.

The Regulation of Japanese Commercial Banks' Securities Operations Overseas

As noted earlier, Article 65 of the Securities and Exchange Law does not apply to Japanese banks' overseas operations. Nevertheless, such overseas activities are constrained not only by virtue of the application of foreign laws but also by MoF administrative guidance. Accordingly, since the early 1970s, Japanese banks have only been allowed to engage in such activities through merchant bank subsidiaries incorporated overseas. Moreover, the precise type and nature of the permissible activities have been strictly defined.

In the early days, the merchant bank subsidiaries engaged primarily in euromarket activities, such as underwriting corporate and sovereign bonds, but even here the so-called 'three-bureau' guidance precluded them from lead-managing issues for Japanese companies.[57] They were allowed, however, to lead-manage euroyen issues for non-Japanese borrowers and also for Japanese corporate subsidiaries located overseas provided that the issue was made on the strength of the subsidiary's name and did not involve the issue of a parental guarantee. Restrictions also prevented them from selling euroyen bonds directly into Japan within 90 days of the issue date.

The traffic was not all one way, however. For example, in October 1986 the MoF gave permission for the banks' overseas securities subsidiaries to deal in commercial paper issued overseas – this is denied to the Japanese banks' overseas branches – and in January 1989 the Industrial Bank of Japan, with the agreement of the MoF, became the first Japanese bank to engage in equity market-making overseas (hitherto it had confined its overseas activities to debt and equity warrant activities but the new plans involved making markets in ten leading Japanese stocks), although it was prohibited from dealing with Japanese clients from its London operation.

Apart from their success in London, merchant bank activities also proved popular in Switzerland, West Germany (both 'universal banking' centres) and the USA, with the last-mentioned also proving a popular site for the establishment of mergers and acquisitions boutiques.[58] These US activities followed on from the acquisition of primary dealerships[59] and the setting up of trust companies, brokerage subsidiaries[60] and leasing operations[61] in the late 1980s.

In the UK, while the underwriting of new eurobond issues and the selling and trading of eurobonds remain their core business, some of the longer-established firms offer a fuller range of services, including investment management, loan syndication, market-making (for example, in equity warrants, Japanese equities, ECU Treasury bills[62]), swaps, and mergers and acquisitions business. And, aided by the MoF's easing of the restrictions on Japanese corporations issuing euroyen commercial paper in the mid-1980s, many of the subsidiaries are now also active in these markets in addition to dealing in the sterling commercial paper market.[63] Finally, it is worth noting that a Japanese regional bank, the Bank of Yokohama, secured entry into the UK merchant banking industry through a successful bid for Guinness Mahon in 1989.

The Regulation of Overseas Financial Companies' Operations in Japan

Overseas banks' securities operations in Japan

The establishment of foreign-owned securities companies in Japan is governed by two securities laws: the Law on Foreign Securities Firms of 1971 and the Securities and Exchange Law. The former law was designed to administer the entry and regulation of foreign securities firms although it relates primarily to the establishment of a *branch*, which requires an MoF licence. The establishment of a *representative office*, which is not allowed to conduct business, requires prior notification being given to the MoF; while a firm contemplating the setting up of a *subsidiary* has to comply with the provisions of the Securities and Exchange Law.[64]

The acquisition, or takeover, of a Japanese securities firm is regulated by Japanese anti-monopoly law, and approval from the Japan Fair Trade Commission has to be secured for all holdings in excess of 5 per cent of the outstanding equity.

As for supervision, the companies fall within the purview of the Securities Bureau of the MoF and most hold all four securities business licences: the licence to underwrite security issues, the licence to distribute securities, the licence to deal in securities as a principal, and the licence to deal in securities as an agent.

The first foreign banks to be allowed to establish securities subsidiaries in Japan were Deutsche Bank and Security Pacific National Bank. They both received the green light in December 1985. Prior to this date, foreign banks' securities affiliates had been refused permission by the MoF to establish offices or branches in Japan on the grounds that banking and securities business were legally separated in Japan. Following pressure from those countries, notably West Germany, entertaining Japanese banks engaged in securities activities, however, the MoF eventually relented and decided that bank affiliates in which the parent bank holding did not exceed 50 per cent could conduct securities business in Japan. The reasoning behind this approach was that a legally independent entity could not be held to be in breach of Article 65 of the Securities and Exchange Law. Other foreign banks soon followed in the footsteps of the Deutsche Bank and the Security Pacific National Bank (see Exhibit 3.8) and one was even allowed to enter in its own name and not through the restricted equity-holding route. By the end of 1986, 12 US investment banks had licences to operate securities branches in Japan, together with a number of British and European commercial banks.

Another source of contention for overseas firms and governments was access to the Tokyo Stock Exchange. Although numerous securities-broking licences had been awarded to foreign-owned companies prior to 1986, this involved the overseas companies in the payment of 27 per cent of the commission received on the buying and selling of shares to member Japanese securities companies. Not unnaturally, and especially in the light of the asymmetry in the national treatment of foreign securities companies, foreign companies, often backed by their governments,[65] campaigned vociferously for easier access to the Tokyo Stock Exchange. The Japanese authorities eventually relented and in 1986 foreign firms were admitted for the first time.[66] Foreign membership has been expanded at periodic intervals since then, with further admissions occurring in 1988 and 1990.[67]

In addition to securities broking and dealing,[68] foreign firms (including banks) have successfully entered the following markets in Japan: trust banking (since 1985);[69] government bond auctions;[70] funds management;[71] and investment advisory services.

Overseas securities firms' banking operations in Japan

Apart from engaging in much the same range of securities operations in Japan as do the overseas banks (for example, securities underwriting, trading and broking, investment management and advisory services), foreign securities firms may also engage in banking operations. The precedent was created in January 1991 when the MoF granted the European-based banking subsidiaries of three US-based securities houses – Morgan Stanley, Salomon Brothers and Goldman Sachs – preliminary licences to open branches in Japan to offer banking services. The foreign securities houses, however, are limited to a 50

*Exhibit 3.8   Foreign securities companies' operations in Japan at 31
December 1988*

Date of branch opening	Company	Membership of TSE
July 1972	Merrill Lynch	✓
December 1978	Merrill Lynch – Osaka	✓
November 1985	Merrill Lynch – Nagoya	
March 1988	Merrill Lynch – Yokohama	✓
October 1978	Citicorp Vickers	✓
January 1980	Prudential Bache	✓
June 1980	Smith Barney	✓
May 1981	Jardine Fleming	✓
September 1982	Salomon Brothers	✓
June 1983	Kidder Peabody	✓
September 1987	Kidder Peabody – Osaka	✓
November 1983	Goldman Sachs	✓
June 1984	Morgan Stanley	✓
January 1985	S.G. Warburg	✓
March 1985	W.I. Carr	✓
July 1985	First Boston	
December 1985	Drexel Burnham	
December 1985	Kleinwort Benson	✓
March 1986	Schroder	✓
April 1986	Hoare Govett	✓
April 1986	Paine Webber	✓
May 1986	DB Capital Markets (Deutsche Bank)	✓
May 1986	Shearson Lehman	✓
June 1986	Cazenove	✓
September 1986	Baring	✓
October 1986	Dresdner ABD Securities (Dresdner Bank)	
October 1986	SBCI (Swiss Bank Corporation)	
October 1986	County Natwest	
December 1986	DG Securities (DB Bank)	
February 1987	SoGen Securities (Société Générale)	
February 1987	UBS Phillips and Drew	
April 1987	Morgan Grenfell	
June 1987	James Capel	
June 1987	Commerz Securities (Commerzbank)	
June 1987	Amro (Amsterdam–Rotterdam Bank)	
June 1987	WESTLB Securities (Westdeutsche Landesbank)	

Exhibit 3.8 *(continued)*

Date of branch opening	Company	Membership of TSE
June 1987	Paribas Capital Markets (Banque Paribas)	
June 1987	Chase Manhattan Securities	
June 1987	Midland Montagu	
October 1987	BT Asia (Bankers Trust)	
October 1987	BV Capital Markets (Bayerische Vereinsbank)	
November 1987	JP Morgan (Morgan Guaranty Trust)	
December 1987	Credit Lyonnais Finanz	
December 1987	Manufacturers Hanover Asia	
February 1988	BHF Securities (Berliner Handels und Frankfurter Bank)	
February 1988	Chemical Securities (Chemical Bank)	
April 1988	Smith New Court	
June 1988	BNP Securities (Banque Nationale de Paris)	

Note: All branches are established in Tokyo unless otherwise indicated. Each firm is listed in order of its first branch opening in Japan, thereafter each branch of a given firm is listed in date order.

Source: Trenchard (1990), p. 119.

per cent stake in their banking units. The banking services planned comprised mainly foreign exchange dealing and currency and interest-rate swaps.

SUMMARY

Despite a fairly extensive legislative framework, the separation of banking and securities business in Japan was far from complete. This was due partly to the exemptions and exclusions from the legal prohibitions on the joint offering of banking and securities services, partly to the administrative decisions made by the MoF,[72] and partly to the natural evolution of the financial marketplace, which had witnessed a general fusion of banking and securities business, as in many parts of the globe. Like their US counterparts, the Japanese authorities tolerated, while not actively encouraging, their securities firms'[73] and commercial banks' diversification into a wide range of overseas banking and securities activities, respectively. Their treatment of foreign companies – be they banks or securities firms – in Japan diminished the case for continued strict separation of banking and securities business for domestic concerns in Japan.[74] As in the USA, commercial banks could and actively did participate in many securities activities.[75]

The Case for Reform

In attempting to establish a case for reform of the legislative framework surrounding commercial banks' involvement in securities business, a convenient starting-point is a reassessment of the original rationale for the establishment of the relevant primary legislation.[76] Of particular interest, given America's influence in the drafting of the legislative provisions of Article 65 of the Securities and Exchange Law, is the Glass–Steagall Act of 1933.

In respect of the Glass–Steagall Act, a thorough review has already been conducted by Benston (1990). He identifies seven[77] reasons which have been or might possibly be advanced for continuing with the separation of commercial and investment banking effected under the Glass–Steagall Act of 1933:

(i)   to help protect customers from conflict-of-interest abuse (for example, from receiving biased investment advice);
(ii)   to reduce individual bank risk;
(iii)   to remove the temptation for banks to make loans to support the price of securities held (or underwritten) directly or by affiliates;
(iv)   to help stabilize the banking system (that is, to reduce systemic risk through routes (ii) and (iii);
(v)   to reduce taxpayer exposure and to prevent the misallocation of resources which intervention might entail (a requirement to limit banks' engagement in riskier activities is deemed necessary because of their access to the so-called federal safety net through discount window borrowing and deposit insurance arrangements, implicit guarantees and so on);
(vi)   to ensure competitive equity prevails between the banks on the one hand and securities brokers and underwriters on the other (again, this is held to warrant the limiting of banks to traditional commercial banking operations because of their privileged access to the federal safety net which, it is alleged, provides access to cheap deposits which can be used for cross-subsidization); and
(vii)   to avoid an excessive concentration of power and reduction in competition which abolition of the existing restrictions might eventually lead to.

Each of these arguments, however, can be challenged.

(i)   On the issue of the need to shield consumers from conflict-of-interest abuse, it should be noted that there may be alternative and more cost-effective means available than the option of outright prohibition on the undertaking of certain activities (Hall, 1987), assuming, of course, that the maintenance of a good reputation is an insufficient incentive for the institutions to refrain from taking advantage of their customers.

(ii)   On the subject of risk, it is not intuitively obvious that securities activities are inherently more risky than traditional, or even more modern commercial banking activities (for example, operations in the swaps, options and futures markets). Even if they were shown to be so, their returns might still justify investment in them.[78] Secondly, whatever the riskiness of individual activities, it should be remembered that, in principle, diversification into such areas may offer the prospect of a reduction of overall portfolio risk, where this is measured as the variability in portfolio returns (Jensen, 1972).[79]

(iii)   The problem of banks being tempted to support security prices can be dealt with adequately in differing ways. For example, the appropriate use of firewalls (such as the Federal Reserve Board's rules 23A and 23B),[80] codes of conduct, monitoring and sanctions for breaches of the rules and regulations should reduce the temptation and the associated potential risks for both the banks and the wider system.

(iv)   With regard to preserving the stability of the banking system, it can be argued that stability is best promoted by allowing commercial banks the widest possible freedoms in the longer term, subject to necessary checks and safeguards to protect consumers from possible conflict of interest and other abuse, to ensure the prudent operation of the business,[81] and to prevent abuse arising from excessive concentration of economic and political power (see below).

(v)   In respect of the need to contain taxpayer exposure and reduce the chances of resources being misallocated through official intervention, there is no *a priori* reason why allowing banks to engage in a wider range of securities activities should lead to adverse results on either front.[82] This is because such diversification need neither result in an increase in risk nor in an institution's propensity to take risk. Indeed, if diversification did lead to a reduction in risk, the impact in the two areas of concern would actually be positive. Moreover, the regulatory authorities could always take restraining measures (such as through manipulation of the risk-based solvency requirements – see Hall, 1989) should they wish to deter certain kinds of activity.

(vi)   On the thorny subject of competitive equity, it is not clear that provision of an official safety net confers a competitive advantage on commercial banks. For example, costs, both explicit and implicit, are borne by those covered by the safety net in the form of: insurance premiums (albeit mispriced);[83] examinations; supervision; regulations; reporting requirements; fees; interest-free loans (that is, required reserves) to the central bank; and the lodging of security against discount window lending. It should also be appreciated that there probably already exists (implicitly if not explicitly: actions taken in the wake of the stock market crash of October 1987 point to the latter) a federal safety net for securities firms, which is almost certainly underpriced, to the benefit of such firms.

(vii)   Finally, on the subjects of concentration and competition, the existing concentration in the securities underwriting industry might lead one to support reduction of the barriers to entry imposed on commercial banks. But even if the worst fears of the anti-reform lobby are realized and, perhaps because of their competitive advantages (federally derived or otherwise) and the existence of potentially large and unexploited economies of scale and scope, 'universal banks' come to dominate the financial arena, remedies remain for dealing with any undesirable consequences. For example, the risk of failure could be reduced through expeditious use of risk-based capital requirements and other supervisory techniques, and 'appropriate' resolution policies;[84] anti-trust laws can be used to deal with the problems arising from the concentration of power; and the existing array of legal and market remedies, such as Chinese Walls,[85] for handling conflicts of interest, backed up, if necessary, by more intensive monitoring and stiffer penalties for abuse, can be employed to deal with the likely increase in conflict-of-interest situations that banks would face.

In short, little of the original rationale for enforcing the separation of commercial and investment banking stands up to scrutiny, and any legitimate fears that remain can be adequately dealt with through alternative, and more cost-effective, means. The defenders of the *status quo* in Japan, however, stressed their concerns about the proliferation of conflicts of interest that reform would induce, the imbalances in competitive conditions[86] that might favour banks with expanded powers, with concomitant implications for concentration[87] and competitiveness in the financial sector, and the possible damage that reform might do to the stability of the banking sector.

Apart from the weakness of the traditional case for continuing with the enforced separation of securities and banking business, yet further pressures for reform emerged. These embrace, *inter alia*: the banks' desire to meet changing client requirements as the distinction between banking and securities business becomes increasingly blurred and technological advances in communications and computing systems dramatically increase the range of possible business options; the desire of banks (and regulators, for stability reasons) to be given access to new sources of revenue because of the impact of competition, deregulation and securitization on their traditional lending margins;[88] the authorities' wish to deal with the competitive and regulatory anomalies which have emerged because of the differential treatment of foreign and domestic financial institutions' activities in the home market and of domestic institutions' home and overseas activities;[89] and the regulators' need to respond to underlying structural changes in their domestic markets as a result of structural changes in their economies. Above all, governments were keen to improve the efficient functioning of financial institutions and markets,[90] the former being aided by allowing institutions to reap economies of scope and by enhancing their risk-management capacity (for example, by allowing for further diversification and access to additional hedging mediums), and the latter benefiting from promotion of competition and financial innovation.

The Options for Reform

The alternatives
The major alternative routes[91] to reform would appear to embrace the following:

(i) require banks to offer securities business through wholly owned, non-bank securities subsidiaries. This could involve the banks in offering securities business through direct non-bank subsidiaries, either multifunctional or functionally separated by type of non-banking business (the Canadian approach) or through subsidiaries of bank holding companies (the 'section 20' route adopted in the USA for extending bank powers within the confines of the Glass–Steagall Act);

(ii) allow banks to offer securities facilities direct to the general public through their existing branch networks (the universal banking model);

(iii) gradually extend the range of exceptions to the general prohibition on banks engaging in securities business (the so-called piecemeal approach). This was the approach adopted pre-1993, allowing diversification to financial institutions on a balanced basis within the confines of the existing legally segmented system.

The relative merits of the different options are set out in Exhibit 3.9.

Exhibit 3.9   A comparison of the relative merits of different options for reforming Article 65

Option	Merits	Demerits
1. Bank's securities business to be conducted within wholly owned non-bank securities subsidiaries[a] (i) where the subsidiaries are *direct subsidiaries of the bank*; or (ii) where the subsidiaries are *subsidiaries of bank holding companies*.	1. (i) Legal separation maximizes protection of the payments and settlement system and minimizes the potential scope for abuse arising from conflict-of-interest situations, whilst allowing the parent access to new income sources. (The holding company route is clearly preferred on these grounds.) (ii) Allows for isolation of the securities operation from explicit and implicit government guarantees and facilitates functional supervision. (iii) Minimizes disturbances caused to the balance of competitive equality by preserving the existing vertical separation of the various types of business conducted by the parent companies. (The holding company route is the least preferred on this count.)	1. (i) Legal separation of the banking and securities business does not insulate the banking operation from all adverse reactions associated with the poor performance of the securities operation; moral responsibilities (with or without the coercion of supervisory authorities) and market realities will ensure that the fortunes of the two separate operations are inextricably linked. (ii) It is a high-cost option for the banks and one which limits the potential benefits to be reaped from economies of scope, according to the restrictiveness of the firewall structure adopted. (On efficiency grounds, the multifunctional, direct subsidiary option is clearly preferred.)
2. Banks allowed to offer securities facilities themselves direct to the general public through their branch networks (the so-called *universal banking*	2. (i) Allows the banks maximum flexibility in the choice of operation, thereby maximizing the potential gains reaped from economies of scope and diversification as well as	2. (i) Conflict-of-interest situations would abound, creating the potential for wide-scale abuse. (ii) Banking operations are more directly exposed to possible cross-

model, applied in Germany and elsewhere).

(ii) Would best promote the internationalization of Japan's capital market as most financial centres are following the lead of Europe towards the adoption of universal banking principles.

(iii) The best way of promoting competition in the financial services sector, with concomitant benefits for the economy and the consumer.

3. Gradually extending the range of exceptions to the general prohibition on banks' involvement in securities activities (the so-called *piecemeal* approach).

3. (i) Minimizes market disturbances and 'turf' disputes, thereby appeasing vested interests.

operational efficiency.
contamination from securities operations, thereby possibly threatening the stability of the banking system and increasing taxpayers' exposure via the deposit insurance system and the official support programme.

(iii) The risk of excessive concentration of power and business within bank hands is highest.

(iv) Potentially highly disruptive for the domestic financial system, at least during a transitional phase.

(v) Arguably[b], this approach would best serve the interests of the banks, thereby upsetting the balance of 'competitive equity'.

3. (i) At best, delays, and at worst, reduces the scale of, the enjoyment of economic benefits.

(ii) Likely to artificially distort capital markets.

Notes:

[a] These subsidiaries may be multifunctional. (i.e. allowed to engage in a wide range of non-banking business) or restricted to engaging solely in securities business.

[b] This presupposes, of course, that the net effects of external regulations and supervision (embracing, *inter alia*, monitoring and reporting, capital and liquidity requirements, reserve requirements, moral suasion, balance sheet restraints, implicit and explicit government guarantees, etc.) are a positive benefit to banks, a situation which is not at all clear.

Assessment of the Reform Options

A useful starting-point is the interim report by the Second Financial System Committee of the Financial System Research Council (Financial System Research Council, 1989) wherein the Committee argued that the following factors should be taken into account when assessing the relative merits of reform proposals:

(i) Users' requirements. The relevant questions to be answered are: to what extent will reform promote competition, thereby contributing to an increase in consumer choice, an improvement in product quality and/or to cuts in product prices/service charges?; will reform promote innovation and contribute to the growth and vitality of markets?; will reform allow institutions to diversify away risk?

(ii) Internationalization requirements. The relevant issues are the extent to which changes will facilitate market entry by overseas users, prevent the hollowing of domestic markets and permit the exercise of responsibilities commensurate with Japan's international standing. The compatibility of the reformed financial system with overseas systems is another important consideration.

(iii) The maintenance of financial stability. Here the concern is with the continuing protection of depositors and maintenance of an orderly credit system. Solutions to any problems posed on either front must be found before reform can be contemplated.

(iv) Preservation of the integrity of the capital market. Here the concern is to ensure that changes do not undermine public confidence in the operation of the capital market through, for example, inducing wide-scale abuse of conflict-of-interest situations.

(v) 'Competitive equity'.

Using this framework, the Second Financial System Committee evaluated five conceivable formulas (the 'five formulas' – see Exhibit 3.10) for revising the Japanese financial system. It came out in favour of the wholly owned subsidiary route to reform,[92] which envisages either functionally separated subsidiaries or a single, multifunctional subsidiary, possibly engaged solely in wholesale finance (that is options B and C of the 'five formulas'), for the following reasons:

(i) Although the holding company route does offer the prospect of substantial economic gains and does provide a degree of effective protection against conflicts of interest, it would require repeal of Article 9 of Japan's Anti-Monopoly Law which is not deemed desirable in the light

Exhibit 3.10   The 'five formulas' for reform in Japan

A. Piecemeal approach	To keep the basic system as it is and handle specific problems associated with particular financial instruments separately, allowing various types of banks and securities companies to gradually encroach on each other's business areas.
B. Separated subsidiaries	To authorize banks and securities companies to establish wholly owned subsidiaries in each of the specified financial areas (e.g. Canada).
C. Multifunctional subsidiary	To allow each bank and securities company to set up anew a wholly owned subsidiary which can (exceptionally) engage in a wide range of securities and banking activities within a certain limited field (e.g. wholesale).
D. Holding company	To allow banks and securities firms to create holding companies which have various types of financial subsidiaries, e.g. US Proxmire Financial Modernization Act.
E. Universal bank	To introduce a European-type universal banking system, which does not distinguish between banking and securities businesses, e.g. Germany, France, UK and other EU countries, Switzerland, etc.

Source: Financial System Research Council (1989), p. 51.

of the concentration of economic and political power which might result (Japan's prewar experience with the *zaibatsu* provides a salutary reminder of the potential dangers).

(ii) Although the least disruptive, continuation of the piecemeal approach would make it difficult to improve user services or to build an internationally acceptable or compatible financial system.

(iii) Although the universal banking model (adoption of which would require repeal of Article 65) offers the greatest potential economic gains, doubts persist about the authorities' ability to deal adequately with the resultant conflicts of interest and about the possibly destabilizing impact on the banking system and the wider financial system in Japan. However, in recognition of the possibility that, depending on the environment and nature of the new operations, the establishment of a new subsidiary might inflate overhead costs whilst bringing few benefits to users, the Committee recommended that consideration be given to discussing ways 'to ease regulations affecting the operating spheres of parent financial institutions' (p. 50).

Of the two subsidiary routes to reform, the Committee noted that both approaches posed relatively few problems for Japan, at least in the short run. Thus, either singly or as a combination (or, alternatively, institutions might be left to select their mode of operation), both approaches were acceptable in principle.

In comparing their relative merits, however, the Committee noted that the multifunctional subsidiaries approach had the comparative advantage of lower spending costs and greater flexibility and shared the customer service advantages of universal banking. Offset against this, however, is that it would be more difficult than in the separated subsidiaries scenario to ensure sound banking and prevent conflicts of interest; and it would further complicate matters by introducing a new type of financial institution, the multifunctional subsidiary.

Although noting in its second interim report (Financial System Research Council, 1990, p. 25) the widespread belief that the separated subsidiaries route is the less desirable of the two options on competitive equity grounds, because it might favour banks by virtue of their relative advantages in terms of capital strength and privileged position *vis-à-vis* access to the official safety net and information on their customers, the Committee nevertheless favoured formula B over formula C on the grounds that it represented the superior formula for mutual entry from the standpoints of achieving a level playing field, preventing harmful conflicts of interest, protecting depositors, preserving the stability of the banking system, and internationalizing Japan's financial system. Formula C's comparative advantage was deemed to lie in the maximization of efficiency gains and user benefits.

Such, then, represented the deliberations of the Second Financial System Committee of the Financial System Research Council.

The Outcome

Whatever the respective merits of the universal banking route to reform, the Japanese authorities (though, somewhat ironically, not the ruling Liberal Democratic Party), like their US counterparts, ruled it out of court because of their concerns for stability, depositor and consumer protection, and competition. Similarly, fears about the likely ensuing degree of concentration precluded sponsorship of the holding company option. Given an acceptance of the need for reform and an official eschewal of a continuation of the piecemeal approach, this left of the five options considered only the subsidiary routes for further consideration; and, for the reasons given earlier, it is the separated rather than the multifunctional subsidiaries formula which received the seal of approval. Accordingly, in June 1992 the Diet agreed on proposals incorporated within the Financial System Reform Bill to allow banks and securities companies to engage in each other's areas of activity through wholly owned, separately capitalized subsidiaries. Brokerage, however, would still be denied to the banks – at least for the time being, because of the parlous state of the securities industry – and an appropriate set of firewalls[93] would be placed between the parents and their subsidiaries. In this manner, ordinary banks would be allowed into trust banking and securities business, trust banks into securities business, securities firms into ordinary and trust banking, and long-term credit banks and the specialized bank for foreign exchange into ordinary banking, trust banking and securities business. Cross-sectoral entry involving insurance business would be effected at a later date. The new Act came into force in April 1993.

The Development of Cross-Sectoral Entry Under the Financial System Reform Act of 1993

Since enactment of the new law the pace of reform has been slow, with the authorities determining priorities in the shape of which industry types should be allowed to diversify first (long-term credit banks and trust banks were generally favoured at the expense of ordinary banks, for example)[94] and the institutions themselves treading wearily because of the costs and perceived risks associated with rapid and wide-ranging diversification. Moreover, the deregulation proved to be more limited than planned. The securities subsidiaries of private banks, for example, apart from being banned from brokerage, were restricted in their underwriting/trading activities to the underwriting and trading of straight corporate bonds, public bonds, bank debentures, and investment securities, and to the underwriting of convertible bonds and bonds with warrants.[95] (Such restrictions did not apply to the activities of overseas banks' securities subsidiaries in Japan.[96]) In other words, they were excluded from equity-related activities altogether and from trades in convertible bonds and bonds with warrants. (They were, however, allowed to deal in CP, CDs placed overseas, housing-loan trust certificates and car-loan trusts.) Similarly, the trust banking subsidiaries of securities companies and banks,[97] in order to protect the beleaguered trust banks, were denied access to both 'large-lot'

Exhibit 3.11   The development of cross-entry by financial institutions under the Financial System Reform Act of 1993

A.   The establishment of securities subsidiaries by banks

Parent institution	Subsidiary created	Date operational
Industrial Bank of Japan	IBJ Securities	July 1993
Long-Term Credit Bank of Japan	LTCB Securities	July 1993
Norinchukin Bank	Norinchukin Securities	July 1993
Mitsubishi Trust & Banking	Mitsubishi TB Securities	November 1993
Sumitomo Trust & Banking	Sumitomo Trust Securities	November 1993
Asahi Bank	Asahi Securities	July 1994
Yasuda Trust & Banking	Yasuda Trust Securities	August 1994
Dai-Ichi Kangyo Bank	DKB Securities	November 1994
Sakura Bank	Sakura Securities	November 1994
Fuji Bank	Fuji Securities	November 1994
Bank of Tokyo–Mitsubishi	Tokyo–Mitsubishi Securities	November 1994
Sanwa Bank	Sanwa Securities	November 1994
Sumitomo Bank	Sumitomo Capital Securities	November 1994
Tokai Bank	Tokai International Securities	March 1995
Hokkaido Takushoku Bank	Hokkaido Takushoku Securities	April 1995
Mitsui Trust & Banking	Mitsui Trust Securities	May 1995
Toyo Trust & Banking	Toyo Trust Securities	November 1995
Bank of Yokohama	BOY Securities	November 1996
Zenshinren Bank	Shinkin Securities	November 1996
Daiwa Bank	Cosmo Securities[1]	September 1993

Note: [1]   Created via an acquisition.

Source: Federation of Bankers' Associations of Japan (1997).

B. The establishment of trust bank subsidiaries[1] by banks and securities companies

Parent institution	Subsidiary created	Date operational
Nomura Securities	Nomura Trust and Banking	October 1993
Daiwa Securities	Daiwa International Trust Bank	October 1993
Nikko Securities	Nikko Trust and Banking	October 1993
Yamaichi Securities	Yamaichi Trust and Banking	October 1993
Bank of Tokyo – Mitsubishi	Toyo Trust Bank	October 1993
Zenshinren Bank	Shinkin Trust Bank	April 1994
Nippon Credit Bank	Nippon Credit Trust Bank	April 1994
Tokai Bank	Tokai Trust and Banking	September 1995
Norinchukin Bank	Norinchukin Trust and Banking	September 1995
Industrial Bank of Japan	IBJ Trust and Banking	November 1995
Dai-Ichi Kangyo Bank	Dai-Ichi Kangyo Trust and Banking	December 1995
Sanwa Bank	Sanwa Trust and Banking	December 1995
Sakura Bank	Sakura Trust and Banking	January 1996
Asahi Bank	Asahi Trust and Banking	March 1996
Fuji Bank	Fuji Trust and Banking	June 1996
Sumitomo Bank	SB Trust Bank	July 1996
Long-Term Credit Bank of Japan	LTCB Trust and Banking	December 1997
Bank of Tokyo—Mitsubishi	Nippon Trust Bank[2]	November 1994

Notes:
[1] The Act also permits regional banks, member banks of the 'Second Association' of regional banks and *shinkin* banks to enter into trust business directly or indirectly by acting as an agent for trust banks. As of end April 1997, 17 such banks deal with trust business directly and 180 banks indirectly.
[2] Created via an acquisition.

Source: Federation of Bankers' Associations of Japan (1997).

129

securities trusts (the so-called *tokkin* funds) and the special loan trusts in which public funds are invested.

Notwithstanding these difficulties, by the end of 1997 some 20 banks were operating securities subsidiaries, with 18 major financial concerns operating trust bank subsidiaries (see Exhibit 3.11). And in September 1996, life assurance companies and non-life companies were allowed to enter each other's business through wholly owned subsidiaries.

NOTES

1. No separate working guidelines were given for the issue of foreign-currency-denominated foreign bonds (*shogun* bonds) in Japan with the result that, from November 1985, the rules applying for yen-denominated foreign bonds were recognized as applicable.
2. That is, those with a good record of issuing yen-denominated foreign bonds.
3. Impact loans of less than one year's maturity were prohibited until June 1979 and Japanese foreign exchange banks were not permitted to make impact loans until March 1980. Euroyen impact loans were not authorized until June 1984.
4. Non-corporate residents were allowed for the first time to hold up to ¥3 million with banks abroad, and residents in general were free to invest abroad in foreign securities and to make foreign loans (subject to prior reporting). Before 1986, the purchase of foreign securities by non-bank institutional investors had been severely restricted (see Osugi, 1990, Table 5, p. 19).
5. The ¥3 million limit on non-corporate resident holdings of foreign currency deposits with Japanese banks was abolished in December 1980 and the Japanese foreign exchange banks' freedom to accept foreign currency deposits (from residents and non-residents) and make foreign currency loans was enhanced.
6. Non-residents could issue bonds in Japan, subject to prior reporting. They could also purchase and sell Japanese securities without possessing a licence and hold non-resident bank accounts, reducing the 'non-resident free yen accounts' of the Japanese banks.
7. A third, Fitch Investors' Service, was added in July 1987.
8. *Unrated* private corporations, however, were still eligible if they satisfied certain size-related criteria relating to minimum capitalization and other balance sheet ratios (see JCIF, 1988, pp. 58–9).
9. In June 1986 five types of product were available: floating-rate notes; zero coupon bonds; deep discount bonds; currency conversion bonds; and dual-currency bonds. Prior to this date, only fixed-rate products with a minimum term of five years were recognized. And finally, in June 1987, restrictions on euroyen bonds with a four-year maturity were lifted.
10. On condition that the banks exercised self-restraint and refrained from channelling the funds back into the country.
11. Under the Foreign Exchange and Foreign Trade Control Law of 1980, non-residents of Japan had to obtain the approval of the MoF before issuing yen-denominated bonds outside Japan. The MoF's practice had been to grant this approval on an issuance-by-issuance basis (except for issuance under the 'medium-term note' (MTN) programme, when 'blanket approval' had earlier been made available). With effect from 1 April 1995, a blanket approval, which remained effective for one year, was generally available to such issuers of bonds, whether or not the bonds were issued under the MTN programme
12. Under the previous rules, applicable to both resident and non-resident euroyen bond issues alike, resale (i.e. 'flow-back') into Japan was prohibited for 90 days (180 days for dual-currency bonds).
13. Under the Securities and Exchange Law, an issuer who intends to issue securities by way of a public offering must, as a general rule, file a securities registration statement with the

MoF. A 15-day waiting period then becomes operable (although this can be shortened in certain circumstances). However, if an issuer satisfies certain criteria set out in the law, it is able to use a 'shelf registration system', which enables it to make issues, at times of its own choice, within the shelf registration period without the need for further notification/ approval. Relaxation of these criteria allowed more foreign issuers – sovereign and corporate – to take advantage of the shelf registration system.

14. With the result that, by the end of the first quarter of 1986, the share of yen-denominated loans in international bank lending rose to nearly 17 per cent. This meant that the yen had become the second most commonly used currency (after the American dollar) in international lending by that date. (For subsequent developments and data on the use of the yen in other capacities, see Exhibit 3. 1.)

15. In line with the recommendations of the Foreign Exchange Council, a consultative body for the MoF, which called for its early establishment in a report issued in 1985. The recommendations of the Council's Special Committee (Foreign Exchange Council, 1985) were duly accepted by the MoF which, in July 1986, announced the necessary amendments to the Foreign Exchange and Foreign Trade Control Law and the Special Taxation Measures Law.

16. These related to maximum issue amounts and the eligibility of issuers, the latter subject first arising in July 1972 following the interest stimulated by the Asian Development Bank's foray – the first of any issuer – into the market.

17. The higher one's credit rating, the higher the limit. The term of the issue was also regulated in this way, that is, the higher one's rating, the longer the permitted term. Ceilings on both amounts and maturities were eventually abolished in July 1989 although the restriction on minimum maturities remained.

18. From any one of the following rating agencies: Standard & Poors, Moody's, the Fitch Investors' Service, the Nippon Investors' Service, the Japan Bond Research Institute and the Japan Credit Rating Agency.

19. Unrated corporations could also qualify by satisfying certain financial ratio requirements (see JCIF, 1988, pp. 49–51, for further details).

20. Sovereign issuers who had previously floated yen-bond public offerings in Japan were automatically qualified to make further issues.

21. Previously, only foreign corporates, governments and government agencies had been allowed to do so because of the rules restricting Japanese commercial banks' access to the domestic bond market (i.e. bond issuance by banks was restricted to the issue of debentures by long-term credit banks and foreign exchange banks).

    Although such funding restrictions on commercial banks are programmed to disappear in the second half of fiscal 1999, under Japan's 'big bang' programme of reform (see next chapter), it is likely that sales of bonds will be confined to institutional investors, in order to preserve the principle that short-term funds of the commercial banks are principally raised from bank deposits, not debentures. This, of course, would hand the market in bond issues to individual investors in Japan to foreign players.

22. The ceilings were substantially higher for foreign banks operating in Japan than Japanese banks, so that, somewhat ironically, the abolition of the ceilings *reduced* the comparative advantage enjoyed by the foreign banks.

23. Resident-owned foreign currency deposits plus a portion of non-resident-owned yen-denominated deposits were not subject to interest-rate controls, however.

24. With the scrapping in April 1979 of the 'quotation system' on call rates, under which a uniform rate for all transactions was established, and in October 1979 on bill discount rates (see Suzuki, 1987, pp. 155–6).

25. The maximum term for large time deposits was only increased to 3 years in November 1991. After that date, liberalization took the maximum term to 4 years in October 1993 and to 5 years in October 1994, with the ceiling finally being eliminated in October 1995. Similarly, it took until April 1988 for the maximum term of CD issues to be extended from 1 to 2 years, with the ceiling finally being raised to 5 years in October 1995.

26. Under this system, the call money market dealers set rates, which applied to all market participants, according to supply and demand considerations and after a consensus be-

tween the major borrowers (city banks) and lenders (other financial institutions) had been reached.

27. This was introduced not only because of the demands made by foreign banks active in the markets but also because of the official desire to internationalize Japanese financial markets, which had already resulted in the liberalization of the euroyen and other markets.

28. That is, bills whose maturities cross three month-ends.

29. That is, those that are due on the corresponding day of the month succeeding the month of the transaction or within 15 days of the day after that corresponding day. This means they can mature any time between 30 and 45 days after issue. Two-months bills can mature any time between 45 and 75 days after issue; three-months bills any time between 75 days and 100 days after issue; four-, five- and six-months bills, however, mature on the precise days implied in their titles.

30. Until June 1978 financial institutions had to hold such bills for at least a month before reselling and, even then, direct sales to other institutions were not permitted – dealers had to purchase them first.

31. Today, there are two basic types of bill which are eligible for discount in the bill market: cover bills (*hyoshi tegata*) and other bills. Cover bills are simply bundles of other bills (e.g. high-grade commercial and industrial bills, trade bills, high-grade promissory notes and yen-denominated fixed-term export and import bills) which are grouped together and used as collateral for bills underwritten by the institutions themselves with money market dealers as payees. Because the underlying securities may not be in perfect order nor in round sums, most transactions are in the form of cover bill trades.

32. That is, a circular entitled *Concerning the Dealing of Conditional Transactions in Bonds* issued on 30 March 1976. The guidance covers the following areas: (i) eligibility of participants; (ii) eligibility of securities which can be traded in the market; (iii) price limits for the range of agreed prices; (iv) maximum allowable term of transactions (i.e. under one year); and (v) individual guidance to be given to each company concerning its appropriate trading balance (not to be 'disproportionately large' in relation to its financial position).

33. Eligible securities comprise: national bonds; local bonds; government agency bonds; and corporate bonds (including yen-denominated bonds of foreign countries and companies and, since June 1984, foreign-currency-denominated bonds).

34. All bills of exchange traded in the market must be underwritten by a bank and originate from an exporter's or importer's settling of a trade transaction. In practice, there are five types of bill which may be issued or traded in the yen BA market: yen-denominated, fixed-term bills of exchange; 'accommodation' bills; *jikihane* bills; refinance bills; and 'cover' bills (for further details, see Suzuki, 1987, p. 124). And to be 'eligible' they must satisfy the following conditions: (i) they must be accepted within 30 days of the loading of the ship (45 days for non-Japanese exporters); (ii) the date of maturity must be within six months of loading (some allowance is also made for mailing); and (iii) a minimum unit issue size of ¥100 million must be met.

35. Sales back to the issuers are prohibited.

36. Because the yield offered on other short-term government securities (i.e. 'financing' bills) is set below the official discount rate, and hence market rates, almost all of the issues are held by the Bank of Japan.

37. One factor retarding its growth is the treatment of withholding tax (no transactions tax is levied). As for other discount bonds, tax is withheld at the time of issue but is later deductible from the companies' corporate tax payments. This arrangement complicates matters for overseas purchasers, although foreign central banks from countries that have signed a tax treaty with Japan are compensated at the time of purchase rather than at the maturity of the bills.

38. Claims outstanding at the end of March 1990 totalled ¥13.3 trillion. By end-January 1997 this figure had fallen to ¥10.4 trillion.

39. Adherence to the principle of non-deficit financing, laid down in the Finance Act of 1947, had precluded the issue of government bonds as a means of supplementing annual revenue until January 1966.

40. Banks, however, may not act as brokers but only as principals.
41. The most infamous are: the bribery and corruption share scandal – the Recruit affair – of 1988, which eventually brought down the then Prime Minister Nakasone the following year; and the revelations of June 1991 that two of Japan's top broking houses, Nomura and Nikko Securities, had compensated favoured corporate clients for stock trading losses (leading to significant tax evasion) and had close business dealings with the criminal fraternity in Japan. Both company presidents subsequently resigned in recognition of the responsibilities they bore, although both remained on the respective boards.
42. Although, it has to be said, it took a long time for the damage done by such scandals to sentiment within the retail investing community to be repaired. This did little to dampen the apparently inexorable rise in significance of the institutional investor, at the expense of the personal investor.
43. A further boost to the with-warrant bond market was provided during fiscal 1995 with the sanctioning of public offerings for companies whose shares were registered with the Japan Securities Dealers' Association.
44. And even for convertible debentures issues, the overseas market may be preferred because of the greater speed of conversion into stocks that overseas issues allow.
45. No collateral, of course, is required in the eurobond market.
46. General industrial bonds are distinct from the bonds issued by the nine electric power corporations, which are all floated through public subscription. They are issued through either public subscription or private placement.
47. For the electric power companies there is no specified collateral, although the investors in the bonds have first claim in respect of the repayment of interest and principal. For the other industrial issuers, the firm's factories, equipment or other assets are usually put up as collateral.
48. Five-year maturities were ruled out of court so as to avoid competition with the debenture issues of the long-term credit banks.
49. Defined under Article 2.8 as:

     (i)   the buying and selling of securities;
     (ii) acting as a broker, or agent or a proxy with respect to the buying and selling of securities;
     (iii) acting as a broker, or agent or a proxy with respect to entrusting of buying or selling transactions on the securities market;
     (iv) underwriting securities;
     (v)   effecting secondary distribution of securities;
     (vi) handling an offering or secondary distribution of securities.

50. The sale of medium-term public bonds was sanctioned in October 1983.
51. Although banks were still required under both the Banking Law and the Securities and Exchange Law to obtain a licence prior to engaging in the retail sale of newly issued public bonds.
52. The move was taken for a number of reasons. These included an official desire to: (i) promote wider ownership of government bonds; (ii) reduce the banks' funding burden due to their extensive government bond underwriting activities; (iii) allow banks to reduce capital losses on their government bond holdings; and (iv) allow banks to reap economies of scope (e.g. through offering new savings instruments). Prior to this move, liquidity in the government bond market was provided by the Bank of Japan through its willingness to purchase them one year after issue. The banks' share of secondary market trading in government bonds amounted to some 12 per cent in fiscal 1996.
53. Initially, such activities were restricted to bonds with maturities of less than two years, but in 1985 this restriction was removed.
54. Because commercial paper was defined in legal terms as a promissory note it lay outside the scope of the Securities and Exchange Law restrictions, thereby allowing banks to engage freely in activities in this market since its inauguration in 1987. (Japanese banks have been permitted to issue and deal in certificates of deposit since 1979.)

55. Under the regulatory framework established in 1988 as an amendment to the Securities and Exchange Law:

    (i)   Japanese banks (and securities firms) are allowed to trade government bond futures on the Tokyo Stock Exchange (the market was established in October 1985) and, since 1989, have been allowed to *broke* government (domestic and foreign) bond futures but not stock index futures. (Nor are they allowed to broke the underlying cash government bonds although, in practice, this is done by passing client orders once they are through their own accounts.)

    (ii)   Japanese banks have unlimited access to the domestic financial futures exchange to trade both futures and options, both on their own account and as brokers.

    (iii) Japanese banks (and securities firms) are allowed to use overseas options and futures markets but may not act as brokers in foreign currency or stock index options.

56. Securitization of bank loans to local governments and corporates was sanctioned in July 1989 and March 1990 respectively.

57. Co-managements are less desirable as they are less profitable.

58. For example, that set up by the Industrial Bank of Japan in the USA in September 1990, known as the Bridgeford Group.

59. For example, the Long-Term Credit Bank of Japan bought a stake in Aubrey G. Lanston in 1986.

60. For example, Dai-Ichi Kangyo opened a brokerage subsidiary in New York to deal in and underwrite 'bank-eligible' securities in 1989.

61. For example, the Industrial Bank of Japan took a 20 per cent stake in D'Accord, a US leasing specialist, in May 1989.

62. For example, Bank of Tokyo Capital Markets has made markets in ECU-denominated Treasury bills since November 1989.

63. Sumitomo Bank's London securities offshoot was the first to obtain such a licence in July 1986; and since then many other Japanese commercial banks (e.g. Dai-Ichi Kangyo, Fuji, Mitsubishi, Sanwa, Mitsui) have also acquired licences.

64. Overseas banks' Japanese securities subsidiaries were first sanctioned in December 1985, with overseas securities companies achieving success in 1986.

65. A notorious example of this was the stalling by the Bank of England, on the prompting of the Treasury, of the award of primary gilt dealerships to Japanese firms until the dispute over the admission of certain British firms to the membership of the Tokyo Stock Exchange had been resolved. The dispute was duly settled in 1990.

66. In fact the foreign investment banks concerned – Warburgs, Jardine Fleming, Merrill Lynch, Goldman Sachs, Morgan Stanley and Vickers da Costa – were informed of their successful applications in November 1985.

67. The British firms Barclays de Zoete Wedd, Kleinwort Benson, Schroders, Baring Brothers and County Natwest subsequently became members.

68. Dealing licences in Japanese government bonds were first granted to foreign concerns in 1986.

69. Permission for foreign banks to establish trust banking subsidiaries in Japan required waivers from the Japan Fair Trade Commission.

70. Foreign *commercial* banks were first admitted as participants in 1986.

71. Corporate pension fund management was first opened up to foreign companies (banks) in 1985, with a requirement that it be conducted within wholly owned trust bank subsidiaries. Investment management (excluding pension fund business) licences were first granted to foreign companies in 1987 and investment trust (i.e. mutual) fund management licences in 1990. Public pension fund management was not permitted (for foreign trust banks) until 1989.

72. Apart from the MoF's acquiescence in, if not promotion of, Japanese banks' securities aspirations, a number of important decisions were also taken which furthered the securities companies' inroads into banking. Thus, while they could not take deposits or make loans other than for securities purchases in Japan, they could nevertheless: make loans

collateralized by local government bonds; buy and sell yen-denominated certificates of deposit (CDs), foreign CDs and commercial paper; operate in the yen-based bankers' acceptance market; offer money market funds, and deposit accounts linked to medium-term government bond investments, which compete with banks' short-term deposit accounts; trade freely in stock exchange futures as well as on the financial futures exchange (except spot currency option trading).

73. Nomura, for example, obtained a deposit-taking licence in London in 1986, and has stakes in Banco Santander, the Spanish bank, and Matuschka, the West Germany investment bank. It also has a Swiss banking licence.

74. It was becoming increasingly difficult for the authorities to champion the principle of separation, given their attitudes to the overseas activities of their own commercial banks and the treatment granted to overseas firms in the Japanese marketplace. Competitive distortions, which weigh against their own firms in domestic markets, abounded as a result of the asymmetry in regulation of domestic and foreign financial firms.

75. Some of the remaining irritations facing the city banks comprised: (i) the prohibition on participation in the retail sector of the equity brokerage business; (ii) the inability directly to underwrite corporate bonds; and (iii) the frequent need to use trust banks for both underwriting public bond issues and for selling shares to the public.

76. Before the Second World War, the separation of banking and securities business was not enshrined in law in Japan. Under the Banking Law of 1927, banks were permitted to invest in equities and public bonds on their own behalf, to act as securities agents (e.g. accept money for equities payment, pay principal and interest for securities, etc.) and to lend securities. Indeed, the large banks played a significant role in public bond underwriting, particularly in government bonds, where the underwriting syndicate was composed exclusively of banks.

77. This excludes the possibility that regulators are susceptible to 'special pleading' from interested parties, keen to maintain barriers to entry to their industries.

78. It is the *risk-adjusted* rates of return which are relevant.

79. Benston (1990, p. 149) contends that this is not the most appropriate measure of risk but rather 'the probability that a bank will become insolvent and impose costs on the FDIC, other banks, and the economy'.

80. This is assuming that banks, in a deregulated environment, would not be allowed to offer securities services directly, a policy which finds favour with Benston (1990, ch. 2) as a means of minimizing risk.

81. This is part of the rationale for the so-called prudential controls widely applied to banking organizations around the world.

82. Traditional commercial banking activities probably already expose banks to the levels of individual risk that new activities entail.

83. The introduction of actuarially sound, risk-based premiums would preclude the extension of the safety net through the medium of federal deposit insurance. Similarly, expeditious use of risk-based capital requirements and resolution policies could be used to avoid extension of the safety net through the other mediums.

84. For example, forcing a reorganization *before* their economic capital falls below zero (Benston, 1990, p. 184).

85. That is, institutional measures designed to prevent the leakage of information acquired in the course of performance of business in one section of an organization to other sections of the organization.

86. The concern about the comparative advantages (*vis-à-vis* securities companies) possessed by commercial banks is more marked in Japan compared with the USA because of the differing institutional and legal frameworks applying in the two countries. Thus, Japanese commercial banks, unlike their US counterparts, can hold client firms' shares up to a certain degree (i.e. up to 5 per cent of total outstanding stock), capital ties which are often considerably strengthened through the holdings of the said stock by the banks' affiliates, which are not governed by the 5 per cent limitation (although *group* holdings are restricted by the exercise of moral suasion by the MoF – see text). While companies have traditionally welcomed these ties as a means of stabilizing shareholdership, thereby allow-

ing them to concentrate on maximizing long-term returns rather than being concerned with short-term defensive moves to stave off predators, etc., some nevertheless regard the situation as unhealthy.

Similarly, institutional arrangements in Japan result in many bank officials sitting on the boards of directors of client companies, and corporate customers looking to their bankers for lender of last resort facilities in tough trading conditions under the so-called 'main bank' relationships. These features, together with privileged access to the official safety net, help to explain the widespread concern felt about the power of banks in the Japanese economy and why many called for, at the very least, *quid pro quo* diversification opportunities (e.g. in banking, trust, foreign exchange – FOREX – and other business areas) to be given to securities companies under any reform package.

87. Pre-1940 experience with the *zaibatsu*, the all-powerful financial and industrial conglomerates, also weighed heavily with administrators who feared the consequences of full-scale deregulation.

88. Deregulation in Japan has led to a narrowing of margins because of an increase in bank deposit rates; and the banks also lost deposit business because of the abolition of the tax exemption on *maruyu* savings accounts (money flowed out into unit trusts) and lending business because of the decision, taken in 1989, to allow companies access to the short- to medium-term (i.e. up to four years' maturity) domestic bond market.

89. In Japan, foreign banks (including US banks, which are prohibited from engaging in such activities at home) are able to engage in securities and trust business in Japan which is not open to Japanese banks; and, through subsidiaries, both Japanese banks and securities firms can engage in activities in overseas markets which are prohibited domestically.

90. An added benefit for the Japanese government of more efficient money and capital markets is that this would facilitate the conduct of official monetary policy through open market operations.

91. It is assumed that we are concerned here with fundamental reform (i.e. allowing banks in principle to engage in all forms of securities activities) rather than with a minor relaxation of the rules to allow, for example, banks greater freedom in the area of private placements of securities products or to receive, as trust banks already do, commission on stock exchange transactions carried out on an agency basis (as permitted under Article 65). Other options, such as allowing interpenetration of banking and securities business through the routing of business through the banks' and securities houses' overseas operations, with associated privileges, are considered in Dale (1990).

92. Thus would require either new legislation exempting wholly owned subsidiaries from the scope of the Anti-Monopoly Law or companies seeking special permission from the Fair Trade Commission.

93. For example, subsidiaries had to be located away from the parents' head offices. Other restrictions were also imposed. Minimum capital requirements – ¥2 billion for the banking subsidiaries of securities companies and ¥10 billion for the securities subsidiaries of private banks – were applied to all newly formed subsidiaries. Restrictions were imposed on the dealings undertaken by the new securities subsidiaries of private banks with companies for which they are the 'main bank'. And there is a general requirement that the new subsidiaries operate profitably within three years.

94. As is evident from Exhibit 3.12, city banks had to wait until at least July 1994 before they were allowed to establish securities subsidiaries (although Daiwa got in through the back door via an acquisition of Cosmo Securities in September 1993), whereas long-term credit banks and trust banks were allowed to do so during 1993. Similarly, city banks had typically to wait until the autumn of 1995 before they were allowed to establish trust bank subsidiaries, whereas the 'big four' brokerage houses were allowed to move in this direction in October 1993.

95. By September 1994, the newly established securities subsidiaries of Japanese commercial banks had captured 6.8 per cent of the market for the underwriting of domestic straight bonds and 4.7 per cent of the market for the underwriting of all corporate bonds. Moreover, by the end of 1997, the securities subsidiary of the Industrial Bank of Japan had overtaken Japan's broking houses to become the largest lead manager in underwriting

domestic corporate bonds, lead-managing ¥1.27 trillion – 16 per cent of the total – of corporate bonds in the first 11 months of 1997.
96. Nor to the operations of Cosmo Securities, acquired by Daiwa Bank in September 1993.
97. Such restrictions did not apply to Nippon Trust Bank, acquired by the Tokyo–Mitsubishi Bank in November 1994.

REFERENCES

Benston, G.J. (1990), *The Separation of Commercial and Investment Banking: The Glass–Steagall Act Revisited and Reconsidered*, London: Macmillan.

Dale, R. (1990), 'Japan's banking regulation: current policy issues', in C.A.E. Goodhart and G. Sutija (eds), *Japanese Financial Growth*, London: Macmillan, pp. 33–45.

The Economist (1986), *Tokyo 2000: The World's Third International Financial Centre?*, London: Economist Publications.

Federation of Bankers' Associations of Japan (FBAJ) (1989), *The Banking System in Japan*, Tokyo: FBAJ.

Federation of Bankers' Associations of Japan (FBAJ) (1992), *Japanese Banks '92*, Tokyo: FBAJ.

Federation of Bankers' Associations of Japan (FBAJ) (1996), *Japanese Banks, '96*, Tokyo: FBAJ.

Financial System Research Council (1989), *On a New Japanese Financial System*, interim report by the Second Financial System Committee of the Financial System Research Council, Tokyo: Federation of Bankers' Associations of Japan.

Financial System Research Council (1990), *On a New Japanese Financial System*, second interim report by the Second Financial System Committee of the Financial System Research Council, Tokyo: Federation of Bankers' Associations of Japan.

Foreign Exchange Council (1985), *The Establishment of the Tokyo Offshore Market*, Report of the Special Committee on the Internationalization of the Tokyo Markets (Special Committee Report), Tokyo: Foreign Exchange Council.

Hall, M.J.B. (1987), 'Reform of the London Stock Exchange: the prudential issues', *Banca Nazionale del Lavoro Quarterly Review*, June, pp. 167–81.

Hall, M.J.B. (1989), 'The BIS capital adequacy "rules": a critique', *Banca Nazionale del Lavoro Quarterly Review*, no. 169, pp. 207–27.

Hanzawa, M. (1991), 'The Tokyo offshore market', in Foundation for Advanced Information and Research (FAIR), *Japan's Financial Markets*, Tokyo: FAIR.

Japan Centre for International Finance (JCIF) (1988), 'The past and present of the deregulation and internationalisation of the Tokyo money and capital market', JCIF Policy Study Series, no. 10, Tokyo: JCIF.

Japan Centre for International Finance (1997), *The International Business of Japanese Banks Over the Last Fifty Years*, Tokyo: JCIF, January.

Jensen, M.C. (1972), 'Capital markets: theory and evidence', *Bell Journal of Economics and Management Science*, **3**(2), 357–98.

Ministry of Finance (1997), *Guide of Japanese Government Bond, 1997*, Tokyo: MoF, May.

Nakaishi, A. (1991), 'The foreign exchange market', in Foundation for Advanced Information and Research (FAIR), *Japan's Financial Markets*, Tokyo: FAIR, pp. 245–59.

Osugi, K. (1990), 'Japan's experience of financial deregulation since 1984 in an international perspective', *BIS Economic Papers*, no. 26.

Postal Savings Bureau (1987), *Postal Banking in Japan: Fiscal 1986*, Tokyo: Postal
    Savings Bureau.
Suzuki, Y. (1987), *The Japanese Financial System*, Oxford: Clarendon Press.
Trenchard, Thomas, 2nd Viscount Trenchard (1990), 'Japan', in W. Kay (ed.), *Mod-
    ern Merchant Banking*, 3rd edn, London: Woodhead-Faulkner, ch. 18.

4. Financial reform under the 'big bang' programme[1]

INTRODUCTION

In November 1996 the Japanese Prime Minister Mr Hashimoto announced plans for an acceleration in and broadening of financial reform in Japan, a process begun in earnest back in the 1970s (see Chapter 3). This package of measures, all of which must be implemented by the year 2001 at the latest, has been labelled 'big bang', although it extends well beyond the confines of the securities-related reforms introduced in London in the mid-1980s under the banner of the UK's 'big bang' (see Hall, 1983). The measures to be implemented – an omnibus 'Financial System Reform Bill', revising 22 laws, is expected to be enacted on 1 December 1998 – emanate from the deliberations, which took account of Diet discussions, of a variety of 'Councils'/ 'Committees',[2] which duly reported in June 1997[3] [see, for example, the Financial System Research Council, 1997 and the Securities and Exchange Council, 1997a].

THE STRUCTURE OF THE REFORM PACKAGE

Despite some inevitable overlap, the reform measures[4] can usefully be divided into the following groupings (this is consistent with Japanese Ministry of Finance (MoF), 1997): (i) those designed to expand *user choice*; (ii) those designed to improve the *quality of service provision* and to promote *competition* amongst intermediaries; (iii) those designed to ensure the development of an '*easy-to-use*' market; (iv) those designed to ensure the establishment of a '*fair*' market; and (v) those designed to help preserve *financial stability* in the face of financial reform and structural upheaval. Each of these 'groupings' will now be addressed in turn.

Measures Designed to Expand User Choice

As with the second grouping of measures – see below – the expansion of user choice is heavily dependent on liberalization which allows intermediaries to

Exhibit 4.1   Financial reform under Japan's 'big bang' and the timetable for reform

Measures	Planned schedule for implementation
Group 1: Measures designed to expand user choice	
(i) Lifting of ban on derivatives transactions:	
• Trading of options on individual stocks to be allowed at stock exchanges.	• Trading commenced at the Tokyo and Osaka Stock Exchanges in July 1997.
• Ban on securities derivatives to be lifted once the conditions are set for allowing over-the-counter trading of securities-related derivatives.	• Legislative bill to be submitted to next (i.e. post-13 July 1997) ordinary session of the Diet.
• Banks to be allowed to engage in over-the-counter trading of securities- and commodities-related derivatives (although they will not be authorized to receive or deliver the underlying assets).	• Legislative bill to be submitted to next ordinary session of the Diet.
(ii) Money management funds to be allowed to introduce asset management accounts.	To be implemented during fiscal year 1997.
(iii) Banks to be allowed to sell securities investment trusts and insurance:	
• Banks will not be required to use the subsidiary route of provision to sell securities investment trust certificates.	• Relevant bills to be submitted to next ordinary session of the Diet.
• Banks will be allowed to lease their office space to investment trust management companies wishing to make direct sales of securities investment trust certificates to the public.	• To be implemented during fiscal year 1997.
• Once measures have been designed to limit potential abuse, banks will be allowed to sell long-term fire insurance and credit life insurance where related to housing loans.	• To be implemented around the year 2001.
(iv) Measures to be adopted to increase the liquidity of assets:	
• Preparation of a legal framework for 'special-purpose companies' (SPCs) which will be allowed to issue asset-backed securities.	• Legislative bill to be submitted to next ordinary session of the Diet.
• Liquidity of money loan trust certificates to be increased by specifying the basis for issuing securities.	• Legislative bill to be submitted to next ordinary session of the Diet.
(v) Liberalization of cross-border capital transactions:	
• Range of investment and borrowing opportunities open to both companies and individuals to increase dramatically once controls on cross-border securities transactions and foreign deposits are liberalized.	• The Diet has already approved major revisions to the Foreign Exchange and Foreign Trade Control Law, to take effect on 1 April 1998.

Group 2: Measures designed to improve the quality of service provision and to promote competition

(i) Measures allowing for the utilization of the holding company system:

- Appropriate legal framework to be created to allow for the use of holding companies and to ensure protection of depositors, investors and policy-holders.

  - Necessary legal framework to be prepared as soon as possible, in line with the implementation of the revised Anti-Monopoly Law.

(ii) Review of the licensing regime applicable to securities companies:

- Present licensing system to be replaced, in principle, by a registration system. Within this framework, a system of 'approvals' will only operate for specific business areas requiring special skills and higher degrees of risk control, e.g. over-the-counter (OTC) derivatives and underwriting.

  - Legislative bill to be submitted to next ordinary session of the Diet.

(iii) Liberalization of controls imposed on the business scope of separate subsidiaries:

- Remaining restrictions on business scope of banks' securities subsidiaries and trust subsidiaries to be lifted.

  - Restrictions to be lifted in latter half of fiscal year 1999.

- Measures to be taken to allow insurance companies and other financial institutions to enter each other's business areas by means of area-specific subsidiaries.

  - To be realized by the year 2001 at the latest.

  Measures to be taken at an earlier date to allow: (a) insurance companies to enter banking, trust and securities business via separate subsidiaries; and (b) securities companies to enter insurance business via separate subsidiaries.

(iv) Abolition of certain operational regulations imposed on ordinary banks:

- Rules supporting the separation of short-term from long-term finance to be relaxed to allow ordinary banks to issue ordinary (corporate) bonds.

  - To be implemented in the second half of fiscal year 1999.

- Foreign Exchange Bank Law to be abolished thereby ending the specialized foreign exchange bank system.

  - Related bills to be submitted to next ordinary session of the Diet.

(v) Allowing securities companies to diversify their business operations:

- System of obligatory specialization to be abolished, allowing securities companies to engage in whatever range of securities-related activities they want, as well as to engage in non-securities-related activities.

  - Legislative bill to be submitted to next ordinary session of the Diet.

Exhibit 4.1 (continued)

Measures	Planned schedule for implementation
(vi) Total deregulation of brokerage commissions levied on stock trading.	Liberalization to be completed by the end of 1999. As an intermediate step, the transaction value up to which the current fixed commissions apply to be reduced from over ¥1 billion to ¥50 million in April 1998.
(vii) Promoting the development of electronic money and electronic payments systems: • Necessary measures to be taken to promote new entry, to clarify related legal aspects and to ensure the protection of users.	• Consideration of steps necessary to promote programme to be undertaken 'promptly', with a view to ensuring speedy implementation of the necessary measures.
(viii) Diversifying non-bank financial intermediaries ('non-banks') funding sources: • Legal restrictions on non-banks issuing of (corporate) bonds and commercial paper to be abolished.	• Legislative bill to be submitted to next ordinary session of the Diet to deal with those items requiring revisions to existing laws.
(ix) Reform of the 'rating organization system' used by the non-life insurance industry: • Obligation on member insurers of a rating organization to use the premium rates calculated by the rating organization to be abolished.	• Reform to be implemented by July 1998 provided that the Diet passes the necessary revisions to the relevant laws.
(x) Liberalization of foreign exchange business: • Authorized foreign exchange bank system (see above), money exchanger system and designated securities firm system to be abolished. Free entry into and exit from foreign exchange business to ensue.	• Relevant amendment to the Foreign Exchange and Foreign Trade Control Law has already been approved by the Diet, to take effect on 1 April 1998.

Group 3: Measures designed to ensure the development of an 'easy-to-use' market

(i) To promote the use of financial futures:

- Measures to be adopted to enhance the development of new products, improve the environment for transactions and enhance investor protection.
  - Spread transactions associated with short-term Japanese yen interest-rate futures to be introduced in 1998.

(ii) Development of the short-term money market:

- Trading practices to be reassessed and Bank of Japan netting (BOJ-NET) to be placed on a real time gross settlement (RTGS) basis.
  - BOJ-NET to be placed in a RTGS basis by the end of the century.

(iii) Liberalization of cross-border capital transactions:

- The approval and prior notification requirements to be abolished, in principle, for external settlement and capital transactions.
  - Proposed revisions to the Foreign Exchange and Foreign Trade Control Laws have already been approved by the Diet, to take effect on 1 April 1998.

(iv) Abolition of the restrictions imposed on off-exchange trading of listed securities:

- Restrictions to be lifted once rules have been established to ensure 'fair' trading off-exchange.
  - Legislative bill to be submitted to next ordinary session of the Diet.

(v) Liquidity of the registered OTC JASDAQ (Japanese Securities Dealers' Automated Quotation) market to be improved:

- Status of the registered OTC JASDAQ market to be reassessed. Secondary market capacity to be enhanced.
  - Measures to be taken after fiscal year 1997.

(vi) Lifting of the ban on the trading and intermediating of unlisted and unregistered securities by securities companies.
  - Ban lifted in July 1997.

143

Exhibit 4.1 (continued)

Measures	Planned schedule for implementation

Group 4: Measures designed to ensure the establishment of a 'fair' market

(i) Information disclosure requirements to be strengthened:

- System of consolidated financial statements to be reviewed with a view to ensuring disclosures based primarily on consolidated accounting. Fundamental review of consolidation procedures to be undertaken.
  - New system to be implemented in stages, starting in March 1999.

- Accounting standards for financial instruments to be reviewed, including use of mark-to-market valuation methods for securities and derivatives.
  - Revised standards to be introduced shortly after Business Accounting Council reports on the subject (due by summer of 1998).

(ii) Enhancement of (external) audit process:

- Practice and system of auditing to be made comparable with international norm, including a requirement that auditing procedures be reviewed by other firms or accounting organizations.
  - Reforms to be implemented shortly after the Certified Public Accountants Examination Committee has made its recommendations on the subject.

(iii) Review of definition of 'securities' to enhance investor protection:

- Definition of 'securities' in the Securities and Exchange Law to be reviewed to ensure it covers new products. This is necessary to ensure investor protection rules extend to those new products.
  - Legislative bill to be submitted to the next ordinary session of the Diet (part of this to be implemented by Cabinet Order).

(iv) Rules in the Securities and Exchange Law to be broadened:

- Rules concerning conflicts of interest, market manipulation, and insider trading, etc. need to be broadened to cope with developments such as wider scope of business conducted by securities firms, expansion of electronic trading through the Internet, and the introduction of new transactions such as in OTC derivatives.
  - Legislative bill concerning 'netting agreements' to be submitted to next ordinary meeting of the Diet.

(v) Enhancement of the systems of inspection, surveillance and enforcement, and review of the penalty system for violation of rules:

- Inspection, surveillance and enforcement to be reinforced, including strengthening of the Securities and Exchange Surveillance Committee. Penalty for insider trading to be increased.
  - To be promoted after fiscal year 1997.

(vi) Enhancement of system for dealing with civil disputes:

- To include, *inter alia*, establishing a legal basis for mediation by self-regulating organizations.

  - Legislative bill to be submitted to next ordinary session of the Diet.

(vii) Enhancement of user protection:

- Enactment of a unified consumer credit protection law to be considered.
- Measures to be taken to prevent the misuse of consumer credit information.

  - Conference for the Protection and Use of Individuals' Credit Information to make recommendations on this shortly.

- Rules to be formulated regarding disclosure requirements to be imposed on vendors of non-deposit products.

  - To be implemented shortly after fiscal year 1997.

- Payment system to be placed on an RTGS basis.

  - To be implemented by end of the century.

(viii) Enhancing investor protection in face of securities companies' failures:

- Client assets to be strictly separated from securities companies' own assets and the Securities Deposit Compensation Fund scheme to be strengthened.

  - To be implemented during fiscal year 1997.

(ix) Mechanism to allow for the effective imposition of economic sanctions etc. when called for by the international community.

  - Legislative bill to be submitted to the next ordinary session of the Diet.

(x) Strengthening of anti-money-laundering requirements:

- Banks and money exchanges to be legally required to verify identity of recipients of foreign remittance. Customs authorities to become involved in cases of export or import of means of payment such as cash.

  - Covered in the revisions made to the Foreign Exchange and Foreign Trade Control Law, which take effect on 1 April 1998.

Exhibit 4.1 *(continued)*

Measures	Planned schedule for implementation
Group 5: Measures designed to help preserve financial stability	
(i) Introduction of 'prompt corrective action' (PCA):	
• PCA, based upon capital adequacy ratios, to be introduced, whereby supervisory authorities are mandated to take administrative action in a transparent and timely fashion when institutions get into difficulty.	• To be implemented in April 1998.
(ii) Reduction of settlement risk:	
• BOJ-NET to be moved on to an RTGS basis.	• BOJ-NET to be placed on an RTGS basis by end of the century.
• Private sector encouragement to promote the reduction of risk in the existing private sector clearing system.	
• Legislative validity of 'close-out netting agreements' to be clarified.	• Legislative bill to be submitted to next ordinary session of the Diet to deal with netting agreements.

Sources: Ministry of Finance (1997a, 1997b and 1997c); Financial System Research Council (1997); Securities and Exchange Council (1997a and 1997b).

146

choose which activities to engage in and which products/services to supply according to their perceived comparative advantage. Accordingly, banks[5] will be allowed to sell securities investment trust certificates through their branch networks and, at the same time, money management funds will be allowed to introduce asset management accounts. Both measures will assist in the development of the relatively small investment trust industry in Japan, the former by broadening the sales channels,[6] thereby making investment trusts more accessible to the general public and enticing new customers into securities investment, and the latter by enhancing the scope of investment trusts.[7] Eventually, once appropriate safeguards[8] have been established, banks will also be able to offer certain insurance products (for full details and the timetable for reform see Exhibit 4.1).[9]

Another set of measures to be introduced under this banner relate to those concerned with the lifting of the ban on derivatives transactions.[10] The use of derivatives is to be actively encouraged in order to promote sound risk management, by intermediaries and businesses alike (this emphasizes the role of derivatives as hedging mediums), to improve the allocation of risk within the national economy, to extend the risk/return spectrum of choice for investors, to encourage financial innovation, and to enhance the international competitiveness of Japan's financial markets. As noted in Exhibit 4.1, the first reform to be made under this heading – the trading of options on individual stocks – has already been implemented,[11] with over-the-counter trading of securities-related and commodities-related derivatives, including by banks,[12] to follow shortly.[13] The supervisory authorities, however, will be keen to ensure that sound risk management policies and appropriate levels of capital are maintained by those engaging in such activities so as to try to ensure that Japanese institutions do not repeat the mistakes made all too often in the Western world.

A further set of initiatives designed to enhance intermediaries' risk (and balance sheet) management capabilities relate to attempts to increase the liquidity of loans and other assets. These measures, such as those designed to promote the issue of asset-backed securities (ABS) (that is, securitization),[14] also enhance the general efficiency of financial intermediation by unbundling the functions of initial credit review, credit extension, loan management and risk management, potentially allowing efficiency gains through the adoption of individual functions by those best suited to the tasks involved. Measures to be taken on this front include preparation of a legal framework[15] for special-purpose companies (SPCs), the issuers of such securities, to protect investors' interests, particularly in respect of protection against third-party claims.[16] Consideration will also have to be given to granting SPCs privileged tax treatment *vis-à-vis* corporations if they are to flourish.[17] An attempt to increase the liquidity of money loan trust certificates will also be made by

*Exhibit 4.2   Revisions to the Foreign Exchange and Foreign Trade Control
Law approved in 1997*

Area of reform	Reform measures to be undertaken
1. Liberalization of cross-border capital transactions	1. (i) Permission and prior notification requirements in respect of capital transactions and foreign settlement to be abolished. (ii) Settlement of export–import payments through overseas deposits to be permitted. (iii) Multilateral netting of settlements to be recognized. (iv) Foreign exchange transactions (including spot, futures, swaps and options contracts), with residents and non-residents to be sanctioned.
2. Liberalization of foreign exchange business and abolition of the authorized foreign exchange bank system	2. (i) Market participants, both bank and non-bank, to be allowed to engage freely in foreign exchange business (previously, only 'authorized' foreign exchange banks could do so). (ii) Designated securities firm system and money exchanger system to be abolished. (iii) Foreign currency positions in future to be governed by the Banking Law and bank-related laws once the market risk assessment proposals of the Basle Committee have been implemented.
3. Development of an *ex-post facto* reporting system on cross-border capital transactions	3. (i) Under the new system, the reporting burden will be reduced, and reporting procedures will be streamlined and simplified (ultimately, a paperless reporting system is envisaged) to ensure concise content. (ii) For those reports necessary for the achievement of legal objectives, an appropriate set of legal obligations (and penalties for violations) will have to be established.
4. International requirements	4. (i) An appropriate system will have to be retained to ensure Japan is able to take part in any international agreement on the

Exhibit 4.2   (continued)

Area of reform	Reform measures to be undertaken
	imposition of economic sanctions against third parties.
	(ii) A mechanism must also be available to allow for the imposition of restrictions in times of national emergency.
	(iii) In order to assist in the prevention of money laundering, the following measures need to be introduced: – prior reporting to the Customs authorities of the export or import of means of payments such as a large amount of cash; – banks and money exchangers to carry out identity checks when foreign remittance and money is involved; – tax offices to consider what appropriate measures they should take.
5. Direct investment	5. (i) Prior notification requirements for general business (excluding certain industrial sectors – but *not* banking, cultured-pearl production or fibre manufacturing/ processing – and business conducted in countries subject to economic sanctions) to be abolished and replaced by an *ex-post facto* reporting system, as will be the case for other capital transactions.
	(ii) Remaining permission and prior notification requirements for direct domestic involvement to be liberalized in due course, in line with discussions held at the OECD.
6. Other	6. (i) A reporting system suited to cross-border transactions using electronic money to be developed.
	(ii) The development of the offshore market to be reviewed, possibly with a view to allowing securities transactions to be conducted within it.

Source: Ministry of Finance (1997d).

specifying measures which enable the issuance of securities based on money loan trust certificates, thereby circumventing the 'designated asset transfer' system.

The final, but by no means least important, measure to be taken in the name of increasing user choice is the liberalization of cross-border transactions. As noted in Exhibit 4.1, the range of investment and borrowing opportunities open to both companies and individuals will increase dramatically once controls on cross-border securities transactions and foreign deposits are liberalized on 1 April 1998. (For a review of the revisions to the Foreign Exchange and Foreign Trade Control Law, which will lose the word 'Control' from its title, already approved by the Diet, see Exhibit 4.2.)

Measures Designed to Improve the Quality of Service Provision and to Promote Competition in the Financial Services Sector

The measures to be taken to promote competition and raise the quality of service provision in the Japanese financial sector embrace a raft of liberalizing proposals which will, *inter alia*, allow intermediaries to diversify their business operations and funding sources, give them greater freedom in the choice of organizational structure to be adopted and abolish certain price-fixing arrangements. Accordingly, opportunities for diversification through subsidiaries for all intermediary types will be greatly increased, securities companies will have greater freedom in their choice of what securities-related activities to engage in, foreign exchange business will be opened up to all, new entrants to the electronic payments system will be encouraged, ordinary banks will be allowed to issue ordinary (that is, corporate) bonds, non-bank financial intermediaries will be allowed to issue corporate bonds and commercial paper, brokerage commissions will be totally deregulated, non-life insurance premiums will become more flexible, and intermediaries will be allowed to adopt holding company structures if they so choose. Some of these initiatives merit further discussion (further detail on those initiatives not addressed below feature in Exhibit 4.1).

The belated decision to allow for the use of holding companies – the Second Financial System Committee of the Financial System Research Council had rejected the idea when it evaluated the 'five formulas' for financial reform in 1989 (Financial System Research Council, 1989 – reviewed in Hall, 1993, pp. 253–8) – reflects the authorities' new-found willingness to revise the Anti-Monopoly Law[18] in the face of demands for a more efficient financial system. Concerns about the concentration of economic and political power are, in the current environment, subordinated to the need for intermediaries to maximize economies of scope and synergistic benefits, although remaining conflict-of-interest concerns still render the *universal banking* style of operation common in Western Europe unacceptable to the authorities (for a comparison of the relative merits of the two operational structures see Hall, 1993, Table 9.6, p. 257). Indeed, conflict-of-interest concerns will play an important role in shaping the facilitating legal framework allowing for the use of holding company structures. Accordingly, while it is envisaged that holding companies will be allowed to own a bank,[19] with the non-bank subsidiaries of the bank being allowed to operate as separate subsidiaries of the holding company, they will not, at least for the time being, be allowed also to own commercial entities. Moreover, an appropriate set of 'firewalls'[20] will have to be devised, to operate alongside a strict regime of information disclosure and reporting requirements and tight supervisory controls, to ensure depositors, investors and policy-holders are all adequately protected from potential abuse.[21]

A determination to hasten and broaden the reforms taking place through subsidiaries under the Financial System Reform Act of 1993 (see Chapter 3) is evident in the proposals for liberalizing the controls placed on the business scope of intermediaries' subsidiaries. Under the latest reform plan, the remaining restrictions on the business scope of *banks'* securities and trust subsidiaries will be lifted in the latter half of fiscal 1999 (in line with the Government's Deregulation Program of March 1997);[22] and banks, securities companies, insurance companies and trust companies will have complete freedom to enter each other's business areas by means of area-specific subsidiaries by the year 2001 at the latest.[23]

Finally, it is worth noting that the government's attempts to stimulate price competitiveness in the financial sector are due to take place in the not-too-distant future. Reform of the 'rating' system used to set (non-life) premium rates is provisionally scheduled for July 1998, in line with the 'Supplementary Measures by the Government of Japan and the Government of the United States regarding Insurance' agreed in December 1996; while the phased deregulation of brokerage commissions, an essential ingredient of the reforms implemented on Wall Street and at the London Stock Exchange in the mid-1970s and mid-1980s, respectively, is due for completion by the end of 1999.

Measures Designed to Ensure the Development of an 'Easy-To-Use' Market

One of the first areas to be addressed under this banner is the financial futures market. Although such a market has operated at the Tokyo International Financial Futures Exchange since 1989, complaints have surfaced concerning the extremely limited range of financial futures products available, the lack of investor protection available in the event of a failure of a financial futures broker, and the declining international competitiveness of the Japanese market. As a result, measures are to be adopted which enhance the development of new products – spread transactions in short-term Japanese yen interest-rate futures will commence in 1998 – improve the environment of financial futures transactions to meet international standards, reduce transactions costs (including the possibility of removing the transactions tax) and enhance investor protection. A possible extension of trading hours and linkages with foreign markets may also be examined.

As for the development of the securities markets, the Securities and Exchange Council appears to be getting most of what it asked for (SEC, 1997a, p. 14):[24] off-exchange trading of listed securities will be encouraged; the liquidity of the registered over-the-counter (OTC) Japanese Securities Dealers' Automated Quotation (JASDAQ) market is to be increased; and securities companies are to be allowed to trade and to intermediate in unlisted and unregistered securities. Likewise, trading practices in the short-term money market are to be reassessed in order to enhance the development of the market. In particular, market capacity is to be increased through, for example, enhancing the role of the yen–TIBOR (Tokyo Inter-Bank Offered Rate) as Japan's effective interest-rate indicator and, possibly, enlarging the Treasury bill market and reviewing the procedures for the issuance of financing bills (see Chapter 3). Improvements in efficiency will be highly dependent upon reviews of the legal framework for products, of market practices – especially those relating to promissory notes, to the methods used to calculate interest rates in call transactions, and to cash-collateralized loan transactions in bonds – and of the fiscal system affecting transactions in the short-term money market. And security is to be improved by placing BOJ-NET (Bank of Japan netting – the current designated-time, gross settlement system used to settle most short-term money market transactions – see MoF, 1997e, ch. 4) on a real-time gross settlement basis by the end of the century.

Finally, the liberalization of cross-border capital transactions to be implemented under the revised Foreign Exchange and Foreign Trade Control Law on 1 April 1998 will bring about the abolition, in principle, of the approval and prior notification requirements for external settlement and capital transactions. As a result, the Japanese financial system will become more open, and Japanese companies and citizens will enjoy the freedoms currently experienced by much of the Western world.

Measures Designed to Ensure the Establishment of a 'Fair' Market

The authorities' determination to ensure a 'fair' market reflects a number of concerns: first, that the introduction of a 'free' market should not be allowed to undermine the soundness of the market. Cessation of the traditional approach of ensuring soundness through the regulation of the business activities of intermediaries necessitates a new regulatory philosophy based upon enhanced disclosure, surveillance, enforcement, and so on. Second, given the importance of retail operations in the Japanese securities market, it is vital to regain the trust of small investors by ensuring that they are no longer disadvantaged *vis-à-vis* institutional clients, be this as a result of limited access to information or unfair discrimination on price or other terms. Strengthening of the 'rules' should ideally accommodate higher business ethics if trust is to be fully restored. And, third, a set of clear and transparent rules, rigorously enforced, must be on offer if business between market professionals is to be stimulated.

To satisfy these needs, a wide-ranging set of reforms has been drawn up. These reforms include, *inter alia* (full details are provided in Exhibit 4.1): a strengthening of information disclosure requirements (to be secured through a review of consolidation procedures and accounting standards);[25] enhancement of the audit process (to bring it up to international standards); revisions to the Securities and Exchange Law to extend the scope of investor protection in the face of product development and to broaden the rules concerning conflicts of interest, market manipulation and insider trading to accommodate developments such as the widening of the scope of business conducted by securities firms, the growing use of the Internet and the introduction of new types of transactions; enhancement of the systems of inspection, surveillance and enforcement; a revision of the system of penalties imposed for rules violations; improvement of the system available for settling civil disputes; and enhancement of investor protection in the consumer credit area and in the face of securities companies failures.

Measures Designed to Help Preserve Financial Stability

The final group of measures, comprising those designed to assist in the struggle to help preserve financial stability, build upon the new regulatory environment to be established to promote a fair marketplace. Thus, in addition to enhancing disclosure requirements and the inspection, surveillance and enforcement systems, plans are afoot to reduce settlement risk (for full details see Exhibit 4.1) and to enhance the efficacy of the supervisory effort via the introduction of so-called 'prompt correction action' (PCA) (see Exhibit 4.3).[26] These developments will serve to reinforce the measures already taken to improve the soundness of the financial system through the promotion of a speedy disposal of non-performing assets by financial intermediaries (see Yamawaki, 1996)[27] and the encouragement given to intermediaries to upgrade risk management systems.

Exhibit 4.3   Japan's version of prompt corrective action[1]

Class of action	Capital adequacy ratio trigger		Action to be taken
	BIS standard[2]	Adjusted[3] national standard[4]	
1	Less than 8%	Less than 4%	To order the formulation and implementation of a management improvement plan.
2	Less than 4%	Less than 2%	To order such measures or implement such restrictions as:

- formulation of a plan to increase capital;
- restraint on the increase of total assets or reduction of total assets;
- prohibition on entering new business fields;
- curtailment of current business operations;
- prohibition on opening new offices and curtailment of offices currently operated;
- curtailment of business activities of subsidiaries and overseas affiliated companies, and prohibition on establishing such entities;
- restraint or prohibition on paying dividends;
- restraint on paying bonuses to directors and other senior officers;
- restraint or prohibition on taking deposits at high interest rates.

| 3 | Less than 0% | Less than 0% | Usually,[5] to order the suspension of some or all of the business activities.[6] |

Notes:
[1]   The scheme will be reviewed in the year 2000.
[2]   To be adopted by banks operating overseas whether through branches or subsidiaries.
[3]   The current 'national standard' ratio is calculated as the sum of capital plus certain reserves as a percentage of the daily average of total assets less some special reserves. Under the proposed revisions, the numerator would include debt raised through the issue of subordinated debentures but would exclude specific reserves and unrealized gains on securities holdings. Moreover, the denominator would henceforth be represented by the 'total of weighted risk assets', as calculated under the BIS 'rules' (see Hall, 1993, p. 189).
[4]   To be adopted by those banks without foreign branches or subsidiaries.
[5]   The second class of actions, however, cannot be taken in the following cases: (i) if the net value of assets, as with unrealized gains of the financial institution, is positive; and (ii) even when the net value of assets, as with unrealized gains, is negative but is expected to become positive once allowance is made for implementation of management improvement plans and other specific measures, the rates of business income and expenditure, profitability and bad-debt ratios.
[6]   A business suspension can also be ordered, even when a financial institution does not belong to this class, when the net value of assets, including unrealized losses, is negative (or when it is clearly expected to become negative) or because of a lack of liquidity.

Source: Ministry of Finance (1996).

NOTES

1. This chapter rests heavily on Hall (1997).
2. Namely, the Securities and Exchange Council, the Business Accounting Council, the Financial System Research Council, the Insurance Council and the Committee on Foreign Exchange and Other Transactions. Representatives from each of these bodies also sat on the Financial System Reform Consultation Committee to discuss issues of mutual concern.
3. An earlier report (January 1997) of the Committee on Foreign Exchange and Other Transactions resulted in an amendment to the Foreign Exchange and Foreign Trade Control Law, which was passed by the Diet in May 1997 and will become effective on 1 April 1998. (For further details see Exhibit 4.2.) In due course, other laws and regulations will have to be revised in order to allow for the implementation of the remainder of the reform plan. The tax system is also to be reviewed.
4. For a summary of the proposed measures and the planned timetable for reform see Exhibit 4.1.
5. At the moment, the Securities and Exchange Law confines sales channels to investment management companies and securities firms.
6. The Insurance Council wanted insurance companies also to be allowed to sell investment trusts (MoF, 1997c, p. 3).
7. The Securities and Exchange Council (SEC) also argued for the private placement of investment trusts to be allowed and for consideration to be given to the introduction of investment company type funds (SEC, 1997a, p. 11).
8. The Financial System Research Council (FSRC) was concerned about the possibility of banks using undue influence to promote insurance sales or unfairly using information gleaned from the conduct of banking business to conduct insurance sales, and that the risks run by the purchasers of insurance products might not be fully understood by the latter (FSRC, 1997, p. 23).
9. Banks would, of course, also become subject to the regulations applied under the Insurance Business Law.
10. Reform will require revisions to the following pieces of legislation: the Securities and Exchange Law; the Commodity Exchange Law; and the Financial Futures Exchange Law. It must also be made clear that the Criminal Code on gambling does not apply to such transactions.
11. Trading in individual stock options began on 18 July 1997 on both the Tokyo Stock Exchange and the Osaka Securities Exchange. Thirty-three stocks, in total, were covered, seven of which (i.e. Torray Industries Inc., Nippon Steel Corp., Hitachi Ltd, Sony Corp., Industrial Bank of Japan, and Bank of Tokyo–Mitsubishi) were listed on both exchanges. Both exchanges use European-style options trading (i.e. ones with a fixed exercise date) and both operate on a stock delivery rather than cash settlement basis. Prior to this liberalization, only stock index options trading had been sanctioned by the MoF on the grounds that trading in individual stock options would be too speculative and hence potentially destabilizing.
12. They will not, however, be authorized to receive or deliver the underlying assets.
13. Following consideration of the Securities and Exchange Council's report on the subject, delivered in May 1997 (SEC, 1997b).
14. Currently, banks are allowed to issue commercial paper to gain liquidity from assets, and both banks and securities companies can securitize loan receivables from home loans under the investment trust method.
15. This will require revisions to both the Commercial Law and Civil Law.
16. A report on the subject by a private research group of the Director General, Civil Affairs Bureau, of the Ministry of Justice – the 'Study Group on the Legal System Affecting Asset Transfers' – was published in April 1997. The necessary legal measures, based on this report, are likely to be introduced in 1998.
17. The Financial System Research Council would also like further consideration (it has

already been considered by the government's Consolidated Conference on Real Estate Collateral which produced a report entitled 'The Comprehensive Package to Stimulate Real Estate Liquidity' in March 1997) to be given to promoting the securitization of real-property collateral, both to deepen Japan's financial markets and to assist local intermediaries in their disposal of non-performing assets (FSRC, 1997, pp. 17–18).

18. A bill revising the Anti-Monopoly Law, which has prohibited the establishment of, or transformation of corporate structures into, holding companies for the past 50 years, was passed in the 140th Diet during 1997. Under the revisions, Article 9 would be repealed, thereby lifting the general ban on holding companies. However, holding companies deemed to result in an 'excessive' concentration of economic power would be prohibited. Once total corporate assets reach ¥15 trillion, approval by the Fair Trade Commission (FTC) will be necessary; and holding companies must notify the FTC once their assets total ¥300 billion. Moreover, restrictions on the ownership of both financial and non-financial companies will remain. The prohibition under Article 11, on banks, securities firms and other financial companies holding more than 5 per cent (10 per cent for insurance companies) of another, unrelated company's stock will remain.

   Notwithstanding the repeal of Article 9, unless the Japanese Ministry of Finance relents and allows 'consolidated taxation' for holding companies, the attempt to stimulate their development may be stymied.

19. Similar restrictions are to be applied to holding companies owning insurance companies or securities companies.

20. For a discussion of those adopted in the USA in respect of the 'Section 20' non-bank subsidiaries of banks see Hall (1993), pp. 222–4 and 240–51. (Note, however, that some of these have since been relaxed or abolished.)

21. The Securities and Exchange Council would also like to see banks reducing or eliminating their large holdings of company shares once the holding company system becomes a reality.

22. Under this plan, emanating from the report entitled 'Regarding the Revision of the Plan for Promoting Deregulation', in the latter half of fiscal 1997, securities companies were to have been allowed to conduct virtually all types of securities businesses, and trust bank subsidiaries were to have been able to conduct all money trust business except for pension trust and joint money trust business.

23. Insurance companies' diversification into non-insurance business and securities companies' entry into insurance will, however, be favoured by the phasing of reform.

24. No mention, however, was made in the Ministry of Finance's communiqué of the SEC's demands for: abolishing the requirement for the order flow for listed securities to be consolidated; broadening access to transaction and quote information; improving the clearing and settlement system for securities; and improving the share-lending market.

25. For example, in July 1996 the MoF introduced the following disclosure requirements in respect of *derivatives* trading: all types of derivatives, including futures and options, forward exchange contracts and swap transactions, traded on authorized exchanges and on the over-the-counter market, must be stated as notes in the securities report disclosed to the public; the information which is disclosed must cover volume of derivatives trading and the content, trading policy, purpose, risk and risk management of each derivatives transaction; disclosures relating to the volume of transactions must, for each transaction, also cover the contract amount or expected principal amount, the market value, and the basis used to calculate that market value; all the information mentioned above must also be audited by an accounting firm. The new rules took effect on 1 March 1997.

26. PCA is a device borrowed from the Americans (see Hall, 1993, pp. 72–4) which is used to promote sound management and to ensure that problems incurred by (depository) intermediaries are dealt with in a timely and appropriate fashion. It uses a system of penalties and rewards to induce banks to hold more capital, and embraces a set of rules designed to ensure that prompt corrective action is taken to address problems as capital levels decline, and certainly well before a position of insolvency is reached. In part, it reflects strong disapproval of the traditional approach of forbearance adopted by supervisory authorities around the world (for an appraisal of recent Japanese policy in this area see Yamawaki, 1996).

In the Japanese version of PCA, introduced in April 1998 (at least for internationally active banks – a delay of one year applies to those with only a domestic presence), PCA operates at three levels. Once a bank's capital adequacy ratio falls below 8 per cent on the BIS risk-adjusted basis (Hall, 1993, Exhibit 8.1, p. 189) (or below 4 per cent on an 'adjusted' national basis for those banks without overseas branches or subsidiaries), the authorities must intervene to order management to formulate a management improvement plan and to implement it. Once the capital ratio falls below the 4 per cent (2 per cent) threshold, the authorities are obliged to order the bank's management to implement a variety of remedial measures and to impose a variety of restrictions on their activities (for full details see Exhibit 4.3). And, finally, once the ratio passes the 0 per cent (0 per cent) threshold, the authorities are usually (see Exhibit 4.3) obliged to suspend all or part of the bank's activities.

27. This was a component of the financial reform introduced under the so-called 'Three Acts' in June 1996. The first 'Act' was concerned with the introduction of prompt corrective action and the enhanced monitoring of credit co-operatives. The second and third 'Acts', concerned with facilitating the smooth and swift disposal of failed institutions, embraced amendments to the Deposit Insurance Act which would, *inter alia*, result in the creation of the Resolution and Collection Bank to assist in the orderly disposal of failed credit co-operatives, guarantee *all* deposits until the year 2001, allow the supervisory authority to petition for the initiation of reorganization or bankruptcy procedures, and involve an extension in the rights of the Deposit Insurance Corporation during reorganization and bankruptcy proceedings.

REFERENCES

Financial System Research Council (1989), *On a New Japanese Financial System*, interim report by the Second Financial System Committee, Tokyo: Federation of Bankers' Associations of Japan.

Financial System Research Council (1997), *Regarding the Reform of the Japanese Financial System – Contributing to the Vitalization of the National Economy*, Tokyo, 13 June.

Hall, M.J.B. (1983), *The City Revolution: Causes and Consequences*, Basingstoke, UK: Macmillan Press.

Hall, M.J.B. (1993), *Banking Regulation and Supervision: A Comparative Study of the UK, USA and Japan*, Aldershot, UK and Brookfield, US: Edward Elgar.

Hall, M.J.B. (1997), 'Financial Reform in Japan: Japan's "Big Bang"', *Journal of International Banking Law*, **13** (2), 58–70.

Ministry of Finance (1996), *Summary of the Interim Report by the Study Group on Prompt Corrective Action*, Tokyo, December.

Ministry of Finance (1997a), *Financial System Reform: Towards the Urgent Achievement of Reform*, Tokyo, 13 June.

Ministry of Finance (1997b), *Summary of the Report 'Regarding the Reform of the Japanese Financial System'*, unofficial English translation, Tokyo, 13 June.

Ministry of Finance (1997c), *Outline of the Report by the Insurance Council entitled 'Regarding the Review of the Insurance Business'*, unofficial English translation, Tokyo, June.

Ministry of Finance (1997d), *Concerning the Amendment of the Foreign Exchange and Foreign Trade Control Law: Toward the Further Activation of the Financial and Capital Market in Japan*, provisional English translation of the report of the Committee on Foreign Exchange and Other Transactions, Tokyo, January.

Ministry of Finance (1997e), *Guide to Japanese Government Bond 1997*, Tokyo, May.

Securities and Exchange Council (1997a), *Comprehensive Reform of the Securities Market – For a Rich and Diverse 21st Century*, unofficial and provisional English translation, Tokyo, 13 June.

Securities and Exchange Council (1997b), *Concerning Securities-Related Over-the-Counter Derivative Transactions*, Tokyo, May.

Yamawaki, T. (1996), 'The forbearance policy: what went wrong with Japanese financial regulation?', *Loughborough University Banking Centre Research Paper*, No. 106/96, November.

5. Supervisory reform

SUPERVISORY INITIATIVES TAKEN TO DEAL WITH THE BANKING SECTOR'S PROBLEMS

The authorities' response to the banking industry's plight has been tardy and piecemeal. Until recently, a policy of 'forbearance' applied whereby time was perceived to be the ultimate healer, that is, given time, interest and fee income, trading profits, and new capital raisings could be used to write off bad debts and restore balance sheet strength. Only when emergencies or crises arose were the authorities jolted into action, albeit through the development of *ad hoc* solutions.

A more considered, consistent and enduring response to the industry's problems, however, is evident in the authorities' recent[1] attempts to facilitate the orderly disposal of banks' bad debts. The establishment of the 'Resolution and Collection Bank', the resolution of the *jusen* crisis, the stimulus given to the 'securitization' process, the reform of the deposit insurance arrangements, the proposed introduction of 'prompt corrective action', and the encouragement given to speedy bad-debt write-offs are all positive signs. These topics are addressed below.

Failure Resolution Policies

Problem banks
Given the gravity of the situation facing the Japanese banking industry in the early to mid-1990s it was unsurprising to see so many problem cases emerging affecting the city bank, trust bank, long-term credit bank and regional bank sectors as well as the smaller institutions, such as credit co-operatives (see Exhibit 5.1). The Japanese authorities' initial response was to fall back on the tried and trusted approach to resolving problem cases – calling on healthier institutions, in the interests of collective health and the national good, to bail out the weak by taking them over and absorbing the losses. In this manner, all depositors were fully protected.

Despite the obvious attractions of this policy option from the authorities' point of view – no costs imposed on taxpayers, financial system stability assured, and so on – the deterioration in banks' balance sheets, even for the

Exhibit 5.1 Chronology of the emergence and resolution of 'problem' banks in Japan: 1991–97

Troubled financial institution: nature of problem	Date troubles announced by authorities	Resolution policy adopted	Assistance given by DIC (¥)	Other organisations giving support
Toho Sogo Bank Large non-performing loan to a shipping company which went bankrupt	July 1991	Taken over by Iyo Bank in April 1992 in an 'assisted merger'	8 billion	The Secondary Regional Banks Association of Japan; Bank of Japan
Toyo Shinkin Bank Fraud	August 1991	Taken over by Sanwa Bank in October 1992 in an assisted merger	20 billion	Local *shinkin* banks; the Zenshinren Bank; the Industrial Bank of Japan
Taiheiyo Bank Loan exposure to property speculator Mogami Kosan which went bankrupt	May 1992	¥110 billion of low-interest loans made to the bank over next 10 years	None	Sakura Bank (30%); Fuji Bank, Tokai Bank and Sanwa Bank (70%)
Kamaishi Shinkin Bank Became insolvent due to weak local economy	October 1993	Liquidated and performing assets transferred to Iwate Bank in October 1993	26 billion	Local regional banks and *shinkin* banks; the Zenshinren Bank; local association of *shinkin* banks
Osaka Fumin Credit Co-operative Problems due to weak local economy	November 1993	Taken over by Osaka Koyo Bank in an assisted merger in November 1993	20 billion	Osaka Prefectural Government; Fuji Bank; Daiwa Bank; Zenshinkumiren Bank; local association of credit co-operatives
Gifu Shogin Credit Co-operative Problems due to weak local economy	1994	Taken over in March 1995 by Kansai Kogin Credit Co-operative in an assisted merger	2.5 billion	Gifu Prefectural Government; Zenshinkumiren Bank; local association of credit co-operatives; and others

Institution	Date	Outcome	Amount	Sources of support
Kizu Credit Co-operative Collapsed because of crippling bad loans, which represented about 60% of total loans	August 1994	Business suspended in August 1995. Performing assets eventually transferred to the Resolution and Collection Bank (established in September 1996); kept active in the short run (i.e. until August 1995) by assistance from local government, the Bank of Japan and banks with relationships with the co-operative	1.034 trillion	Under the rescue package agreed in December 1995: Sanwa Bank, the Long-Term Credit Bank and Tokai Bank were asked to contribute as much as they could; the Osaka Government was also asked to contribute; and the Bank of Japan agreed to provide short-term liquidity, via ¥359 billion of special loans (this figure rose to ¥910.5 billion at its peak)
Nippon Trust Bank Weakened by huge amount of non-performing property-related loans	October 1994	MoF-approved takeover by Mitsubishi Bank in November 1994	None	None
Tokyo Kyowa Credit Co-operative; Anzen Credit Co-operative Brought to knees by huge amount of non-performing loans, especially those made to EIE International, a troubled property group	December 1994	Liquidated and performing assets transferred to newly established Tokyo Kyodo Bank in March 1995. (This bank was reorganized into the Resolution and Collection Bank in September 1996)	40 billion	Bank of Japan (¥20 billion); all financial institutions in Japan; Tokyo Metropolitan Government; local association of credit co-operatives; and others
Yuai Credit Co-operative Problems due to weak local economy	July 1995	Liquidated and performing assets transferred to a labour credit co-operative in July 1995	3 billion	Kanaga Prefectural Government; Yokohama Bank; Zenshinkumiren Bank; local association of credit co-operatives

Exhibit 5.1 (continued)

Troubled financial institution: nature of problem	Date troubles announced by authorities	Resolution policy adopted	Assistance given by DIC (¥)	Other organisations giving support
Cosmo Credit Co-operative Business suspended in the wake of a deposit run sparked by fears over use of aggressive interest-rate bidding for funds and scale of non-performing loans	July 1995	Liquidated and performing assets transferred to Tokyo Kyodo Bank in March 1996	125 billion	Bank of Japan (¥198 billion at its peak); Tokyo Metropolitan Government; Zenshinkumiren Bank; local association of credit co-operatives and others
Hyogo Bank Collapsed due to huge amount (¥800 billion) of bad loans	August 1995	Business suspended in August 1995. Subsequently liquidated and performing assets transferred to the newly established Midori Bank in January 1996	473 billion	Bank of Japan (¥612 billion at its peak); all financial institutions in Japan; local enterprises
Fukuiken Daiichi Credit Co-operative Problems due to weak local economy	December 1995	Liquidated and performing assets transferred to Fukui Bank	0.6 billion	Fukui Prefectural Government; Zenshinkumiren Bank
Ibaraki Chuo Credit Co-operative	December 1995	Taken over by the Joyo Bank	None	None
Osaka Credit Co-operative Crippled by non-performing loans	December 1995	Liquidated and performing assets transferred to Tokai Bank in summer of 1996. Non-performing loans transferred to the Resolution and Collection Bank	252 billion	Osaka Prefectural Government; Zenshinkumiren Bank; National Federation of Credit Co-operatives

162

Bank	Date	Action	Amount	Assistance
Taiheiyo Bank Collapsed under weight of huge amount (¥170 billion) of non-performing property-related loans	March 1996	Liquidated and performing assets transferred to the newly established Wakashio Bank, a wholly owned subsidiary of Sakura Bank, which began operations in September 1996	117 billion	Sakura Bank; Fuji Bank; Sanwa Bank; Tokai Bank
Musashino Shinkin Bank Crippled by bad loans which amounted to over 50% of loan book	September 1996	Assisted takeover by Oji Shinkin Bank	None	Zenshinren Bank; Tokyo Association of Shinkin Banks; *shinkin* banks based in Tokyo
Hanwa Bank Crippled by non-performing property-related loans	November 1996	Business suspended in November 1996. Bank liquidated. A new 'bridge bank' was established for the (temporary) purpose of paying out depositors, recovering performing loans and disposing of performing loans and disposing of collateral. Irrecoverable non-performing loans transferred to the Resolution and Collection Bank	57 billion	Bank of Japan (to make up any shortfall in deposits – amounted to ¥269 billion at its peak); governmental financial institutions responsible for small businesses
Nippon Credit Bank Large stock of non-performing loans and rumours of a liquidity crisis	April 1997	MoF reassured the markets by announcing a restructuring plan which involves, *inter alia*: disposal of ¥460 billion of non-performing loans; fixed-asset disposals; withdrawal from overseas operations; financial institutions to subscribe to ¥300 billion of newly issued capital	Assistance to be given from the Financial Stabilization Fund	Bank of Japan (¥124 billion taken from the funds earmarked to help resolve the *jusen*'s problems); long-term credit banks; main shareholder banks; life and non-life insurance companies

163

Exhibit 5.1 (continued)

Troubled financial institution: nature of problem	Date troubles announced by authorities	Resolution policy adopted	Assistance given by DIC (¥)	Other organisations giving support
Hokkaido Takushoku Bank Burdened by huge amount (>¥900 billion) of bad loans	April 1997	MoF-approved merger with Hokkaido Bank planned for April 1998. (Subsequently delayed for at least six months.) New bank, tentatively named the Shin Hokkaido Bank, to withdraw from overseas operations	None	None
Naniwa Bank; Fukutoku Bank Both weakened by high proportion of non-performing loans	October 1997	MoF-approved merger took place at the end of October 1997	Some assistance may be given	None
Kyoto Kyoei Bank Became insolvent because of burden of non-performing loans (which amounted to nearly 40% of total loans at end September 1997)	October 1997	Assisted takeover by Kofuku Bank	Assistance provided via purchase of non-performing loans from Kofuku Bank	Bank of Japan (via provision of emergency assistance until business transferred to Kofuku Bank – by October 1998)

164

Hokkaido Takushoku Bank Overburdened with non-performing loans. Collapse precipitated by liquidity crisis in wake of announcement to postpone the planned merger with Hokkaido Bank	November 1997	Business (i.e. deposits and performing assets) in Hokkaido region to be transferred to Hyokuyo Bank. Business in the Honshu area to be transferred to other financial institutions	Assistance to be provided via purchase of non-performing assets. All deposits to be protected. Will eventually repay all Bank of Japan loans	Bank of Japan to provide the bank with the necessary funds (under Article 25 of the Bank of Japan Law) until its business is transferred to the transferee institutions. Hokkaido Prefectural Government, public financial institutions and other commercial banks to be asked to provide assistance
Tokuyo City Bank Overburdened with non-performing loans. Collapse precipitated by liquidity crisis in wake of nervousness generated by collapse of Yamaichi Securities	November 1997	Bank eventually to be allowed to close its doors	None	Bank of Japan to provide assistance as necessary until the final resolution of the bank

Sources: Yamawaki (1996); press reports (various).

strongest institutions, from the early 1990s onwards, stiffened the resolve of
the industry leaders to resist such demands. As a result, 'sweeteners' were
often required, in the form of financial assistance from the Deposit Insurance
Corporation (DIC) and/or others, to induce the would-be rescuers to play
ball. Such 'assisted mergers' are evident in the rescue operations mounted in
1991 to deal with the problems at Toho Sogo Bank and Toyo Shinkin Bank
(full details of these, and other rescues are given in Exhibit 5.1) and, later, in
the rescue of the Osaka Fumin Credit Co-operative (1993), the Gifu Shogin
Credit Co-operative (1994), the Musashino Shinkin Bank (1996) and the
Kyoto Kyoei Bank (1997). In the case of Mitsubishi Bank's takeover of
Nippon Trust Bank in 1994, the incentive was provided by MoF's willingness
to allow the former to operate a full trust bank service, post-acquisition, at a
time when all other city banks were severely constrained by MoF-imposed
restrictions on the business activities of the city banks' trust bank subsidiaries. The MoF-inspired 'restructuring package' organized for Nippon Credit
Bank in April 1997, however, whereby reluctant private sector institutions
were cajoled into participating in the rescue operation,[2] suggests that the old
ways die hard. The 'rescue' was justified on the grounds that a collapse of the
bank, which, as a long-term credit bank, was one of the top 20 institutions
covered by the blanket guarantee given earlier by the MoF, would destabilize
domestic and international financial markets, and that there was a strong
chance that a reconstruction of the bank would prove successful. Contrari-
wise, the Hokkaido Takushoku Bank, the tenth largest bank in Japan and a
city bank, was allowed to go to the wall in November 1997 notwithstanding
the government's earlier pledge to preserve the country's top 20 banks!

A variant on the assisted merger, or subsidized takeover, solution also
emerged in the early 1990s in the form of a liquidation of an insolvent
institution and subsequent transfer of its ongoing business to another bank or
to a new bank especially created for that purpose. The resolution of problems
at Kamaishi Shinkin Bank (1993), the Tokyo Kyowa Credit Corporation
(1994), the Anzen Credit Co-operative (1994), the Yuai Credit Co-operative
(1995), the Cosmo Credit Co-operative (1995), Hyogo Bank (1995), the
Fukuiken Daiichi Credit Co-operative (1995), the Osaka Credit Co-operative
(1995), and Taiheiyo Bank (1996) provides examples of this. In some cases,
the bank to which the performing assets were eventually transferred was a
bank – called the Resolution and Collection Bank, which emerged from a
reorganized Tokyo Kyodo Bank in September 1996 – specifically set up for
the purposes of repaying the depositors of failed institutions, disposing of
their irrecoverable loans and attempting to collect on other non-performing
loans. This institution duly ended up with the residues of the Kizu Credit Co-
operative, the Tokyo Kyowa Credit Co-operative, the Anzen Credit
Co-operative, the Cosmo Credit Co-operative, the Osaka Credit Co-opera-

tive, Hanwa Bank, and the *jusen*. In the case of Hanwa Bank, no fully fledged bank was involved in the running of Hanwa's sound operations prior to the Resolution and Collective Bank's involvement.

Finally, there are occasions when the results of a merger are perceived to be mutually beneficial to both parties, although it is not always clear to what extent the MoF was involved in bringing the two parties together. Hokkaido Bank's planned merger with the then weakest city bank, Hokkaido Takushoku Bank, to form a 'super-regional bank', must have been warmly welcomed by the authorities, long concerned with the scale of the latter's non-performing loans (which eventually precipitated the bank's collapse in November 1997). Similarly, the agreed merger between the regional banks Naniwa Bank and Fukutoku Bank and the planned rationalization of joint activities would appear to be an ideal solution to the non-performing loan problems experienced by both, although DIC assistance is likely to be provided to 'oil the wheels'.

The *jusen*

In the late 1960s and early 1970s, banks, insurance companies and others established eight non-bank institutions, principally to engage in the provision of housing loans to individuals. These housing loan corporations, the *jusen*, subsequently shifted their focus towards commercial real-estate lending when the founding institutions moved into the residential housing market in their own right in the early 1980s. During this decade, the *jusen* rapidly expanded their lending to the commercial real-estate market financed in large part by borrowing from other financial institutions, especially the large banks and financial institutions linked to agricultural co-operatives. The bursting of the asset 'bubble' in Japan, in 1990–91, duly left the *jusen* nursing huge stocks of non-performing loans causing them, in turn, to default on their borrowings from financial institutions. This was the background to the *jusen* crisis, which so exercised politicians and financiers in the mid-1990s.

The authorities' first response was to ask the *jusen*'s creditors to cut the interest charged on their debts: the 'mother banks' (that is, the founding banks) were asked to cut interest charges to zero; other banks with a special relationship with the *jusen* were asked to cut their interest charges to 2.5 per cent per annum; and agricultural co-operatives were asked to reduce interest charges to 4.5 per cent per annum. In the event this plan, drawn up in the spring of 1993 by the MoF and the Ministry of Agriculture, Forestry and Fisheries, soon collapsed.

In December 1995, the Cabinet decided that the remaining *jusen* should be liquidated immediately to maintain confidence in the Japanese financial system. This followed the liquidation of Jyosu, one of the eight *jusen*, by Japan's seven trust banks in October 1995. In December 1995, it was estimated that, out of a total loan book of ¥10.7 trillion, ¥6.27 trillion would prove irrecoverable, with other losses of ¥0.14 trillion anticipated. The liquidation plan involved establishing a 'Jusen Resolution Corporation' (later named the 'Resolution and Collection Bank'), based on the Resolution Trust Corporation established in the USA to facilitate the orderly disposal of the assets of failed savings and loans associations, which would purchase the assets of the *jusen* and seek to recover the loans. The ¥6.41 trillion of expected losses would be disposed of at the time of purchase of the assets in accordance with the following: mother banks would be asked to relinquish all claims on their ¥3.5 trillion of outstanding loans to the *jusen*; other banks would be asked to abandon ¥1.7 trillion of their ¥3.8 trillion worth of claims outstanding on the *jusen*; and agricultural financial institutions would be asked to contribute ¥530 billion and provide low-interest loans to the Jusen Resolution Corporation, although they would be repaid in full their ¥5.5 trillion of outstanding loans (see Exhibit 5.2). The remaining 'hole' in the accounts, of ¥685 billion, would be met by the government, using taxpayers' money, via payments made into a '*jusen* account' at the Deposit Insurance Corporation (DIC) (see Chart 5.1). Any future losses incurred by the Jusen Resolution Corporation – a figure of ¥1.24 trillion was already being talked about – would be met, in part, by the government. (Any profit would be returned to the government.) A

Exhibit 5.2   *Balance sheet profile of the seven* jusen *companies at 19 December 1995*

Assets (¥ trillion)	
Normal assets	3.49
Non-performing assets deemed 'recoverable'	3.29
'Irrecoverable' bad loans	6.27
'Other' loan losses anticipated	0.14
Possible future losses on disposal	1.24
Liabilities (¥ trillion)	
Loans outstanding from founder banks	3.5
Loans outstanding from lender banks	3.8
Loans outstanding from agricultural financial institutions	
● Norinchukin Bank	0.8
● Prefecture Credit Federations of Agricultural Co-operatives	3.3
● National Mutual Insurance Federation of Agricultural Co-operatives and Prefecture Insurance Federations of Agricultural Co-operatives	1.3

Source: Ministry of Finance (1995).

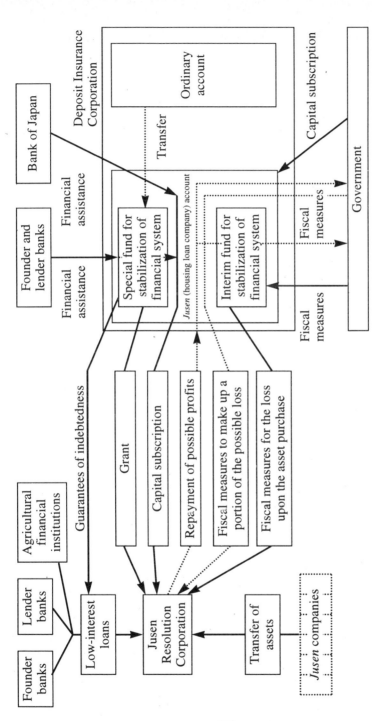

Source: Ministry of Finance (1996a).

Chart 5.1 Jusen *disposal scheme*

¥5 billion capital subscription would also be made by the government in fiscal 1996 to strengthen the DIC; and the Bank of Japan would also be asked to make a capital subscription to the DIC and to make a financial contribution to its *jusen* account.

The announcement of the liquidation plan led to a public outcry against the use of public funds, ¥685 billion of which had already been promised, plus a portion of any future losses (a figure of ¥1.24 trillion, likely to prove a gross underestimate, had already been mentioned) incurred by the Jusen Resolution Corporation. The government had originally hoped to avoid the use of public funds by leaning on the agricultural co-operatives to contribute more, but the latter's political muscle – many politicians are elected in rural areas – ensured that their contribution was kept to a minimum. The founder banks, too, were far from happy, given that they were being asked to abandon all their claims on the *jusen*, although this was sweetened by the government's decision to make the losses fully tax-deductible so long as the banks abandoned claims on the companies to which the *jusen* had also lent.

To assuage public opinion, the government declared its intention to ensure that all those responsible for the débâcle, officials and management alike, would be duly 'punished', and the Administrative Vice-Minister for Finance, Mr Shinozawa, resigned later that month in acceptance of the Ministry's failings in this case.[3] Public dissent, however, continued unabated, not least because of the government's subsequent confirmation (Ministry of Finance, 1996a) that it proposed to shoulder *half* of any losses[4] incurred by the Jusen Resolution Corporation, with the commercial banks shouldering the other half (via the investment income deriving from a fund, of about ¥1 trillion, to be established by them at the DIC).[5] Moreover, allegations began to emerge in the local press concerning the extent to which former MoF officials had been employed, on retirement, as presidents or chairmen at the *jusen*, and the involvement of the *jusen* in lending to property companies controlled by the *yakuza*, Japanese gangsters. Buoyed up by public dissent, opposition parties proceeded to prevent discussion of the government's budget proposals for fiscal 1996 by physically blocking entry to the committee room used for such discussions. A temporary truce, however, was called in April 1996 to allow for discussion of the Budget Bill, the issue of the *jusen* rescue being put on hold. Finally, on 18 June 1996, the Diet passed the controversial bill concerned with the liquidation of the *jusen* following official assurances that the financial institutions would 'pick up the tab', at least for the secondary losses, previously destined for the general public. And that same month, the former head of Nippon Housing Loan, the largest *jusen*, and six others were arrested on suspicion of authorizing loans to an insolvent Tokyo property developer without bothering to take collateral and in full knowledge that the money would never be repaid.

Under the Bill, which became known as the Law Concerning Special Measures to Promote Liquidation of the Assets and Liabilities of Designated Housing Loan Companies, a 'Housing Loan Administration Corporation' (HLAC) would be set up to take over the assets of the *jusen*. The HLAC would be capitalized with ¥100 billion from private financial institutions and ¥100 billion from the Bank of Japan. Private financial institutions and agricultural co-operatives would also be asked to provide low-cost loans to the HLAC to finance the purchases of assets from the *jusen*. The 'primary losses' are to be shared out in accordance with the previous agreement outlined above. A special '*jusen* account' would be set up within the DIC, and this would receive the ¥680 billion in public funds held in the 'Emergency Financial Stabilization Fund' and the ¥1 trillion of funds supplied by private financial institutions and held in the 'Financial Stabilization Contribution Fund', investment earnings from which will cover secondary losses. The HLAC would be established through a ¥100 billion investment by the latter fund. A 'New Financial Stabilization Contribution Fund' would also be established at the DIC through contributions (of approximately ¥900 billion) from private financial institutions and the Bank of Japan.

On 22 July 1996 the Financial Stabilization Fund was duly established within the DIC with ¥1.007 trillion of contributions from private financial institutions.[6] On 22 July 1996, the Bank of Japan provided the DIC with ¥100 billion in funding and the HLAC was established with a ¥200 billion cash investment from the DIC, funded by the contributions noted above. And on 20 August 1996, the MoF paid ¥680 billion into the Emergency Financial Stabilization Fund. The seven *jusen* were formally closed on 31 August 1996 and the HLAC assumed the *jusen*'s sound and recoverable loans, totalling ¥6.78 trillion, on 1 October 1996. Meanwhile, on 27 September 1996 the New Financial Stabilization Contribution Fund was established.

Reform of Deposit Insurance Arrangements to Help Stabilize the Financial Sector

Following the revisions made to the Deposit Insurance Law in May 1986, the premiums paid by private depository institutions were raised from 0.008 per cent of insured deposits to 0.012 per cent, insurance coverage was raised from ¥3 million to ¥10 million per depositor, the limit on Deposit Insurance Corporation (DIC) borrowing from the Bank of Japan was raised from ¥50 billion to ¥500 billion, and DIC borrowing from private financial institutions was sanctioned. At the same time, the DIC was empowered, with MoF approval, to provide financial assistance to facilitate mergers or the acquisition of failed institutions (Hall, 1993, ch. 6). As noted in Exhibit 5.1, however, it soon became apparent that even this degree of reform would not prove sufficient to accommodate the degree of carnage that was evident in the banking sector. The 'rescue' of the Kizu Credit Co-operative, the second largest credit co-operative in Japan, in the winter of 1995 was the catalyst for further reform.

Then, in December 1995, the MoF announced that a Bill revising the Deposit Insurance Law would be sent to the Diet in January 1996. The main purpose of the revision was to enhance depositor protection by putting the DIC on to a sounder footing. In fact, in May 1996 two Bills were considered by the Diet. The first, the Bill for the Special Procedure for the Reorganiza- tion of Financial Institutions, was designed to facilitate the disposal of failed institutions at minimum cost and disruption to the economy by allowing the DIC to undertake 'reorganizations' on behalf of depositors when institutions go bankrupt. More formally, it was proposed that: the supervisory authority be able to apply for the initiation of a company reorganization or bankruptcy procedures; the DIC be allowed to exercise depositors' rights on their behalf during such reorganizations, and so on; and that a 'deposit purchase' system be introduced under which the DIC would provide depositors with the amounts of money (over and above the *de jure* limit of ¥10 million per depositor) which are expected to be available for disbursement after the conclusion of court procedures.

The second Bill, the Amendment Bill to the Deposit Insurance Act, was designed to do two things: first, to facilitate solution of the non-performing loans problem, in part by refining the mechanisms available for disposing of ailing and failed financial institutions; and second, to provide the financial resources to underwrite the government's commitment to protect *all* deposits for the next five years, a commitment given in the light of the inadequate information disclosure made by banks and the current fragility of the finan- cial system. Specifically, the Bill (Ministry of Finance, 1996b) embraced the following proposals:

(i) Increasing the premiums paid by private depository institutions by a factor of 7, that is, from 0.012 per cent of insured deposits to 0.084 per cent. Of this 700 per cent increase, 300 per cent (that is, a 0.036 per cent levy, to be reassessed in 1999) would go towards the creation of 'special accounts' at the DIC, which are designed to cover the costs incurred beyond the 'pay off' cost, and 400 per cent (that is, a 0.048 per cent levy) would constitute the new 'ordinary' premiums, to be held in the 'ordinary account' at the DIC (see Chart 5.2). The new level of premium contribu- tions would raise the depository institutions' level of contribution to the DIC to around ¥490 billion, approximately equal to 8 per cent of net earnings, and if this still proves insufficient to fund bail-outs, the govern- ment would extend public support, but only in the case of credit

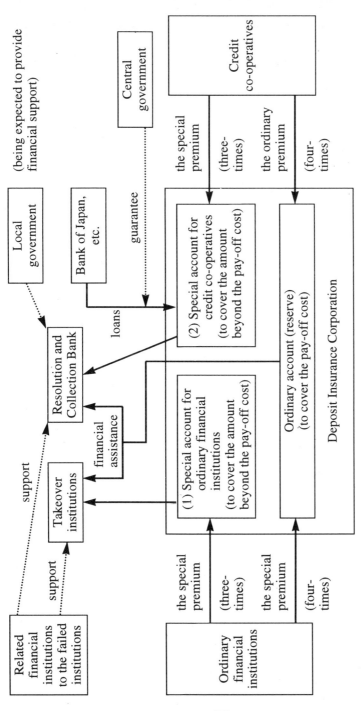

Source: Ministry of Finance (1996b).

Chart 5.2   Deposit insurance reform: 1996. The scheme of specified duration to ensure a sound financial system (for five years)

co-operatives – any additional costs incurred in resolving commercial bank failures would fall upon the commercial bank sector itself.

(ii) Establishing a 'Resolution and Collection Bank' as an institution that can facilitate the smooth disposal of any failed credit co-operatives (see details above).

Both Bills were duly passed by the Diet in June 1996.

As anticipated, the strains involved in resolving institutional crashes, notably that of the Kizu Credit Co-operative (see Exhibit 5.1), proved immense and, in June 1997, the DIC was forced, for the first time in its 26–year history, to borrow from private financial institutions to repay loans taken from the Bank of Japan (BoJ). In June 1997, the DIC owed the BoJ ¥546 billion but, given anticipated premium income for the special account of ¥100 billion by the end of that month, planned borrowing of ¥450 billion was deemed sufficient.

Next, in October 1997, the Cabinet approved a bill revising the Deposit Insurance Law yet again. The revision, which was approved by the Diet in December 1997, will enable the DIC to provide assistance for bank mergers, which will be necessary if the proposed merger of the two ailing second-tier regional banks, Fututoku Bank and Naniwa Bank, is to go through as planned. (Currently, the DIC can only assist the takeover of a troubled bank by a healthy bank.)

Finally, in December 1997, further proposals were put forward for reforming the deposit insurance arrangements as part of a package of emergency measures designed to stabilize the financial system in the wake of the nervousness generated by the collapse of Yamaichi Securities and other financial intermediaries during the previous month. The proposals, which were confirmed the following month (MoF, 1998a), envisaged a further strengthening of the financial base of the DIC through the injection of public funds and conferment on the DIC of the power to issue bonds. The DIC's ability to collect bad loans would also be strengthened; and a new account would be set up within the DIC to allow for the stabilization of the financial system in times of financial crisis by providing the DIC with resources to purchase preferred stocks and subordinated bonds issued by financial institutions, thereby recapitalizing the banking/financial sectors.

Specifically (see Chart 5.3), the Deposit Insurance Law would be amended to allow for the following:

(i)   the integration – they are currently separated for credit co-operatives and other financial institutions – of the existing 'special accounts' held at the DIC (which were set up as a temporary measure to last until the end of March 2001 – see Chart 5.2);

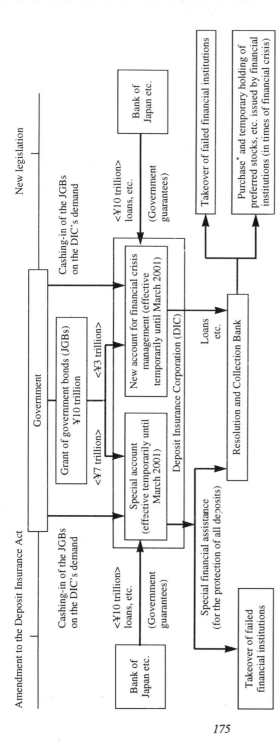

Notes:

* A unanimous approval, after a thorough review by a newly established neutral 'examining body', is necessary.

1. The special account is to protect individual deposits that exceed ¥10 million. The new account for financial crisis management is newly established to purchase and hold temporarily preferred stocks issued by financial institutions, aiming to stabilize the financial system.

2. In addition to the accounts mentioned above, the DIC has the ordinary account that serves to protect deposits up to ¥10 million.

Source: Ministry of Finance, (1998a).

Chart 5.3 Framework of emergency measures for stabilizing the financial system

(ii) the delivery of ¥7 trillion of government bonds to the newly integrated special account of the DIC, to be cashed in to meet any losses arising from resolving financial failures (that is, resolution costs not covered by the special account deposit insurance premiums and possible secondary losses arising from the disposal of acquired assets);

(iii) the DIC being empowered to issue bonds;

(iv) ¥10 trillion of public funds being given to the DIC to allow for the purchase of assets from failed financial institutions;

(v) an extension in the powers of the Resolution and Collection Bank (RCB) to allow it to take over the financial business of *any* failed financial institution (rather than, as at present, being confined to dealing with failed credit unions);

(vi) an enhancement in the DIC's ability to collect bad loans through, for example, an expansion in its investigative powers (it may be given the power to impose penalties, and will also be required to apportion blame for financial failures);

(vii) the establishment of a 'new account for financial crisis management' at the DIC, with ¥3 trillion in government bonds being delivered to the new account, which can be cashed in by the DIC to finance the purchase, until end March 2001, of preferred stocks and subordinated bonds issued by financial institutions and to compensate for any losses incurred in the subsequent sale of such instruments (the DIC will entrust the said purchasing operations to the RCB);

(viii) the DIC being provided with an additional ¥10 trillion worth of government guarantees to ensure the smooth operation of the new account; and

(ix) the establishment of an 'examining board' – comprising three experts from the private sector, the Minister of Finance, the Commissioner of the Financial Supervisory Agency, the Governor of the Bank of Japan and the Governor of the DIC – to ensure that the purchase of preferred stocks and subordinated bonds is conducted on a fair and proper basis and in accordance with a prescribed set of objective criteria. (A decision to engage in such purchases also requires the unanimous approval of the examining board and the consent of the Cabinet; and any institution receiving such assistance in this way must submit, and have approved by the DIC, a programme designed to ensure its continued solvency. Only 'healthy' institutions, whose insolvency is not foreseen at the time of purchase, may participate in the sales of such debt instruments to the DIC.)

The reform proposals were duly passed by the Diet in February 1998. Later that month an economics professor, Ms Sazanami, was appointed Chairwoman of the Examining Board. A fairly loose set of criteria (few banks were disqualified from applying as a result) for determining the eligibility of applicants for funding under the scheme providing for DIC purchases of subordinated debt and preferred stock was also published that same month. Banks would only be barred from applying if they had recorded a loss for the previous three years or had failed to pay dividends. The provision of assistance would also be dependent upon submission of a viable restructuring plan; and the management of any bank with international business would have to resign if their capital adequacy ratio fell below 4 per cent on a risk-adjusted basis. (This is additional to the other measures which must be complied with from 1 April 1998 under the policy of 'prompt corrective action' – see Chapter 4). Finally, on 5 March 1998, 18 of Japan's largest banks, plus three regional banks, formally applied for funding under the scheme to the tune of about ¥2000 billion in aggregate.[7] A mixture of subordinated bonds, subordinated loans and preferred shares were used to generate the funding requested. (The scheme will also be used to inject capital in the spring of 1999 into the bank created from the merger of Hanshin Bank and the troubled Midori Bank, the latter having become enfeebled since its assumption of the bad debts of the now-defunct Hyogo Bank in 1995.)

Financial Deregulation

Given the fiscal crisis that emerged in government finances in the mid-1990s and the record loosening of monetary policy noted earlier, the Japanese government was forced to fall back on 'liberalization', or supply-side policies, as the solution to the economy's woes. Such policies, however, if successful, will only reap benefits in the medium to longer-term and so cannot be viewed as providing the stimulus to growth that is so urgently required in Japan today. While deregulation is thus unable to revive the immediate fortunes of the banking industry through regeneration of the domestic economy, there are signs that the reforms embraced are beginning to have some beneficial effects.

As far as resolution of the banks' bad debts problems is concerned, the most obvious beneficial reform is the fillip given to the securitization process (see Chapter 4). And the other freedoms introduced since April 1998, under, for example, the liberalization of the Foreign Exchange and Foreign Trade Control Law and the Anti-Monopoly Law, and the extension of cross-sectoral powers under the Financial System Reform Law (for full details see Chapter 4), offer the prospect of increased risk-adjusted rates of return, for some at least. But, as noted earlier, the 'threats' posed by financial deregulation render such liberalization very much a 'double-edged' sword for the banking industry, but one which is unavoidable.

ENHANCEMENT OF EXTERNAL SUPERVISION

A number of initiatives have recently been adopted to try to enhance the efficacy of external supervision. These include, *inter alia*, the introduction of 'prompt corrective action' (PCA), an overhaul of inspection and supervisory procedures and the creation of a new supervisory agency. Each of these issues is addressed in turn below.

Impetus for a review of supervisory arrangements operating in Japan was provided by the widespread feeling that the chief supervisory authority, the Ministry of Finance (MoF), had 'underperformed' in respect of its obligations to ensure the safety and soundness of the financial system. The large number of banking failures, supervisory 'failings' and the unfortunate Daiwa incident conspired to undermine the credibility, both at home and abroad, of the MoF as a supervisory body. This loss of confidence ultimately led to the proposed transfer of supervisory powers to a new agency.

The starting-point for a review of recent developments in this area is the statement made by the MoF in December 1995 on measures it was proposing to take to improve banking inspection and supervision. Acknowledging the deficiencies of the traditional 'convoy' style of banking administration, and accepting that it had placed too much trust in financial institutions (which led to inadequate checks of management and internal control functions) and that banking supervision had not been transparent enough, the MoF proposed a raft of changes based upon two principles: first, that henceforth the management of financial institutions exercise more *self-responsibility*; and second, that supervision be more *transparent* and based on *market discipline*. Specifically, the MoF proposed the following (Ministry of Finance, 1996b):

(i)   that Japanese financial institutions reinforce their risk management and internal control functions;
(ii)   that supervision and inspection procedures be revised to allow for the introduction of PCA, the greater use of external audit, and an overhaul of the procedures relating to the treatment of wrongdoing in financial institutions;
(iii)   that on-site inspections be strengthened; and
(iv)   that the exchange of information with overseas supervisory authorities be increased.

In respect of the demand that institutions reinforce their risk management and internal control functions, institutions were advised to reinforce their in-house inspections, encouraged to carry out external audits of their overseas branches, asked to enhance their internal audit and compliance functions (especially in respect of overseas operations), and urged to improve their risk management systems for market-related operations. To facilitate this, the MoF promised to release guidelines on both in-house inspections (covering quality of assets, internal controls (including compliance with laws and regulations), risk management for market-related businesses (including derivatives), and computer systems) and market risk control (covering basic policies on risk control, institutional arrangements promoting sound risk management (including the checking of functions and the independence of risk management sections), and procedures for controlling risks (including the measurement of risks, reporting to the Executive Board, and assignment of risk limits or stop-loss limits)). In addition, the MoF promised that it would monitor closely institutions' in-house inspections and demanded that those institutions carrying out market-related business on a global basis adopt the most advanced risk management systems available.

As to the revision of the MoF's operational procedures, by far the most significant development was the introduction of PCA in April 1998 (at least in respect of internationally active banks – those with only a domestic presence have been given one year's reprieve). Under this scheme, the supervisory authority has lost much of its flexibility as it is mandated to intervene in a prescribed fashion once an institution's capital falls below certain thresholds, and certainly well before a position of insolvency is reached. Accordingly, once an institution's capital adequacy ratio falls below 8 per cent on the BIS risk-adjusted basis (see Hall, 1993, Exhibit 8.1, p. 189) (or below 4 per cent on an 'adjusted' national basis for those banks without overseas branches or subsidiaries) the authorities must intervene to order management to formulate a management improvement plan and to implement it. Once the ratio falls below the 4 per cent (2 per cent) threshold, the authorities are obliged to order the bank's management to implement a variety of remedial measures and to impose a variety of restrictions on their activities. And, finally, once the ratio passes the 0 per cent (0 per cent) threshold, the authorities are usually obliged to suspend all or part of the bank's operations (for full details see Chapter 4).

Apart from implementing PCA, the MoF promised to enhance its inspection and monitoring functions and to make use of external audits in reviewing the banks' self-assessments of asset quality. Moreover, in its revised treatment of wrongdoing, the MoF will require the following: that financial institutions notify the relevant authorities (including those overseas) immediately of any wrongdoing; that institutions report to the supervisory authorities in writing, in accordance with specified deadlines, within 30 days of acknowledging such wrongdoing; that independent divisions, such as an in-house inspection section, be used in any in-house investigations; and that institutions disclose any wrongdoing that is judged likely to have a 'significant effect on the institution' in a timely manner. In addition, the MoF proposed expanding the scope of reporting requirements on wrongdoing to include subsidiaries with more than 50 per cent shares of stock or investments owned by financial institutions.

Strengthening of (domestic) on-site inspections is to be secured through the introduction of a new inspection system, built around PCA, and reinforcement of inspections of risk management and control functions. The former, which is to be based on self-assessment by the institutions and external audit, will involve the Ministry in formally *rating* an institution according to capital strength, the accuracy of its self-assessment and the appropriateness of its policies on provisioning and write-offs. Low-rated institutions would then suffer more frequent and intensive (pre-announced) inspections focusing on asset quality. The latter, which revolves around the monitoring of institutions' management systems (covering risk management, operations, and compliance with laws and regulations) and in-house inspections, will also involve the promulgation of formal ratings by the MoF. And, once again, low-rated institutions would be subject to more frequent and intensive inspection, but in this case regarding their risk management and internal control functions. More inspectors will also be employed. As far as overseas offices are concerned, the MoF is to increase both the frequency and intensity of inspection. Inspection of offices in New York, London and other financial centres will be conducted at the same time as the inspection of the Japanese headquarters; and stand-alone inspections of branches located in Asia, the west coast of the USA and other places will also take place. As for the inspection process itself, inspectors will be required to verify directly transaction slips and booked accounts, and inspection of risk management, operations, and compliance will have to be carried out in accordance with an MoF checklist. To facilitate these developments, the MoF is to increase the number of inspectors that it employs (raising the overall complement from 420 to 490 officers) and expand the duration of such inspections. A specialist team of overseas inspectors, concentrating in this area, is also to be set up. Training for all inspectors will also be enhanced; and 'experts' from the private sector will be used in the inspection process.

Finally, with a view to promoting a closer exchange of information with overseas supervisors, the MoF promised to adhere to the principles enshrined in the 'Basle Concordat', to provide the necessary information to host supervisors in a prompt fashion, to hold *ad hoc* meetings (in addition to the usual annual bilateral meetings) with overseas authorities when necessary, to increase mutual visits by senior staff, and to increase the exchange of information concerning the inspection of overseas offices.

Subsequent to this MoF-inspired overhaul of banking supervision, in August 1996 the Bank of Japan (BoJ) ordered several leading Japanese banks to improve the quality of their management of their overseas branches. This followed the BoJ's inspection of the banks' New York offices in December 1995 and the spring of 1996, during which it unearthed shortcomings in fraud prevention (for example, in electronic transactions) and in basic risk management and internal control functions (for example, failure to separate 'front' – trading – from 'back' – settlement – office functions). This move was designed to avoid a repetition of a Daiwa-style incident. Since then, the BoJ has reorganized its Bank Supervision Department, in an attempt to increase the cost-effectiveness of supervision and enhance the quality of on- and off-site supervision. Like the MoF, it is now more concerned with validating banks' 'self assessments' than evaluating asset quality; but, unlike the MoF, it has become much more focused on risk-based assessment and risk management systems.

The final development on the supervisory front[8] is the imminent arrival of a new supervisory agency, the Financial Supervisory Agency (to be headed by Mr Masaharu, a former prosecutor), which will assume most of the supervisory functions currently exercised by the MoF (see below). It remains to be seen if such structural reform improves supervisory 'performance'.

STRUCTURAL REFORM

The Need for Change

The decision to review the supervisory structure governing financial intermediaries in Japan was taken back in February 1996 by Prime Minister Hashimoto. The prime motivation for ordering such a review was to placate the electorate who had become disenchanted at the MoF's handling of financial crises. The most vociferous popular backlash was prompted by the MoF's decision to use public money in the liquidation of the insolvent housing loan companies (the *jusen*), but popular concern was also expressed at the MoF's failure to prevent, and subsequently to deal adequately with, the dramatic deterioration in the balance sheets of banks and other financial institutions. In particular, its policy of 'forbearance' – allowing an institution to try to trade out of financial difficulty as an alternative to implementing 'prompt corrective action' (see Chapter 4) – was heavily criticized (Yamawaki, 1996). Dismay was also expressed at its handling of the Daiwa crisis, which led US regulators to allege that it was actually misled by the MoF (see Chapter 2).

Apart from such supervisory 'failings', a range of other considerations prompted calls for a review of the functions performed by the MoF. First, many criticized the sheer extent of its powers, which roam across the broad areas of, *inter alia*, budgetary considerations, taxation, financial supervision and the management of state-owned assets (including privatizations).[9] No ministry elsewhere in the world has such wide-reaching powers. Second, because of the scope of its activities, it was charged with being an inefficient, unwieldy, monolithic and unaccountable bureaucracy. Third, again because of the scope of its activities, it was widely felt that it faced impossible conflicts of interest to resolve, not least on the financial front.[10] Fourth, and notwithstanding its postwar success in helping to regenerate the Japanese economy, its autocratic style of management was no longer deemed suited to the needs of the twenty-first century, where willingness to listen to outside advice and to accommodate international concerns are seen as positive virtues. Fifth, its policy of frequently rotating staff around its various bureaux was criticized as militating against the emergence of specialists, thereby increasing the risk of policy error. Sixth, it was widely believed that it had badly handled privatizations. And finally,[11] returning to financial matters, it was widely felt that the BoJ needed more independence – see Chapter 6 – and that the regime of 'administrative guidance' enforced by the MoF was not consistent with an open, efficient and deregulated financial sector.

The Creation of a New Independent Supervisory Agency

Following consideration of the review body's findings, the Cabinet, in March 1997, approved a Bill to establish a new supervisory body, the 'Financial Supervisory Agency' (FSA). This body, which is expected to start operations in 1998 following approval of the Bill by the Diet in June 1997, will be independent of the MoF, being part of the Prime Minister's Office. It will assume the MoF's current roles of licensing, inspection, supervision and resolution of problem cases in respect of banks, securities firms and insurance companies. Moreover, it will be responsible for implementing PCA. The MoF, however, will retain responsibility for financial system planning and the drafting of financial law. Moreover, in times of financial crisis, the Commissioner of the FSA is obliged to consult with the MoF over the appropriate course of action to be taken. (For further details of the relationship between the FSA, MoF, BoJ and DIC see Chart 5.4.)

In terms of regulatory structure, the proposed changes will, of course, add a new face to the institutional landscape – see Exhibit 5.3 – but rationalization will result in the Securities and Exchange Surveillance Council being absorbed into the FSA, while the MoF's banking and securities bureaux will be merged to form a new 'Financial Planning' bureau in charge of financial system planning. This new bureau will operate alongside the existing International Bureau and a severely downsized ministers secretariat (following the transfer of financial inspection to the FSA) at the MoF.

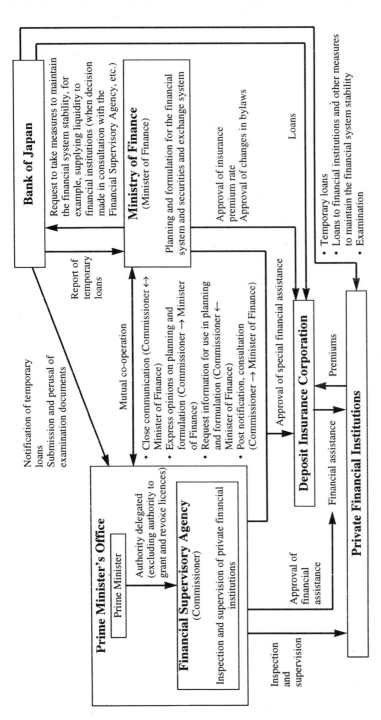

Source: MoF, 1998b.

Chart 5.4 Relationships between the Financial Supervisory Agency, Ministry of Finance, Bank of Japan and Deposit Insurance Corporation

Exhibit 5.3 Current institutional landscape governing the regulation and supervision of financial institutions* in Japan

Industry	Main regulatory bodies involved	Main responsibilities	Governing legislation
A. Banking industry	1. Ministry of Finance		
	(i) Banking Bureau	(i) Licensing, inspection and guidance, supervision of banks' 'banking operations' (by the Commercial Banks and Special Banks Divisions). Supervision of Bank of Japan (by the Co-ordination Division)	(i) Banking Law of 1981; Law Concerning Concurrent Operation of Trust Business by Ordinary Banks 1981; Long-Term Credit Bank Law of 1952
	(ii) Securities Bureau	(ii) Supervision of banks' securities business	(ii) Securities and Exchange Law of 1948; Banking Law of 1981; Trust Business Law of 1922; Financial System Reform Law of 1993; Anti-Monopoly Law of 1947
	(iii) International Finance Bureau	(iii) Licensing and approval of banks' foreign exchange business (by International Banking Division)	(iii) Foreign Exchange and Foreign Trade Control Law of 1947; Foreign Exchange Bank Law of 1954
	2. Bank of Japan	On-site examination of client institutions holding current accounts with it	Bank of Japan Law of 1998
B. Securities industry	1. Ministry of Finance		
	(i) Securities Bureau	(i) Licensing, inspection, supervision and guidance of securities firms	(i) Securities and Exchange Law of 1948; Law Concerning Foreign Securities Firms of 1971; Financial System Reform Law of 1993

(ii) International Finance Bureau	(ii) Enforcing foreign exchange regulations	(ii) Foreign Exchange and Foreign Trade Control Law of 1980
(iii) Securities and Exchange Surveillance Council	(iii) Inspection and supervision of securities firms. Investigation of suspected criminal offences	(iii) Securities and Exchange Law of 1948
2. Bank of Japan	Inspection of securities companies dealing in government securities	Bank of Japan Law of 1998
3. Ministry of International Trade and Industry	Oversees the running of the commodities market in Japan	Commodity Exchange Act
4. Self-regulatory organizations		
(i) Japanese Securities Dealers' Association	(i) Regulation of the broking industry	
(ii) Commodity Futures Association	(ii) Regulation of the commodity trading industry	
C. Funds management and investment advisory industries		
1. Ministry of Finance – via the Securities Bureau	Licensing, inspection, supervision and guidance of investment advisory companies	Law for Regulating Securities Investment Advisory Business of 1986; Securities and Investment Trust Law of 1951
2. Self-regulatory organizations		
(i) Investment Trust Association	(i) Regulation of the funds management industry	
(ii) Japanese Securities Investment Advisers' Association	(ii) Regulation of the securities investment advisory industry	

Note: * Insurance companies are supervised by the Insurance Department of the Banking Bureau of the Ministry of Finance in accordance with the Insurance Business Law of 1996 and the Financial System Reform Law of 1993.

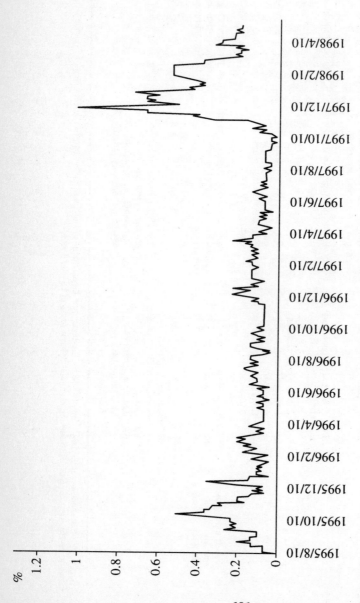

Note: Japan premium is an extra expense Japanese banks must pay for raising funds in overseas financial markets. Japan premium in this chart is calculated as follows: Japan premium = interest rate quoted by Bank of Tokyo-Mitsubishi – interest rate quoted by Barclays Bank in the Eurodollar market (London).

Source: BoJ, 1998.

Chart 5.5 Japan premium: 1995–98 (daily)

NOTES

1. Earlier attempts embraced relaxation of the MoF's restrictions on tax-free reserving and encouragement given to the banking industry to set up a company to which they could sell their bad loans, charging any losses incurred against profits and thus reducing tax bills. The latter initiative led to the formation of the so-called 'Co-operative Credit Purchasing Company' (CCPC) in 1993 whose role was to purchase, at a discount, the bad loans of the banks and then to liquidate the loans by selling the underlying collateral to private investors. As the banks themselves had to foot the bill for the operations of the CCPC, the main advantage to them was that tax relief would, in effect, be brought forward, as reserving against bad loans would, ultimately, have secured the same level of tax relief. A worry for the banks, however, was the extremely limited success achieved by the CCPC in disposing of the underlying collateral.

2. The two other long-term credit banks, the bank's main shareholder banks and life and non-life companies were asked to subscribe to ¥300 billion worth of newly issued preferred and common stock to replenish part of the bank's capital erased by the disposal of non-performing loans. No such coercion, however, proved necessary to bring about the rescue of Yasuda Trust in the spring of 1998; Fuji Bank and four other members of the Fujo *keiretsu* voluntarily injected ¥100 billion of additional capital.

3. The MoF had conducted on-site inspection of the *jusen* in both 1991 and 1992 and so was aware of the scale of their problems (at the latter date, collective non-performing loans stood at ¥4.6 trillion, representing over 38 per cent of their collective loan book). Yet nothing was done. Moreover, when the MoF issued guidelines to financial institutions in 1990 to curtail lending to property-related companies, the *jusen* were for some reason exempted.

4. Although these 'secondary' losses would not be realized until the year 2011 when the government plans to wind up the Jusen Resolution Corporation.

5. Commercial bank loans to the Jusen Resolution Corporation would also be guaranteed by the DIC.

6. The size of the contributions was linked to perceived financial strength: the Industrial Bank of Japan, Bank of Tokyo–Mitsubishi, Fuji Bank, Sumitomo Bank, Sanwa Bank, Dai-Ichi Kangyo Bank and Sakura Bank were each asked to contribute ¥42 billion; the Hokkaido Takushoku Bank and Nippon Credit Bank were each asked to contribute ¥20 billion; regional banks were collectively asked to provide ¥110 billion; life assurance companies were collectively asked to provide ¥50 billion; and brokerage houses were collectively asked to contribute ¥40 billion. The top 20 banks contributed over 80 per cent of the total.

7. The Bank of Japan is thought to have wanted to confine funding to weak banks, but the ruling Liberal Democratic Party didn't want the scheme to be regarded as a 'bail-out' mechanism and so pressurized the stronger banks into participating (the latter were concerned that this might make them vulnerable to political pressure to increase lending and/or support weak companies). In the event, as noted earlier, 21 institutions finally lined up for funding, the only notable absentee being Nippon Trust, which was disqualified from applying because of its recent record of reported losses.

    (Those institutions which did apply comprised the following: Sumitomo Bank (applied for ¥100 billion of funding); Sanwa Bank (¥100 billion); Sakura Bank (¥100 billion); Fuji Bank (¥100 billion); Asahi Bank (¥ 100 billion); Tokai Bank (¥100 billion); Daiwa Bank (¥100 billion); Industrial Bank of Japan (¥100 billion); Long-Term Credit Bank (¥200 billion); Sumitomo Trust (¥100 billion); Mitsui Trust (¥100 billion); Dai-Ichi Kangyo Bank (¥99 billion); Bank of Tokyo–Mitsubishi (¥100 billion); Yasuda Trust (¥150 billion); Mitsubishi Trust (¥50 billion); Toyo Trust (¥50 billion); Chuo Trust (¥60 billion); Nippon Credit Bank (¥290 billion); Bank of Yokohama (¥20 billion); Hokuriku Bank (¥20 billion); and Ashikaga Bank (¥30 billion). In the event, all received funding although the Nippon Credit Bank (¥60 billion) and the Long-Term Credit Bank (¥177 billion) received less than requested. In total, ¥1800 billion of financial assistance was provided.)

8. Apart, that is, from the establishment of an 'accord' with the US authorities in the autumn of 1995 in the wake of apparent investor nervousness about the fragility of the Japanese banking sector. Under the 'accord', which was never confirmed by the Japanese authorities, the US Federal Reserve agreed to provide emergency standby facilities whereby, in the event of a (liquidity) crisis, it would provide unlimited dollar funding directly to troubled Japanese banks at prevailing market rates of interest. The BoJ, in turn, stood ready to guarantee the central bank loans by providing collateral in the form of US securities (mainly Treasury bonds). In this way, the US authorities hoped to avoid the dangers associated with a rapid disposal of dollar-denominated assets by Japanese banks, while the authorities in both countries would benefit from reduced financial instability.

9. Each area is managed through a separate bureau or bureaux.

10. The Daiwa incident was held up as an example of the MoF's unwillingness to be a 'tough' supervisor because of its overriding concern with the stability of the wider banking and financial systems. Its failure to take tough and timely action, however, in the face of the banks' burgeoning bad debts in general and Daiwa's transgressions in particular, backfired on both itself and the system. It became discredited as a supervisor, both at home and abroad, and Japanese institutions suffered through payment of the so-called 'Japan premium' (see Chart 5.5 in the Appendix) in international capital markets because of the market's unease at the way in which the reported figures for bad debts were being calculated.

11. The practice of *amakudari* (Rixtel, 1995), whereby regulatory officials spend their final years of working life in well-paid jobs at the very institutions they had previously been charged with supervising, was also called into question.

REFERENCES

Hall, M.J.B. (1993), *Banking Regulation and Supervision: A Comparative Study of the UK, USA and Japan*, Aldershot, UK and Brookfield, US: Edward Elgar.

Ministry of Finance (1995), *Concrete Measures to Address the Jusen Problem*, preliminary translation of a Cabinet Decision taken on 19 December 1995, Tokyo, December.

Ministry of Finance (1996a), *A Follow-Up of the Cabinet Decision to Address the Jusen Problem*, preliminary translation of a Cabinet Decision taken on 20 January 1996, Tokyo, January.

Ministry of Finance (1996b), *Statement by the Minister of Finance on the Announcement of Measures to Improve Banking Inspection and Supervision*, translation of a Statement made on 26 December 1995, Tokyo, January.

Ministry of Finance (1998a), *Outline of the Emergency Measures to Stabilize the Financial System*, Tokyo, 13 January.

Ministry of Finance (1998b), *Reform to the Financial Regulatory System*, Tokyo, April.

Rixtel, A.A. (1995), 'Amakudari in the Japanese banking industry: an empirical investigation', paper presented at the CEPRWZB Conference, Berlin, mimeo, December.

Yamawaki, T. (1996), 'The forbearance policy: what went wrong with Japanese financial regulation?', *Loughborough University Banking Centre Paper*, no. 106/96, November.

6.   Reform of the Bank of Japan

THE CASE FOR REFORM

The issue of reforming the Bank of Japan was first raised publicly in November 1995 when the Liberal Democratic Party's (LDP) Financial Issues Research Council acknowledged that it was deliberating on the subject. In particular, it was concerned with the transparency of monetary policy-making which, under the then existing arrangements, involved the Bank's 'Policy Board', formally in charge of the decision-taking process, merely 'rubber-stamping' decisions which had been taken at monthly meetings (the so-called 'roundtable') of the Executive Committee. As all the executive directors of the Executive Committee – comprising the governor, a vice-governor and seven executive directors – were appointees of the MoF (indeed, one of them was usually an MoF official!) and as either the governor or vice-governor was formerly an MoF official, the MoF was clearly well positioned to get its own way on policy matters. Accordingly, the Council indicated that it would consider reforming the Policy Board, clarifying and codifying in law its roles. Additionally, it would consider changing the status of the BoJ so that its officials would legally become public servants. In this way, the Council hoped to make the BoJ more immune from political pressure, although some believed the outcome might, in fact, be the exact reverse, with policy-making being taken out of the hands of career BoJ officials and the central bank becoming more subservient to the MoF (Merrill Lynch, 1997).

The proposed reforms, however, did not stop at the issue of independence. There is a price to be paid for greater independence, namely, greater accountability, as recognized by the group of politicians assembled by the three-party coalition in February 1996 to carry forward the discussions. These two issues thus dominated the discussion of a committee – the so-called 'Central Bank Study Group' – comprising mainly academics (but MoF officials were allowed to attend as 'observers') charged with drafting the reform proposals. Their report was released in November 1996 and the MoF was then given the task of drafting legislation to accommodate the proposed reforms. This was completed in February 1997.

PROPOSED CHANGES

In March 1997, the Cabinet approved and submitted to the Diet for consideration a Bill amending the Bank of Japan Law of 1942. The Cabinet accepted that the law should be updated to give the Bank greater independence but, at the same time, it was determined to make the Bank more accountable for its actions. The new law became operational on 1 April 1998, following the Diet's approval of the Bill in June 1997.

The main changes made (Ministry of Finance, 1997) to the Bank of Japan Law comprise the following (see Exhibit 6.1):

(i)   clarification of the BoJ's functions and business operations;
(ii)   increased independence for the Bank;
(iii)   reconstitution of the Policy Board;
(iv)   elimination of the 'roundtable' (leaving the Policy Board to make its own decisions) and publication of Policy Board decisions, thereby increasing the transparency of policy-making;
(v)   clarification of the role of the Policy Board; and
(vi)   increased accountability imposed on the Bank.

Each of these will now be addressed in turn.

Clarification of the Bank's Functions and Business Operations

Under the new law the BoJ, as Japan's central bank, will be required to issue bank notes and to formulate and implement monetary policy. In fulfilling such duties, it is required to 'contribute to the development of a sound national economy through the maintenance of price stability'. Additionally, it is required to 'contribute to the maintenance of an orderly credit system by securing smooth funds settlements for financial institutions'.

In satisfaction of the duties outlined above, the Bank is empowered to engage in the following *ordinary* business operations:

● discounting commercial paper and other bills or notes;
● making loans against collateral in the form of bills or notes, government bonds and government obligations;
● buying and selling of commercial paper and other bills and notes, government bonds and obligations, and other bonds or debentures;
● drawing of bills for sale;
● accepting deposits;
● dealing in domestic exchange;
● accepting custody of articles of value;

- buying and selling of gold and silver bullion;
- performing other business incidental to the businesses enumerated above.

In respect of *government*-related business operations, the BoJ is empowered to undertake the following:

- making unsecured advances to the government (in accordance with Article 5 of the Finance Act), and subscribing to, or taking up, government loan issues;
- making temporary unsecured advances to the government, and subscribing to or taking up the 'financing bills' and other 'accommodation' bills;
- management of treasury funds;
- conducting currency and finance business on behalf of the government.

In respect of *international* business operations, the BoJ may:

- buy and sell foreign exchange, either as agent of the government for the purpose of stabilizing the foreign exchange rate of Japan's currency, or, upon the request of, or with the permission of, the MoF, to co-operate with foreign central banks or other foreign entities;
- receive deposits from foreign central banks or other foreign entities, and undertake operations considered to be appropriate yen-denominated asset investments;
- upon the request of, or with the permission of, the MoF, provide credit and undertake other operations on behalf of foreign central banks or other foreign entities when necessary to co-operate with foreign central banks or other foreign entities in the area of international finance.

With the permission of the MoF, the Bank may also undertake *other* business operations that are not prescribed in this or other laws, whenever it deems it necessary to help in the achievement of its prescribed purposes.

Finally, in seeking to maintain an *orderly credit system*, the Bank may engage in the following:

- making advances of limited duration under special terms and subject to special conditions, to financial institutions that are temporarily unable to meet their payment needs due to problems with their electronic information processing systems, or by reason of other accidents;
- upon the request of the Minister of Finance based on special need, making advances subject to special conditions, or undertake business operations necessary for the maintenance of an orderly credit system, within the scope of the request;

Exhibit 6.1   *Changes made to the Bank of Japan Law of 1942*

Issues	Old law	New law
Monetary policy decisions	Finance Minister could demand BoJ delay a change in policy	Finance Minister can request BoJ delay a change in policy
Policy Board members	7: governor, 4 appointed representatives of various sectors in the economy, 2 non-voting government representatives (from MoF and the EPA)	9: governor, two vice-governors, 6 regular members chosen from 'experts' (N.B. up to 2 government representatives may participate 'as occasion demands') *Advisers to Policy Board members (appointed by MoF) can express their views at Policy Board meetings*
BoJ executives	1 governor, 1 vice governor, 7 directors, up to 2 inspectors	1 governor, 2 vice-governors, up to 6 directors, up to 3 auditors *Elimination of 'roundtable'*
Appointment of Bank personnel	Finance Minister could order the removal of any Bank executive Governor and vice governor appointed by Cabinet Directors and inspectors appointed by MoF	Finance Minister cannot order the removal of any bank executive Governor, vice-governors, and Policy Board members appointed by the Cabinet with the consent of the Diet; auditors appointed by the Cabinet *Directors and advisers (an unspecified few) to Policy Board appointed by MoF*
Making public the proceedings of the Policy Board	No such system	Outline released rapidly, minutes released after slight delay *Deliberations of Policy Board to be submitted to the Diet through MoF*

	Governor spoke to Diet once a year	Governor reports and speaks to Diet twice a year
Reporting to the Diet		
MoF oversight	MoF empowered with broad authority over all Bank operations, could change the Bank's articles of association, could demand on-the-spot inspections and reports	MoF authority to influence Bank operations limited to request for a change if there is an infraction of the law or violation of the Bank's articles of association or if there is fear of such an infraction On-the-spot inspections abolished, but MoF can request inspectors to look into such violations (or 'fears') and request a report on the results of their investigations at short notice *MoF authorization required to change Bank's articles of incorporation and responsibilities (e.g. derivatives, new financial products, new capital settlement system, set up branches, offices, agencies)* *MoF can request information or data regarding BoJ activities 'as necessary'*
MoF authority over Bank's budget	MoF approval needed for all general-affairs budgetary actions by BoJ	*General-affairs budget outlays which do not affect BoJ's monetary policies approved by MoF (wages, transportation, telecommunications); if rejected, reasons must be given* *BoJ must submit financial statements and opinion of auditors to MoF for approval*
Wages and post-retirement employment (*amakudari*)	Wages matched those of city banks: no restrictions on *amakudari*	Wages set according to 'social situation', *notification of MoF required* Rules regarding *amakudari* to be clarified, *notification of MoF required*

Note: Italicized text shows where the MoF retains its influence.

Source: Merrill Lynch (1997).

- on-site examination of client financial institutions on the basis of contracts signed at the time current accounts were opened (such contracts should provide for prior notification to be given by the Bank of its intention to conduct examinations, and for the prior consent to examinations being given by the client institutions; moreover, when conducting examinations the Bank is required to consider the operational burden imposed on financial institutions and, upon request, to submit reports of examinations to the Minister of Finance for review);
- with the permission of the Minister of Finance, undertake business operations of whatever kind deemed necessary to help contribute to smooth payments and settlements among financial institutions.

Increased Independence for the Bank

Under the new law, the BoJ's independence in formulating and implementing monetary policy has to be formally 'respected'. Operationally, this 'independence' is delivered by termination of the 'roundtable' meeting of executive directors, abolition of the Finance Minister's authority to remove Bank officials, including the governor, ending the Minister's right to demand a delay in a change of policy, removal of government representatives from routine meetings of the Policy Board, removing the Minister's authority to 'approve' the Bank's budget outlays arising from monetary policy considerations (see Exhibit 6.1) and ending direct supervision of the Bank by the MoF. As noted below, however, the MoF will continue to exercise considerable power over the BoJ post-reform, and the BoJ will be formally required to 'maintain close communication with the government to ensure there is sufficient mutual understanding to secure consistency between the government's economic policy and its monetary policy'.

Clarification of the Role of the Policy Board

Under the revisions to the BoJ law, the Policy Board has the power to determine the following matters:

- issues concerning monetary policy, such as changes in the discount rate, market operation policies, control of reserve ratios,[1] and the basic evaluation of financial conditions;
- issues concerning management of the Bank's other activities, such as activities contributing to the maintenance of an orderly credit system and examination of financial institutions;
- issues regarding the formulation of basic policy for conducting the Bank's business.

The Board is also required to supervise the Bank's officers in the execution of their duties.

Reconstitution of the Policy Board

Under the new arrangements, the Board comprises nine members – the governor, two vice-governors and six other ('expert') members. 'Where necessary', however, up to two government representatives – the Minister of Finance, or his designee, and/or the Director of the Economic Planning Agency, or his designee – may attend Policy Board meetings and state their opinions, including proposals in respect of monetary policy. They do not have voting rights, however. Moreover, the government representative(s) may table a motion to postpone Policy Board decisions until the following meeting, in which case the Policy Board has to decide whether or not to adopt such a motion. As for the Bank's governors, they are required to carry out their duties as Board members independently at Board meetings.

Increased Transparency of Policy-Making

The changes that have led to increased transparency result from the elimination of the 'roundtable' discussions between executive directors of the Policy Board, leaving the Policy Board itself to take decisions, and the requirements placed on the (chairperson of the) Board to make public a summary of the meeting's agenda and, within a suitable period of time, a record of each meeting's proceedings.

Increased Accountability of the Bank

The main measure designed to increase the Bank's accountability for its actions was the requirement that the Bank report every six months (before, it was only done annually) to the Diet, in the form of a report, which has to be submitted to the Minister of Finance, setting out the Policy Board's monetary policy decisions and the status of their implementation. As before, it is also required to disclose publicly its operational conditions, via financial statements (a balance sheet and a profit and loss statement), at the end of each business period (that is, the financial year 1 April to 31 March). Moreover, the governor, in the future, will have to appear twice (rather than once) before Parliament, and field a wider range of questions than he used to, which by tradition were confined to the issue of the Bank's financial position.

AN ASSESSMENT

In order to assess the merits of the agreed reform it is perhaps best to focus
on its intended objectives with a view to coming to some conclusion about
the likelihood of their being realized. Starting with the issue of independence,
some question whether enough has been done to unshackle the BoJ from the
MoF. For, notwithstanding the relevant changes outlined above, the following
channels of influence remain (see Exhibit 6.1): the Finance Minister is still
able to request a postponement of Policy Board decisions until its next
meeting; under certain circumstances, up to two government representatives
may attend Policy Board meetings concerned with the discussion of monetary policy issues and express their opinions; the MoF is responsible for the
appointment, on the recommendation of the Policy Board, of the Bank's
executive directors and the 'advisers' to the Policy Board members; under
certain circumstances, the advisers may express their views at Policy Board
meetings on any important affairs concerning the operations of the Bank; the
MoF is able to request a change in the Bank's operations if there is an
infraction of the law or violation of the Bank's 'articles of association', or if
there is a fear of such an infraction; MoF authorization is required to change
the Bank's 'articles of association' or responsibilities; MoF approval is still
needed for general-affairs budget outlays which are not associated with the
conduct of monetary policy; the MoF is still able to request information or
data regarding the Bank's activities 'as necessary'; and MoF permission is
still required for the opening of new branches, offices or agencies by the BoJ.
Moreover, even if these numerous channels of influence prove no bar to *de
facto* independence, one still has to ask the question 'will future "performance" on the monetary policy front actually improve in the coming years?'
Unlike in the West (Hall, 1997), the desire for increased independence of the
central bank is not associated with a desire to reduce an inflation premium in
nominal interest rates nor to improve the country's inflation performance –
both have been at record lows for some time now in Japan. Rather, it reflects
a concern about the transparency of policy-making. While increased transparency – see below – may enhance credibility in the longer term, it is far from
certain that the Bank's technocrats, if left to their own devices, will deliver
better results than the MoF's bureaucrats. While most commentators acknowledge that the MoF was wrong to have blocked the BoJ's desire to
tighten monetary policy in the autumn of 1987 – it was forced to delay an
increase in the official discount rate until end May 1989, thereby inflating the
asset bubble – some argue (Merrill Lynch, 1997) that when the BoJ was given
its head, as in the period 1990–93 when the MoF's influence on policy-
making was effectively neutralized by Governor Mieno, it made serious
mistakes also, in the form of an overtightening of policy and a subsequent

failure to loosen policy quickly enough after the collapse of the asset bubble. While the jury is still out on the question of which institution to trust, on the basis of past experience, with interest-rate policy, logic suggests that the administration is right to (try to?) hand over the reins to the technocrats, presumably with the superior expertise in this area.

On the question of transparency of policy-making, it is undoubtedly the case that the reforms will result in major improvements. There are no longer any doubts about where the real power lies, as the Policy Board has become unambiguously the sole decision-taking body on the abolition of the executives' 'roundtable'; and publication, with due lags,[2] of the agenda and minutes of Policy Board meetings, something which had never happened before, will make clear to all interested parties exactly what transpired at such meetings.

On the question of accountability, however, the verdict is less definitive. Increasing the frequency at which the Bank must report to the Diet and the Governor appear before the Diet undoubtedly helps, as does forcing the Governor to field questions other than on mundane issues associated with the Bank's financial position on the occasions he does appear before the Diet. But it remains to be seen how effective the latter proves as a medium for challenging the Bank's wisdom, something which ought to be possible if the Bank is truly to be held responsible for its actions. The Bank of Japan Independence Study Group (1996) has recommended that a new standing committee should be set up within the Diet to facilitate such a development.

Moving away from the main objectives of reform and focusing on the Bank's redefined *raison d'être* (with the emphasis on securing price stability) and operational responsibilities, a number of other concerns arise. First, it remains unclear which body, the BoJ or the MoF, will have the ultimate say in deciding whether or not to activate rescue schemes for ailing financial institutions. While new 'rules' state that the MoF may *ask* (but not compel) the Bank to assist in bail-outs/rescues in order to preserve an orderly credit system, only time will tell if the Bank ever proves willing to refuse such a request. (This will be further complicated by the establishment of the new supervisory agency; see Chapter 5.) Second, it is questionable if the BoJ should be forced to underwrite government financial bills (BoJ Independence Study Group, 1996). And finally, it is arguably preferable that routine operations in the foreign exchange markets be left to the BoJ's initiative (ibid.).

NOTES

1. The Law Concerning Reserve Deposits Requirements was amended to remove the power of the Minister of Finance to fix, change or abolish reserve ratio requirements.
2. The minutes and summaries of the twice-monthly meetings of the Policy Board have to be submitted for approval to the Policy Board at the second monetary policy meeting follow-

ing the monetary policy meeting concerned (i.e. about one month later). They are released on the third business day after they have been approved by the Policy Board. Transcripts providing detailed records of discussions are released after a period of time deemed to be appropriate by the Policy Board. All decisions of Policy Board meetings are announced immediately after the meetings. (Note: The new system was set in motion with the publication of the minutes of the Policy Board's monetary policy meeting of 16 January 1998 on 3 March 1998.)

REFERENCES

Bank of Japan Independence Study Group (1996), *Our Opinion on the 'Reform of the Central Bank System'*, November.

Central Bank Study Group (1996), *Reform of the Central Bank System* ('Torii Report'), November.

Hall, M.J.B. (1997), 'All change at the Bank of England', *Butterworths Journal of International Banking and Financial Law*, **12** (7), 295–302.

Merrill Lynch (1997), 'Special topic: reforming the Bank of Japan', *Japan Economic and Fiscal Income Monthly*, 15 May.

Ministry of Finance (1997), *Report Concerning the Revision of the Bank of Japan Law*, provisional English translation, Tokyo, February.

PART 3

The Consequences of Financial Reform for
Public Policy

7. Implications of financial liberalization for the conduct of monetary policy

CHOICE OF INSTRUMENTS

With a transmission mechanism in mind of the type set out in Exhibit 7.1, one of the first decisions the monetary authorities must take concerns the appropriate mix of instruments to be used in an attempt to secure the end goals of policy (Hall, 1982, ch. 6). In the light of the condition of Japan's postwar economy and the lack of development in its money and capital markets, it is hardly surprising that regulations featured prominently in the monetary authorities' armoury in the early postwar era. The overriding purpose of such regulations, supported by exchange controls, was to promote economic growth through the regeneration of private industry, the promotion of exports and the rebuilding of the public sector infrastructure. This was to be achieved through the channelling of low-cost savings to industry (especially the export sector) via the banking system. The low-interest-rate policy also contributed to growth indirectly by stabilizing the financial system (destructive interest-rate competition was avoided) and promoting indirect finance at the expense of direct finance.

As identified in Exhibit 7.1, the controls and regulations employed at that time embraced exchange controls, interest-rate controls, reserve requirements, 'window guidance' and price and quantity controls on central bank lending to private financial institutions.

The significance of *exchange controls* was that they reinforced the functional separation of finance by isolating the Japanese financial system from the rest of the world. In particular, by denying (city) banks access to foreign sources of funds, the banks were made heavily dependent on the Bank of Japan, the only alternative source of short-term funds to the call money market. This greatly enhanced the effectiveness of monetary policy by increasing the leverage exerted by the Bank of Japan over the banking system both directly, through the determination of its lending policy (see below), and indirectly, because of its pervasive influence over activities in the call money market (see pp. 89–92). Accordingly, changes in bank reserves had a predictable impact on interbank rates.

Interest-rate controls (discussed on pp. 16–17) also played a significant role by limiting the banks' flexibility in the setting of deposit (both demand

Exhibit 7.1   The transmission mechanism of monetary policy in postwar Japan

Instruments of monetary policy	Operational objectives	Intermediate targets	End goals of policy
For example:	For example:	For example:	
(i) transactions in financial markets	(i) interbank interest rates (i.e. call and bill rates)	(i) growth in bank lending (esp. to the non-bank private sector)	(i) Price stability
(ii) lending policy of the Bank of Japan	(ii) bank reserves		(ii) Full employment
• official discount-rate policy		(ii) growth in monetary aggregates	(iii) External balance
• quantitative controls on loans to city banks		(iii) market interest rates	(iv) Maximum (real) economic growth
(iii) reserve requirements			
(iv) 'window guidance' (i.e. quantitative controls on individual banks' lending)			
(v) interest-rate controls			
(vi) exchange controls			

and time) and loan rates, thereby increasing the predictability of monetary policy in terms of the likely effects of changes in the stance of policy on both intermediate and ultimate targets of policy. (For full details see Suzuki, 1987, pp. 332–4.) Changes in interbank (that is, call) rates, for example, brought about by official transactions in the interbank market or by adjustments in central bank lending policy, had a highly predictable impact on the quantity of bank credit supplied to the non-bank private sector (the relevant intermediate target of policy at this time) because of the banks' limited ability to pass on the higher (assuming a monetary squeeze) borrowing costs to their customers.[1] Given the prevailing excess demand for bank credit, itself partly due to the suppression of loan rates, the resultant change in credit supply was effected largely through credit rationing, the speed with which this was effected being influenced by the Bank of Japan's 'window guidance'. This, in turn, had a fairly predictable impact on aggregate expenditure in the economy because of the dependence of the corporate sector on bank credit for satisfying its borrowing needs.

Reserve ratio requirements, involving the holding of non-interest-bearing deposits at the Bank of Japan by commercial financial institutions in proportion to their monthly average of deposit and other liabilities, were first applied in 1959 in accordance with the Law Concerning the Reserve Deposit Requirement System of 1958. Since that date the scheme has undergone a number of revisions, resulting in an extension of the range of institutions[2] and liability types[3] covered by the scheme, an increase in the maximum reserve ratio that could be levied (from 10 per cent to 20 per cent – 100 per cent for foreign-currency-denominated liabilities and liabilities to non-residents), and the application of reserve ratio requirements to *increases* in liabilities. And finally in July 1986, a 'progressive' reserve ratio system (see Suzuki, 1990, p. 325) was introduced under which a progressive scale of reserve ratios is applied (that is, reserve requirements are applied differentially to different tranches of deposits). The purpose of this last reform was to reduce the burden on rapidly expanding institutions as compared with the previous system.

Although frequent changes in reserve ratios were made until 1980 it is questionable how significant a contribution they made to the effectiveness of monetary policy during the high-growth period because of the very low levels at which they were set. Accordingly, active use of reserve requirements as a policy tool was dropped in the early 1980s (Kasman and Rodrigues, 1991), notwithstanding the switch to a 'progressive' system in 1986. The reserve requirements currently applying (they were last changed in October 1991 when they were cut to reduce the burden imposed on institutions) are presented in Exhibit 7.2.

Window guidance refers to the Bank of Japan's 'guidance' given to financial institutions (especially the city banks)[4] concerning the 'appropriate' course

*Exhibit 7.2   Reserve ratio requirements imposed on Japanese banks
(effective from 16 October 1991)*

On the outstanding of yen deposits of residents[a]		Per cent
Banks'[b]		
time deposits[c]	on amounts above ¥2.5 trillion	1.2
	on amounts above ¥1.2 trillion up to ¥2.5 trillion	0.9
	on amounts above ¥0.5 trillion up to ¥1.2 trillion	0.05
	on amounts above ¥50 billion up to ¥0.5 trillion	0.05
other deposits	on amounts above ¥2.5 trillion	1.3
	on amounts above ¥1.2 trillion up to ¥2.5 trillion	1.3
	on amounts above ¥0.5 trillion up to ¥1.2 trillion	0.8
	on amounts above ¥50 billion up to ¥0.5 trillion	0.1
The Norinchukin Bank		
	time deposits[c]	0.05
	other deposits	0.1
On the outstanding of foreign currency deposits of residents'[d]		
	time deposits	0.2
	other deposits	0.25
On the outstanding of securities issuance of ordinary banks, long-term credit banks and foreign exchange banks		0.1
On the outstanding of principal of money trusts (including loan trusts)		0.1
On the outstanding of foreign currency liabilities against non-residents[d]		0.15
On the outstanding of liabilities regarding yen accounts of non-residents[d]		0.15
On the outstanding of fund transfers from the special account for international financial transactions to domestic accounts		0.15

Notes:
[a] Including instalment savings, but excluding the deposits regarding the special account for international financial transactions.
[b] Ordinary banks (including foreign banks in Japan), long-term credit banks, and foreign exchange banks. In addition, *shinkin* banks with deposits of more than ¥160 billion are included.
[c] Including CDs.
[d] Only authorized foreign exchange banks are affected. The liabilities regarding the special account for international financial transactions are excluded.

Source: Press release of the Bank of Japan, 1 October 1991.

for the yen lending of their domestic offices in the period ahead. Such guidance has, in the past, taken the form of directives being issued to keep credit growth, on a monthly or, more usually, a quarterly basis within pre-specified limits, to restrain the growth in lending to trading companies and/or to restrain investment in securities. In recognition of the drawbacks associated with its persistent usage (it is inequitable, distortive and results in a misallocation of resources), it was designed to be used as a short-term supplementary instrument. But after 1982 it assumed an even more limited role as a result of the Bank of Japan's policy of 'accepting' the lending plans of the individual banks (implying a relaxation in the forcefulness of any moral suasion exercised by the former). It was formally abolished in mid-1991.

The final area in which control is exercised in the name of monetary policy, namely in the policies adopted by the Bank of Japan towards its extension of credit to private financial institutions at the lending window, involves the establishment of both price and quantity controls. Price control is effected through the setting of the official discount rate, the rate charged by the Bank of Japan on loans[5] to eligible[6] financial institutions. Changes in the discount rate thus directly affect the borrowing costs of banks and others, thereby eliciting interest-rate and portfolio adjustments which affect both the money supply and real economic activity.[7] Volume or quantity control is effected through the setting of credit ceilings (on a quarterly basis) on loans to city banks, a policy first introduced in 1962 with a view to reducing the city banks' dependence on Bank of Japan funding in the prevailing 'over-loaned' situation.[8] The resultant impact on banks' reserve positions, like discount-rate changes, elicits in turn the familiar interest-rate and portfolio adjustments by both the banks and their customers, with consequences for both the money supply and the real economy.

Such, then, was the nature of the regulatory framework used to support monetary policy in the early postwar period, with changes in the Bank of Japan's lending policy, particularly in respect of the setting of credit ceilings for city banks, and window guidance generally reckoned to have been the most important instruments, especially in the high-growth period from 1955 to 1970 (Katayama, 1985). But what of the Bank of Japan's transactions in financial markets at this time, limited as they were?

Apart from trading in bullion, which ceased in 1978, the Bank of Japan was also involved in transactions in both bills and government bonds.[9] Collateralized[10] loans at official discount rates were replaced by official operations in government and government-guaranteed bonds in November 1962, for example. And in 1972 bill rediscount operations were started to complement the sale of government bills and bills drawn on the Bank of Japan inaugurated in 1966 and 1971 respectively.

Bond transactions were initiated with a view to diversifying the range of monetary instruments at the central bank's disposal and originally they simply represented bilateral trades with financial institutions – ordinary banks, long-term credit banks, foreign exchange banks, *sogo* banks and the Federation of Credit Co-operatives – at fixed rates and on a repurchase agreement basis. The reopening of the bond market in 1966, however, witnessed a switch to the current trading practice of sales at market price without repurchase agreements. Later, the range of counterparties was extended to embrace securities companies (in 1966), the Norinchukin Bank (in 1967) and some *shinkin* banks (in 1978). Despite those and other developments,[11] designed to enhance operational flexibility, however, the bond transactions did not represent open market operations in the true sense of the word as non-banks were still excluded as counterparties.

The *rediscounting* of eligible bills (such as cover bills with less than three months' initial maturity and acceptances) represented a further attempt to broaden the range of policy instruments. Although all client financial institutions were initially able to act as counterparties to the transactions, after 1975 the privilege was confined to the money market dealers.

As far as the official *bill sales* were concerned, the intention was to smooth the impact on the money markets of seasonal fluctuations in the supply and demand for funds. To this end, the Bank of Japan began selling government bills from its own portfolio to money market dealers on a repurchase basis in January 1966. Although such operations ceased in November 1972 they were reactivated in May 1981, with resale to financial institutions (who could then sell on to corporate customers) being allowed. In this way open market operations proper began, although the paucity of government bills militated against further development of the market.

The other type of bill sales undertaken by the Bank of Japan involved the sale of bills drawn on itself. The bills, of up to three months' maturity, were usually sold to the short funds companies but occasionally direct sales to client financial institutions were made.

In summary, the pre-1975 monetary control regime was characterized by a heavy reliance on direct monetary controls. The segmentation of financial markets, at both the long and short ends, secured by interest-rate controls and participation rules and supported by exchange controls, ruled out the option of conducting open market operations on the grounds of ineffectiveness which, at any rate, would have proved impossible because of the dearth of eligible paper in the marketplace.[12]

As shown in Chapter 3, however, the pace of financial liberalization quickened after the mid-1970s. The money and capital markets (both primary and secondary) were broadened and deepened, interest rates were liberalized, participation rules were relaxed and the yen was internationalized as the Japanese government implemented measures to end the isolation of its financial system from the rest of the world. This process of change was, of course, conducive to a switch in emphasis on the part of the monetary authorities away from the use of direct controls and towards the wider use of securities (bond and bill) operations (Yoshitomi, 1985). Accordingly, as noted earlier, less reliance was placed on the use of regulations, such as interest-rate controls, reserve requirements and window guidance, within the monetary policy process, as the Bank of Japan expanded both the scale and variety[13] of its market transactions (Shigehara, 1991). The full transition to an open market operations-based regime, however, took somewhat longer (see Chapter 3), mainly because of the lack of a fully developed Treasury bill market[14] but also because of the remaining restrictions on participation. Moreover, foreign firms complained[15] that they operated at a competitive disadvantage *vis-à-vis* their Japanese counterparts because of the fragmented nature of the interbank market, the associated collateral requirements and the continuing restrictions imposed on access to the Bank of Japan's discount window.

CHOICE OF INTERMEDIATE TARGET

Apart from affecting the choice of monetary instruments, financial liberalization also impinges on the choice of intermediate target (see Exhibit 7.1). 'Operational objectives' were not affected although the priority accorded to the growth objective amongst the end goals of policy was dropped around 1975, with emphasis switching to the control of inflation, which became regarded as a precondition for the maintenance of employment and growth in the medium term. The floating of the yen in 1973 obviously facilitated this move, although, even after this time, concern with the exchange rate occasionally complicated monetary management (Suzuki, 1987, p. 317). The Japanese authorities, in line with most of their Western counterparts, duly switched attention towards the growth in monetary aggregates in the mid-1970s (see Bank of Japan, 1975): M2 initially assumed prime importance although, by 1979, M2 plus negotiable CDs had become the fêted aggregate. Whilst many Western central banks embarked upon monetary targeting (see Hall, 1982, pp. 213–33), however, the Japanese authorities adopted a more pragmatic approach, publishing quarterly forecasts (as opposed to targets) for annualized growth in the chosen aggregate after July 1978. Rigid adherence to such forecasts was not the authorities' main aim, although undoubtedly movements in the selected aggregate relative to the forecasts (that is, the desired movements) heavily influenced official policy at this time. More recently, with the switch in emphasis towards the use of open market operations as a major instrument of policy, market interest rates have assumed greater importance as intermediate objectives of monetary policy, although the unsecured overnight call rate is still the major focus of attention.

The last-mentioned change in policy tack, involving a downgrading of the significance attributed to movements in broad money, deserves further analysis. A wealth of evidence from around the world (see Hall, 1987, ch. 3, for comparison of the UK and Australian experience) suggests that large-scale financial liberalization at the very least severely complicates the task of interpreting movements in broad money, rendering impossible, in all likelihood, monetary targeting. This explains the dropping of money supply targets (at least for broad money) in the mid-1980s in Australia and the UK, for example. And even for those countries which soldiered on with monetary targets, the degree of success achieved in hitting the said targets has left much to be desired, calling into question the very rationale for monetary targeting (Hall, 1982, ch. 7).

The sources of the likely complications are not hard to identify. Any process of liberalization will undoubtedly favour those most adversely affected under the previous regime which, for a number of reasons, are likely to have been the banks. Accordingly, the process of reintermediation will usually follow financial liberalization although the pace, extent and duration of it often prove hard to predict. This reintermediation will, of course, fuel the growth in broad money.[16] Similarly, relaxation of the restraints imposed on the scope of business activities for various intermediaries will naturally lead to potentially significant changes in market shares of (domestic) intermediation, further complicating interpretation of movements in broad money aggregates. Finally, interest-rate liberalization, whether in the form of deposit-rate,[17] lending-rate or bond-rate liberalization, will also cause problems for monetary management by increasing the interest-rate sensitivity of final expenditure because of the greater interest-arbitrage opportunities. The magnitude of the increase and the speed with which it will materialize will, again, prove hard to predict.

To these problems for interpretation must be added the difficulties associated with the switch towards interest-rate control of the *demand* for money and bank credit, which is a prerequisite for running a successful monetary targeting regime in a post-liberalization era. Once again, there is much evidence (for the UK experience see Hall, 1983, chs 4 and 6) from around the globe pointing to the relatively low interest sensitivity of the demand for money[18] and bank credit,[19] with fairly lengthy and unpredictable lags existing between the moment in time when action is taken (for example, through open market operations) and the point in time when the interest-rate effects have run their full course. The implications of this for the conduct of policy are that large and sustained increases in interest rates may prove necessary if the growth in credit demand is to be restrained so as to be consistent with pre-announced targets for broad-money growth; and there can be no presumption that interest rates alone will secure the necessary degree of tightening in the time-scale required by targeting policy. Accordingly, strict adherence to annual targets for the growth in broad monetary aggregates in a fully liberalized environment is likely to result in an increase in both the average level and variability of (nominal) interest interests (see also note 18), with 'overfunding' (that is, the nominal value of net sales of public sector securities being in excess of the size of the public sector deficit) all too often proving necessary if targets are to be hit consistently. Such outcomes, however, with their own attendant costs for the real economy, may be regarded by political administrations as representing too high a price to pay for the control of statistics of dubious significance.[20]

OTHER COMPLICATIONS FOR MONETARY MANAGEMENT

The remaining[21] problems arising from liberalization centre on the implications of the internationalization of the yen (see pp. 67–82). In principle, a perfectly free (as opposed to a managed) float of the yen should have minimized the problems created by external transactions for monetary management but, in practice, certain concerns remained. These arose, at various times, because of the continuation of external imbalances in spite of the floating yen and the tendency for the exchange rate to overshoot its long-run equilibrium level;[22] because of the potential control problems arising from the application of differential reserve requirements on domestic and euroyen deposits; because of the Japanese banks' ability to evade the discipline imposed by window guidance through the extension of yen-denominated loans to Japanese residents via their foreign branches (Osugi, 1990, p. 68); and because of the problems created for defining money by the growth in euroyen business (see Osugi, 1990, pp. 64–6; for further details see Suzuki, 1987, pp. 341–4).

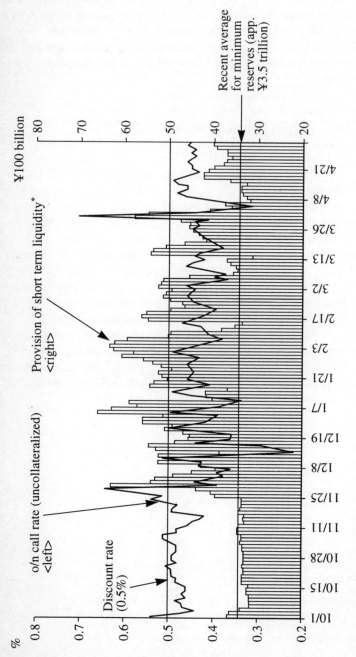

¥100 billion

Provision of short term liquidity*
<right>

o/n call rate (uncollateralized)
<left>

Discount rate
(0.5%)

Recent average
for minimum
reserves (app.
¥3.5 trillion)

Note: * Numbers on a gross basis to reflect day time liquidity.

Source: BoJ, 1998.

*Chart 7.1   Provision of liquidity by the Bank of Japan: October 1997–May 1998 (daily)**

NOTES

1. Despite their limited room for manoeuvre on interest margins the banks could, however, raise effective loan rates to a degree by increasing the required level of compensating balances asked of borrowing customers (see p. 17).

2. Initially, only ordinary banks (including foreign banks), long-term credit banks and the specialized foreign exchange banks were affected, but since then the range of institutions falling within the remit of the scheme has expanded to include: those *shinkin* banks with deposits exceeding a certain level; the Norinchukin Bank; and life assurance companies.

3. Liabilities currently subject to reserve requirements comprise: (i) time deposits, CDs, and other yen-denominated deposits (including instalment savings); (ii) all foreign currency liability accounts of non-residents with authorized foreign exchange banks (excluding guaranteed liabilities) and foreign currency deposits from residents (excluding deposits in the name of the Ministry of Finance); (iii) debentures issued by long-term credit banks; (iv) money trusts with contracts under which deficiencies of principal are recouped (including loan trusts); and (v) the yen deposit liabilities of authorized foreign exchange banks to non-residents.

4. Others subject to such guidance are long-term credit banks, trust banks (in respect of their banking accounts), regional banks, and the larger *shinkin* banks and foreign banks.

5. Although a special lending facility has existed since 1981 whereby loans may be taken at rates other than the discount rate (for money market management reasons), in practice the facility has not been used. Typically, the postwar rate charged by the Bank of Japan on its loans has been below the call rate, thereby fuelling the excess demand for central bank credit (Ichinose, 1991).

6. That is banks of all type, the securities companies, the securities finance companies, the money market dealers, and other financial institutions.

7. These are the so-called 'cost effects' of discount-rate operations which may be distinguished from the 'announcement' or psychological effects which may be associated with discount-rate changes.

8. If loans (confined to periods of less than two weeks) in excess of the agreed ceiling are (unavoidably) made, a penal rate – discount rate plus four percentage points – is charged.

9. Although the yen was not floated until 1973, the Bank of Japan only carried out foreign exchange transactions with the government. It did, however, act as *agent* for the MoF by carrying out foreign exchange transactions with the public, using balances held in the Foreign Exchange Fund special account. It also engaged in foreign exchange trading on behalf of overseas central banks and international institutions in order to promote international financial co-operation.

10. Eligible collateral comprises government and government-guaranteed bonds, government bills, financial debentures and certain local government bonds and corporate debentures and bills.

11. See Suzuki, 1987, p. 321, for details.

12. Due both to the lack of government debt issues and to the syndicate members' policy of holding such securities to maturity in order to avoid sustaining capital losses, which would have resulted because of the government's policy of holding public bond yields below market rates.

13. Operations in government bills (first started in 1981, with 'Treasury bills' featuring after January 1990), CDs (1986), the bond *gensaki* market (1987) and the CP market (1989) complemented the Bank of Japan's traditional activities in the public bond and interbank markets. Moreover, the Bank of Japan concentrated its traditional rediscount operations in bills with a maturity of less than one month (as opposed to those with maturities of between one and three months, the precious focus of policy) after November 1988 with a view to allowing the market a greater say in the determination of one to three months' bill yields. More recently, the Bank of Japan has announced that, with effect from December 1997, transactions in the government bond repo market, inaugurated in April 1996, will displace bill transactions as the main form of market operation, with operations in CP also

212   *The consequences of financial reform for public policy*

being resumed. This is because of the fall in liquidity in the TB market as a result of the fall in claims outstanding.

14. Apart from the dearth of paper available, foreign participation was adversely affected by the problems associated with the application of the withholding taxes (see Chapter 3, note 37).

15. Despite the broadening of the interbank market, the establishment of an offshore market and expansion of the yen swap market, all of which aided those foreign organizations without a retail deposit base in Japan.

16. It should be noted that the effectiveness of monetary policy pre-deposit-rate liberalization *relied upon* disintermediation, which largely resulted from the suppression of bank deposit rates relative to open-market rates, thereby curtailing the growth in bank credit (see Suzuki, 1987, pp. 332–3).

17. Deposit-rate liberalization, along with financial innovation, will also of course complicate interpretation of movements in narrow money such as M1 – notes and coin in circulation plus banks' demand and current deposits. (M2 = M1 plus banks' savings, time and other deposits.)

18. In a fully liberalized financial system this is due to the higher 'own rate' on money which deposit-rate liberalization allows, thereby necessitating a greater absolute change in interest rates in order to achieve the change in interest-rate differentials required to secure the desired change in the demand for money. This implies, of course, that (nominal) interest rates are both higher on average and more variable, *ceteris paribus*.

19. Any tax-deductibility of loan charges will, of course, serve to lower this figure.

20. Evidence casts doubt on any monetary authority's ability to identify stable and enduring demand for money functions. Rather, it would appear that apparently stable demand for money functions (such as those identified by Okina, 1985) break down once the aggregate(s) in question is elevated to the status of a target, particularly if direct monetary controls are employed to assist in the attainment of such targets (this is the so-called 'Goodhart's Law'). While the use of 'private' rather than publicly announced targets might improve the situation somewhat, the wider benefits perceived to derive from the public announcement of targets (see Hall, 1982, ch. 7) would of course be lost. Accordingly, few (if any) from amongst the ranks of those advocating the use of monetary targets would advocate the adoption of such a policy.

21. Apart, that is, from the injection of liquidity necessitated by the financial panic which ensued following the collapse of three financial institutions in November 1997 (see Chapter 2). As Chart 7.1 shows (see Appendix to this chapter), the provision of (gross) short-term liquidity by the BoJ to the market, which is made up of routine open market purchases (of, for example, commercial bills, commercial paper, Treasury bills, and cash-collateralized government bonds on a repo basis) plus Article 33 (collateralized) and Article 38 (uncollateralized) lending to financial institutions, jumped to around ¥6.5 trillion in the immediate aftermath of the collapse of Yamaichi Securities at the end of November, peaking at around ¥7 trillion at the end of fiscal 1997. Of the total, 'emergency' Article 38 loans peaked at around ¥3.8 trillion in November 1997, although the current amount outstanding, of around ¥3 trillion, reflects the continuing weakness of the Japanese financial (especially banking) system.

22. Concerns with exchange-rate instability in Asia and Australia in February 1996 led the authorities in Hong Kong and Singapore (Australia had acted earlier) to develop with Japan formal arrangements whereby the authorities in such countries would intervene in US dollars/yen in their markets on behalf of the Japanese authorities when serious instability threatened. Currency 'pacts' were also agreed with South East Asian governments in the autumn of 1997 in the wake of the currency crises which hit the region.

REFERENCES

Bank of Japan (1975), *The Importance of the Money Supply in Japan*, Tokyo: Bank of Japan.

Bank of Japan (1998), *Main Economic Indicators of Japan*, Economic Statistics Division, Research and Statistics Department, April.

Hall, M.J.B. (1982), 'Monetary targets', in G.E.J. Dennis et al. (eds), *The Framework of UK Monetary Policy*, London: Heinemann, pp. 213–33.

Hall, M.J.B. (1983), *Monetary Policy Since 1971: Conduct and Performance*, London: Macmillan.

Hall, M.J.B. (1987), *Financial Deregulation: A Comparative Study of Australia and the United Kingdom*, London: Macmillan.

Ichinose, A. (1991), 'Why is bank rate below call rates in Japan?', *Okayama Economic Review*, **3/4**, February.

Kasman, B. and Rodrigues, A.P. (1991), 'Financial liberalization and monetary control in Japan', *Federal Reserve Bank of New York Quarterly Review*, **16** (3), 28–46.

Katayama, S. (1985), 'The Japanese economy, the monetary structure, and the monetary policy in Japan after World War II: a comparison between the high economic growth period and the 1970s', *Proceedings of the Seventh International Symposium on Asian Studies*, Hong Kong: Asian Research Service, pp. 201–14.

Okina, K. (1985), 'Re-examination of the empirical study using Granger causality: causality between money supply and nominal income', *Bank of Japan Monetary and Economic Studies*, **3** (3).

Osugi, K. (1990), 'Japan's experience of financial deregulation since 1984 in an international perspective', *BIS Economic Papers*, no. 26.

Shigehara, K. (1991), 'Financial liberalization and monetary policy', in Foundation for Advanced Information and Research (FAIR), *Japan's Financial Markets*, Tokyo: FAIR.

Suzuki, Y. (1987), *The Japanese Financial System*, Oxford: Clarendon Press.

Suzuki, Y. (1990), 'Monetary policy in Japan' in C.A.E. Goodhart and G. Sutija (eds), *Japanese Financial Growth*, London: Macmillan.

Yoshitomi, M. (1985), 'Japan as capital exporter and the world economy', *Group of Thirty*, Occasional Paper no. 18, New York: Group of Thirty.

8. Implications of financial liberalization for prudential policy

The financial liberalization programme was undertaken with a view to increasing efficiency (partly through an accommodation of technological advances) in the face of growing pressures from overseas for the Japanese financial system to be internationalized and for foreign intermediaries to be given reciprocal rights of access to Japanese markets and, domestically, from the intermediaries' desire to meet the changing requirements of their customers. It has serious implications for the conduct of prudential policy.

THE RISKS

At the macro-level, the stability of both the banking and wider financial systems is threatened as a result of: the exposure of individual intermediaries to new risks and to an increase in existing risks (see below); the induced changes in market shares of intermediation services experienced by the different segments of the financial services industry; and the greater variability in profits for the individual intermediaries induced by the intensification in competition faced both at home and overseas and, in the case of banks, by the deregulation of deposit rates.

At the micro-level, and despite the benefits deriving from the wider diversification opportunities created which offer the prospect of a reduction in overall portfolio risk and/or higher risk-adjusted portfolio returns, risk management is at a premium. This is because of the emergence of new risks and an increase in existing risks. *Management risk*, for example, which refers to the management's ability to handle satisfactorily the diversification embarked upon, will be a new phenomenon to many engaged in the financial services sector who have been brought up in, and hence become accustomed to, the traditions of the highly segmented nature of the Japanese financial system. Similarly, the ever-widening use of derivatives in risk management and the growth in off-balance-sheet business poses problems for management (as well as for the wider financial system), who may fail to grasp fully the risks assumed by virtue of their engagement in such activities. The more traditional banking risks may also pose problems. *Credit risk*, for example, is likely to increase in the face of the intensification in competition which all too frequently results in a lowering of creditworthiness assessment standards and a concomitant reduction in risk-adjusted returns on the loan portfolio. The relaxation of collateral requirements will accentuate this problem. *Interest-rate risk* and *foreign-exchange risk* are also likely to increase, as a result of the interest-rate liberalization programme in the former case and the floating of the yen and the internationalization of Japanese intermediaries' activities in the latter case. *Liquidity risk*, too, may increase as the funding mix is changed to embrace the new borrowing opportunities; and *position risk* will also increase as a result of the authorities' willingness to tolerate greater variability in the yields on bonds and other securities. Whilst this is by no means an exhaustive survey of the new risk environment faced by Japanese financial intermediaries, it nevertheless does serve to indicate the seriousness of the situation.

THE POLICY ISSUES

Apart from addressing these issues, the supervisory authorities must also deal with a further set of threats and demands. The threats comprise the damage to the integrity of the financial system (already damaged by the numerous, mainly securities-related, scandals which have surfaced during the last few years – see Chapter 2) that would result from a failure to handle, in an appropriate fashion, the myriad conflicts of interest that result from the relaxation of controls on the scope of business activities that may be undertaken; and the damage to the economy that might result should excessive concentration in the financial sector or overseas domination be the end results of the liberalization programme. The more pressing demands, in turn, relate mainly to concerns about competitive equity. These concerns are expressed both overseas – witness the demands for reciprocity and convergence in the regulation of internationally active intermediaries in the face of the trend towards globalization of finance – and domestically, in the latter case largely because of the dismantling of the participation barriers which has yet further intensified competition in local markets.

Accordingly, and apart from the need to reduce systemic risk, the supervisory authorities have to deliver cost-effective solutions to the problems posed by conflicts of interest, increasing concentration and regulatory anomalies at both the domestic/international interface and the domestic industry/industry interface.

THE SOLUTIONS

Systemic Risk

The chosen solutions of the supervisory authorities (the Bank of Japan and the Ministry of Finance) to handling the systemic risks created by financial liberalization comprise the following elements:

(i)   a controlled pace of deregulation (see Chapters 3 and 4);
(ii)   an expansion in the safety net, in the form of an increase in the level of protection given to depositors under the deposit insurance arrangements and enhanced powers for the Ministry of Finance (MoF) in facilitating bank mergers;
(iii)   the imposition of tougher capital requirements on banks; and
(iv)   enhanced supervision of financial intermediaries (especially banks).

Changes to the *deposit insurance arrangements* were made fairly early on in the liberalization programme. With effect from June 1986 the insurance coverage was increased from ¥3m to ¥10 million; the premiums payable by the intermediaries were increased by 50 per cent (that is, from 0.008 per cent of deposits to 0.012 per cent for banks); the limit imposed on the Deposit Insurance Corporation's (DIC) emergency borrowing from the Bank of Japan was increased from ¥50 billion to ¥500 billion;[1] labour credit associations became subject to deposit insurance; and the range of aid-giving (and failure-preventing) methods available to the DIC was expanded, allowing the DIC to become involved before a declaration of insolvency is made.[2] These changes were introduced through amendments to the Deposit Insurance Law of April 1971 and the corresponding law covering agricultural co-operatives and fishery co-operatives, which resulted in the establishment of the Savings Insurance Corporation for Agricultural and Fishery Co-operatives (SICAFC) in September 1983.

More recently, as noted in Chapter 5, a number of further revisions to the Deposit Insurance Law have been made which resulted in the following: (i) further increases in DIC resources, via increased premiums, the donation of government bonds and the provision of government guarantees; and (ii) the DIC assuming greater powers in respect of its ability to investigate institutional failure, to undertake 'reorganizations' on behalf of depositors when institutions go bankrupt, to provide assistance to facilitate mergers between shaky banks and, in an emergency (subject to the unanimous consent of an 'examining board' and approval by the Cabinet), to purchase the preferred stocks and/or subordinated bonds issued by 'healthy' financial institutions (for full details see Chapter 5).

Enhancement of the MoF's powers to *facilitate bank mergers* also resulted from the 1986 revision to the Deposit Insurance Law. This is because the Law now allows the MoF (the power will transfer to the FSA in June 1998) to initiate merger proceedings even if the institution itself has not applied for assistance. This is authorized under the so-called 'emergency merger' provisions, which provide the MoF with such discretionary powers in situations where a breakdown in the credit system is threatened. To allay fears that it might act precipitately in this capacity, however, the MoF agreed to proposals that the Justice Ministry give prior approval to the activation of the emergency merger procedures and that MoF authorization of a merger should not be given in situations where at least 20 per cent of the shareholders of the troubled institution are opposed to the move.

An early decision to raise banks' *capital requirements* was taken in the spring of 1986. Following the failure of earlier MoF guidance to get banks to observe minimum net worth ratios of 10 per cent, explicit targets were set for raising capital ratios. Banks were asked to observe a minimum 4 per cent ratio of capital to total assets by 1990; and those with overseas branches were given a minimum target ratio of 6 per cent, to be achieved by the end of 1987 at the latest. For the latter set of institutions, 70 per cent of 'hidden reserves' in the form of unrealized gains on securities holdings were eligible for inclusion in the capital base.

Subsequent to this, the Japanese authorities, keen to be seen to be abiding by the spirit if not the letter of the UK/US accord on capital adequacy (see Hall, 1993a, pp. 29–34, for further details), also asked the banks to provide them with regular reports on their risk asset ratios from September 1986 onwards; and, since April 1993, the Japanese banks have been forced to fall into line with the G10 agreement on capital adequacy assessment (see Hall, 1993b, ch. 8). The introduction of 'prompt corrective action' (see Chapter 4) will reinforce the banks' need to be well capitalized.

Enhanced supervision of financial intermediaries has taken a number of guises. An early package of measures aimed at the banking sector was introduced in the spring of 1986 on the recommendation of the Financial System Research Council. Apart from the introduction of a new two-tier system of capital ratio requirements and the reform of deposit insurance arrangements noted above, the package comprised: the imposition of reporting requirements in respect of off-balance-sheet activities (designed to facilitate continuous assessment of off-balance-sheet exposures); the imposition of reporting requirements to cover the activities of overseas subsidiaries (designed to enhance the effectiveness of consolidated supervision); the imposition of requirements relating to the regular submission of data on funding from the money market and holdings of floating-rate instruments (designed to assist in the assessment of liquidity adequacy and interest-rate risk); the imposition of tougher loan-exposure rules – although the limits on loan exposures to single borrowers were raised from 20 per cent of net worth for commercial banks, 30 per cent for long-term credit banks and trust banks, and 40 per cent for the specialized foreign exchange bank to 40 per cent, 45 per cent and 50 per cent respectively, with effect from May 1986 they covered both off-balance-sheet activities as well as loans to corporate customers' affiliates; the introduction of minimum risk asset ratio requirements in respect of external (including off-balance-sheet, securities-related activities) operations[3] – risk-weighted external assets could not exceed 3.5 times net worth after September 1986 (reduced to 2.5 times net worth at the end of 1987); and the use of guideline liquidity ratios in the assessment of liquidity adequacy (to ensure the risks associated with the possible drying up of euromarket sources of funds were accounted for). Inspection procedures were also strengthened, involving an increase in the frequency of inspections for banks' domestic operations and overseas branches (henceforth, for the latter, to be made at three-yearly intervals rather than every eight years, as previously); an extension in the scope of supervision to include, for example, the banks' activities in Hong Kong and Australia for the first time; computerization of monitoring; and an increase in emphasis given to the growth in shareholders' equity, asset quality, earnings, liquidity and managerial skill.

The large number of components of the package concerned with more intensive monitoring of the banks' overseas operations reflected the authorities' increasing anxiety at the rapid expansion in such activities, which lay outside the traditional supervisory framework. The measures duly introduced complemented those already in existence – such as the extensive guidance given after 1983 on what constituted 'appropriate' levels of lending to non-industrialized countries (a limit of 40 per cent of net worth was eventually applied to the aggregate of loans outstanding, excluding debt rescheduling), and the prudential limits on overseas yen lending introduced in 1984 – and were followed by yet further measures later. These latter initiatives involved, *inter alia,* the provision of administrative guidance on the question of what levels of provisions against less-developed country (LDC) debt were appropriate, and the introduction of country lending limits and prudential limits on the net foreign asset positions of the trading banks.

Inspection procedures, too, were kept under constant review and towards the end of the 1980s some further policy adjustments were implemented. First, more importance was attached to the extent and form of capital enlargement, the management of profitability, risk and liquidity, the assessment of asset quality and the review of management and control systems. Second, the authorities determined to tailor their inspections more to the individual characteristics of institutions, taking due account of the risks they faced, in order to increase the flexibility of operations. Third, an attempt was made to enhance the effectiveness of inspection by computerizing procedures as far as possible and by extending the scope of the inspection process to keep pace with the latest developments in international and domestic business, for example the growing use of derivative instruments. Finally, the authorities, in response to the trend towards globalization of finance and as a result of their acceptance of a policy of internationalization, sought to strengthen their liaison with overseas supervisory authorities with a view to fostering greater mutual understanding of each other's policies and facilitating the development of mutually acceptable reciprocity provisions to cover the entry and regulation of foreign firms in local markets. Notwithstanding these improvements, serious deficiencies in the external supervision of financial intermediaries were subsequently revealed – see Chapter 2 – requiring wide-ranging remedial action. Such supervisory reform is still ongoing (see Chapter 5).

Individual Bank Risk

Many of the policies aimed at reducing or at least containing systemic risk also, of course, serve to reduce the probability of an individual bank failure. Higher capital requirements and improved supervision and inspection procedures will all contribute to achieving this goal, as will improved settlement systems and, through its impact on depositor confidence, the extension of the safety net.

Investor Confidence

Such measures however, in themselves, are not sufficient to instil confidence in investors in a deregulated environment, a prerequisite being preservation of the markets' integrity. This is because of their increased exposure to conflict-of-interest abuse following the relaxation or abolition of the participation barriers. Mindful of the efficiency losses associated with preventive measures, such as outright prohibition on the joint undertaking of certain operations, and the doubts surrounding the effectiveness of market-based solutions, based on the alleged restraints associated with the desire to preserve reputation, and self-regulation (for example, the use of Chinese Walls and rule books policed by compliance officers), the Japanese authorities quite rightly sought comfort from legal provisions. These can be used to deter fraud, for example, in the regulation of insider trading under the 1988 amendment to the Securities and Exchange Law, and to elicit adequate disclosure of relevant information (as provided for in the Commercial Law, the Securities and Exchange Law, and the Banking Law), and from external regulation and supervision. (The mix of policies adopted in respect of the joint offering of banking and securities services is highlighted in Hall, 1993b, ch. 9, with a view to illustrating the authorities' attempts to reconcile the often conflicting requirements arising from considerations of equity, efficiency and effectiveness.)

Concentration and Foreign Dominance

Concerns about excessive concentration in the financial services sector can presumably be dealt with by invoking the Anti-Monopoly Law should such fears ever be realized. Similarly, should the spectre of foreign dominance ever appear on the horizon – see Chapter 2 – domestic laws can always be redrafted if necessary to ring-fence the cores of the domestic credit and settlement systems and any other parts of the financial system thought likely to be damaged by foreign dominance, such as the primary government bond market.

Competitive Equity

The final issue to be addressed, namely the need to accommodate demands for competitive equity as far as is practicable, has been taken on board at both the national and international levels. Domestically, deregulation has proceeded at a pace and in a manner designed to satisfy industry demands for 'fairness' without the authorities being required to adjudicate on the fairness of the existing regulatory and supervisory frameworks, for example, through reforms allowing mutual interpretation of different segments of the financial services industry – see Chapters 3 and 4. And at the international level, bilateral negotiations, such as those with the US government and the EC Commission, acting on behalf of EU member states, have been, and continue to be, pursued with a view to promulgating mutually acceptable proposals concerning the licensing and regulation of intermediaries' overseas operations.

NOTES

1. Provisions also allowed the DIC to borrow from other financial institutions to repay the Bank of Japan.
2. Henceforth, the DIC could provide financial aid to a financial institution that merged with or bought another troubled financial institution, if necessary through the purchase of the bad assets of the failed institution in a situation where *all* the assets and liabilities of the failed institution are being assumed.
3. The previous restriction on the growth of external claims took the form of the imposition of a limit of 14 times capital and reserves (reduced from 15 times in May 1985) on the total amount of claims outstanding on non-residents.

REFERENCES

Hall, M.J.B. (1993a), *Handbook of Banking Regulation and Supervision*, 2nd edn, London: Woodhead-Faulkner.

Hall, M.J.B. (1993b), *Banking Regulation and Supervision: A Comparative Study of the UK, USA and Japan*, Aldershot, UK and Brookfield, US: Edward Elgar.

Index

administrative guidance 3, 15–16, 21,
42, 112–15, 182
Anti-Monopoly Law 15, 112, 114, 124,
136, 156, 177, 220

Bank of Japan Independence Study
Group 197
Bank of Japan Law 7
1998 amendments 190–95
an assessment 196–7
case for revision 189
see also central banking
Banking Law 5–6, 15–16, 109, 111,
219
Benston, G.J. 118, 135
'big bang' *see* financial deregulation

central banking 7–8, 190–95
liquidity injection 210, 212
city banks 8
collateral requirements 15, 17–18
commercial banks 5–12
bad debt 'mountain' 29–35
excess capacity and low profitability
39
impost of failure resolution policies
42
problems faced 28–42
threats posed by deregulation 40–41
weakness in domestic property and
stock markets 39–40
weakness in the macro-economy 35–
9, 59–61
Co-operative Credit Purchasing Company 187

Dale, R. 136
Deposit Insurance Corporation 168–71,
182, 187, 216
see also prudential policy; deposit
insurance reform

Federation of Bankers' Associations of
Japan 4, 6, 13, 74, 83, 85, 88, 97,
110, 111, 128, 129
financial deregulation 27–8, 40–41, 67–
158
during the period (1975–97) 67–138
cross sectoral entry under the
Financial System Reform Act
109–30
deepening of domestic financial
markets 89–108
capital market 100–108
money market 89–100
internationalization of the yen 67–
82
internationalization of the
foreign exchange market
81–2
liberalization of the euroyen
market 75–9
liberalization of the foreign yen-
denominated bond market
79–81
liberalization of interest rates
82–9
implications for monetary policy 201–
13
implications for prudential policy
214–21
under the 'big bang' reform programme 27–8, 139–58
measures designed to deliver an
'easy-to-use' market 151–2
measures designed to ensure a 'fair'
market 151–3
measures designed to expand user
choice 139–50
measures designed to help preserve
financial stability 153–4
measures designed to improve
quality of service provision

and to promote competition
150–51
rationale 27–8
financial markets
capital market 14–15, 100–108
bond markets
corporate bond market 106–8
euroyen bond market 75–9
foreign yen-denominated bond
market 79–81
government bond market 20–21,
100–105
equity markets 40, 58–9, 106
futures and options markets 105,
106
foreign exchange market 81–2
insurance market 26–7, 127, 151
money market 12–14, 89–100
interbank markets 89–93
call market 92
commercial bill market 92–3
'Tokyo dollar' call market 93
'open' markets 93–100
BA market 95–6, 99
bond *gensaki* market 94–7, 98
bond repo market 97, 100
CD market 93, 94–7, 98
CP market 96–7, 99, 100
euroyen market 75, 77–9
TB market 95–7, 99
structure 13–15
financial regulation
structure 15–18
financial scandals 43–7, 63
Daiwa 'affair' 45–6, 188
illegal compensation of favoured
clients 43, 45–6
issuing of forged CDs 43
scandals involving MoF/BoJ 46–7
sokaiya related 43–5
Sumitomo 'affair' 46
Financial Supervisory Agency 181, 182
Financial System Reform Law 27, 40,
127–30, 177
Fiscal Reform Law 37
foreign banks 9, 41, 62, 114–15
Foreign Exchange and Foreign Trade
Control Law 3, 67, 130
1997 revisions 148–9, 152, 155, 177
foreign securities firms 41, 62, 115–17

functional separation 3–5

Glass–Steagall Act (USA) 118, 121

Hall, M.J.B. 39, 42, 119, 139, 154, 155,
156, 157, 179, 196, 201, 207, 208,
212, 220
holding companies 124–7, 150–51, 156
Housing Loan Administration Corporation 171

Ichinose, A. 211

Japan Centre for International Finance
13, 74, 85, 91, 97, 104, 131
Japan 'premium' 186, 188
JASDAQ market 152
Joint Japan–US *Ad Hoc* Group 23–4
jusen 'crisis' 31, 42, 159, 187
resolution of 167–71

Katayama, S. 205

labour banks 11
long-term credit banks 3, 9–10

maturity controls 18
Merrill Lynch 189, 196
monetary policy 15, 21, 37
ceilings on loans from Bank of Japan
205
exchange controls 67, 75, 150, 201–3
see also Foreign Exchange and
Foreign Trade Control Law
impact of financial liberalization 201–
13
on choice of instruments 201–7
on choice of intermediate target(s)
207–9
other complications caused 209
interest rate controls 16–17, 82–9
reserve deposit requirements 203–4
transactions in financial markets 205–
7, 211–12
window guidance 203–5

Norinchukin Bank 3, 12, 206

Okina, K. 212
Osugi, K. 91, 209

postal savings system 22, 29, 84–8
'prompt corrective action' *see* prudential
    policy
prudential policy
  capital requirements 217
  impact of financial liberalization 214–
    21
  inspection procedures 178–81, 218–
    19
  'prompt corrective action' 39, 153–4,
    156–7, 177, 178, 179, 180, 182
  reform 159–85
    to deal with the banking sector's
      problems 159–77
      deposit insurance arrangements
        171–7, 216
      failure resolution policy 159–71
        in respect of banks 159–67
        in respect of the *jusen* 167–71
      financial deregulation 177
      to enhance external supervision
        178–81, 217–19
      structural reform 181–5
        creation of a new supervisory
          agency 182–3
  weaknesses in 42
public sector banks 12

regional banks 8–9
Resolution and Collection Bank 159,
  167, 168, 176

samurai market *see* financial markets;
  foreign yen-denominated bond
  market

Securities and Exchange Law 5, 111–15,
  118, 130, 133, 134, 135, 153, 155,
  219
Securities and Exchange Surveillance
  Commission 44
securitization 147
shibosai market *see* financial markets;
  foreign yen-denominated bond
  market
Shigehara, K. 207
special purpose companies 147
supervisory reform *see* prudential
  policy; reform
shinkin banks 3, 10, 105, 206
Shokochukin Bank 11
Suzuki, Y. 6, 13, 15, 16, 24, 74, 105,
  131, 132, 203, 207, 209, 211, 212

Temporary Interest Rate Adjustment
  Law *see* monetary policy; interest
  rate controls
Trenchard, T. 117
trust banks 3, 10

'universal banking' 120, 121, 122, 124–
  6, 150–51

World Trade Organization 27

Yamawaki, T. 28, 39, 42, 153, 156, 181
Yoshitomi, M. 206

Zenshinren Bank 3, 11, 104